James Baldwin

James Baldwin

America and Beyond

Edited by
CORA KAPLAN *and* BILL SCHWARZ

The University of Michigan Press ~ *Ann Arbor*

Published in the United States of America by
The University of Michigan Press
Manufactured in the United States of America
♾ Printed on acid-free paper

2014 2013 2012 2011 4 3 2 1

A CIP catalog record for this book is available from the British Library.

Library of Congress Cataloging-in-Publication Data

James Baldwin : America and beyond / edited by Cora Kaplan and Bill Schwarz.
p. cm.
Includes bibliographical references and index.
ISBN 978-0-472-07152-4 (cloth : acid-free paper) — ISBN 978-0-472-05152-6 (pbk. : acid-free paper) — ISBN 978-0-472-02761-3 (e-book)
1. Baldwin, James, 1924–1987—Criticism and interpretation.
2. African Americans in literature. I. Kaplan, Cora. II. Schwarz, Bill, 1951–
PS3552.A45Z72358 2011
818.5409—dc22 2011014831

Acknowledgments

In June 2007, twenty years after James Baldwin's death, we organized at the School of English and Drama at Queen Mary, University of London, the first major conference to be held on Baldwin in the UK. This formed the basis for the collection that appears here, its European provenance suggesting the "Beyond" of our title, though many transformations have occurred in the original papers between then and now. The formal conference was preceded by a daylong workshop—"Sonny's Blues. Identity/Writing/Politics"—open to the public, free of charge, held at the Rich Mix arts complex in London's East End: we thought it appropriate that our engagement with Baldwin should occur outside, as well as inside, the academy.

None of this could have happened without the commitment of the School of English and Drama at Queen Mary and of our head of school, Julia Boffey. We wish to thank as well, for their generosity and support, the then-vice-principal of arts, laws and social sciences at Queen Mary, Philip Ogden; the Westfield Trust; the Ford Foundation; the British Academy; the Arts Council of England, especially David Cross; James Dunkerley and the Institute for the Study of the Americas; and the European Collegium for African-American Research. Caryl Phillips and Magdalena Zaborowska were early enthusiasts for the project and guided us in our bid to secure funding. Departmental administrative staff, particularly Alistair Daniel and Beverley Stewart, and many students worked tirelessly on our behalf. Ruth Borthwick and Nicole King did much to help us think through the dynamics of the "Sonny's Blues" event, and we are grateful as well to Michael Keith and the Rich Mix team.

We are delighted that Eileen Ahearn, representing the Baldwin estate, was able to join us in London for the duration of the conference and to contribute to our discussions.

Duncan Barrett provided quality help in the last-minute preparation of the manuscript. Pauline Hubner prepared the index quickly and efficiently. Tom Dwyer, Alexa Ducsay, and Christina Milton at the University of Michigan Press demonstrated a wonderful commitment to the volume from the start. In these times when publishers of all stripes face serious difficulties, we thank them. Stephen Long's photograph of James Baldwin appears on the cover with kind permission of the University of Massachusetts.

Colm Tóibín's chapter, based on the plenary he gave at the London conference, first appeared in print in the *Dublin Review;* it appears here with permission.

Our deep thanks, finally, to Sarah Chapman and David Glover.

CORA KAPLAN
BILL SCHWARZ

Contents

Introduction
America and Beyond 1
CORA KAPLAN AND BILL SCHWARZ

PART ONE. *What It Means to Be an American*

1. Stranger at Home
James Baldwin on What It Means to Be an American 35
CHERYL A. WALL

2. Baldwin and "the American Confusion" 53
COLM TÓIBÍN

3. "Over and Over and Over Again"
James Baldwin, *Uncle Tom's Cabin*, and the Afterlife of an American Story 69
BRIALLEN HOPPER

4. "Now Describing You"
James Baldwin and Cold War Liberalism 84
VAUGHN RASBERRY

5. Baldwin, Prophecy, and Politics 106
GEORGE SHULMAN

6. Rendezvous with Life
Reading Early and Late Baldwin 126
ROBERT REID-PHARR

PART TWO. *Stranger in the Village*

7. "History's Ass Pocket"
The Sources of Baldwinian Diaspora 141
KEVIN BIRMINGHAM

8. Separate and Unequal in Paris
Notes of a Native Son and the Law 159
D. QUENTIN MILLER

9. Exile and the Private Life
James Baldwin, George Lamming, and the First World Congress of Negro Writers and Artists 173
KEVIN GAINES

10. From Istanbul to St. Paul-de-Vence
Around James Baldwin's *The Welcome Table* 188
MAGDALENA J. ZABOROWSKA

11. What Is Africa to Baldwin?
Cultural Illegitimacy and the Step-fatherland 209
DOUGLAS FIELD

12. James Baldwin and Chinua Achebe
Transgressing Official Vocabularies 229
ELEANOR W. TRAYLOR

Afterword 241
HORTENSE SPILLERS

Contributors 247

Index 251

Introduction

America and Beyond

CORA KAPLAN AND BILL SCHWARZ

James Baldwin was one of the boldest and most important writers in English of the twentieth century. His radical humanism was eclectic, undogmatic, and interrogative, aiming always to illuminate the psychic elements in the discourses of power. This was a way of thought that—in our view—is of immediate relevance to the international climate of fear and uncertainty in which we now live. Who else in public life has been so eloquent in insisting upon the necessary relations between affect, ethics, and politics?[1]

Since his death Baldwin's public reputation, though, has been complicated (as indeed it was during his lifetime). The great historian Marc Bloch—reflecting on the connections between past, present, and future—once observed that "the traces left by past events never move in a straight line, but in a curve that can be extended into the future."[2] The "past" that concerns us in this volume is Baldwin. Whether we can imagine a human life, or a literary oeuvre, to have been a historical "event" may be open to question. But Bloch's emphasis on what we might call *indirection* is useful. In no department of his life was Baldwin ever won by the concept of "a straight line." We can see evidence of this in his prose, for example, which often works by stealth, in the manner of Henry James, adding subclause to subclause and detour to detour. Even so, when Baldwin was alive many critics were keen to describe the trajectory of his writing life as if it had traveled along a straight line, from A to B. A consensus grew that his literary career represented a diminishment of sensibility, in which the early achievements (A) were followed by literary decline (B). Different versions of this story prevailed. The dominant account came to suggest that, in the era of civil rights and Black Power, Baldwin's art had been undone by his deepening political commitments. By the time of his death in 1987 he seemed, in the public eye, and particularly in the United States, to be a strangely isolated figure, far removed from the aura that had been generated by the blaze of publicity that had accompanied him in the early 1960s. While many admirers continued to rally to him, his location in the national culture of the United States became increasingly problematic. His prophetic voice about the fate of America could sound, during the decade of Reagan Republicanism, ever more apocalyptic and out of touch with the spirit of the times; his later writings were perceived to be diffuse and difficult, oblique in a way that his earlier novels and essays never were; and his statements on sexuality conformed to no publicly recognized convention, unsettling even a significant portion of sexual radicals. Whatever he said appeared to confirm the suspicion that, to the different constituencies that composed his native land, his was an imagination that was too wayward, too given to detours, parentheses, and complexity, and never straight enough.

There was, in our view, nothing rectilinear about Baldwin: neither in his conception of the world nor in the trajectory of his life. And as Bloch acknowledged, the past bequeaths no straight lines. In recent years the movements along which Baldwin's influence can be felt—the means by which his past enters our present—have been deepening. As every year passes he appears a more, not a less, significant figure. He is becoming a more contemporary, maybe even a more complex presence whose capacity to speak to our age remains powerful. As Kevin Gaines once put this, historically we might only now—belatedly—be catching up with him.[3]

For these reasons, in part, there has occurred of late a renaissance in Baldwin studies, recognizing the significance for our own times of his continuing authority. The beginnings of this renewed appreciation can perhaps be marked—to opt for a single occasion—by the publication in 1999 of Dwight A. McBride's edited collection under the emphatic, symptomatic title *James Baldwin Now*. McBride suggested that "a Baldwin revival of sorts" was under way, with a critical mass of younger scholars writing dissertations on Baldwin and doing so with an understanding of "the complicated relationships that not only obtain but are inevitable between race, gender, class and sexuality." Their work was undertaken, McBride argued, when the academy came to realize "the impact of cultural studies on critical thought," allowing, he and his contributors implied, for a more integrated and less tendentious approach to Baldwin's work and politics. In turn this encouraged "the centrality and exemplarity of Baldwin" to emerge and to "come into sharper focus."[4] *James Baldwin Now* was followed a year later by D. Quentin Miller's *Re-Viewing James Baldwin: Things Not Seen,* and a clutch of important studies then appeared in quick succession.[5] In 2009 Magdalena J. Zaborowska's *James Baldwin's Turkish Decade: Erotics of Exile* and Douglas Field's *Historical Guide to James Baldwin* both appeared.[6] The novelist Colm Tóibín has written influential essays on Baldwin's continuing intellectual presence for the *New York Review of Books* and for the *London Review of Books.*[7] There have been large, set-piece tributes at the Lincoln Center (2001)—including, notably, Chinua Achebe—and at the New York Public Library (2008). And in the academic field a series of conferences has been organized in order to take stock of Baldwin and assess the complexities of his multiple legacies: in London in 2007, in Boston in 2009, and in New York in 2011.

Our volume taps into this renewed engagement with Baldwin, bringing together authors who have been prominent in this collective labor of public reappraisal. *James Baldwin: America and Beyond* represents a further staging of this revival, highlighting both the prescience and the complexity of Baldwin's critique of America and his fascinating, if always ambivalent, response to Europe. Although it is not possible to reduce this recent body of work to handy maxims, one thing is clear. A method of interpretation has to be established that refuses the old dichotomies that have customarily characterized the reception of Baldwin. For too long one Baldwin has been pitted against another Baldwin, producing a series of polarities that has skewed our understanding: his art against his politics; his fiction against his nonfiction; his early writings against his late writings;[8] American Baldwin against European Baldwin; black Baldwin against queer Baldwin.[9] Baldwin himself spent a lifetime endeavoring to overcome these oppositions. He sought to establish new ways of being in which he could learn the imaginative and social imperatives required to live with contraries, to live with difference. His eye was always on the potential for establishing connections between contrary phenomena—even as their very contrariness remained in place—rather than forcing disconnections and retreating to the encampments. If we wish to make sense of Baldwin, we have to do the same.

In this volume, for reasons that we will explain, we highlight one of these putative oppositions in Baldwin's life and writing: that between

American Baldwin and Baldwin the expatriate, the Baldwin preoccupied with those "other" lands that lay beyond the United States, places that he came to know either in his own person, through direct experience, or that he came to know only in his imagination. This story is complicated by the fact that he spent a substantial part of his life contemplating the different histories of America and Europe, and there were conspicuous moments when, in his mind, America became the focus for his despair and Europe something of a haven. But as we show, Europe was never exempt from criticism. And the story becomes more complex when we address, as Baldwin himself did, the growing centrality of Africa and Asia. We have taken for our subtitle *America and Beyond.* In choosing this we don't mean to imply any necessary, given polarity between the two: between America and its others. As ever with Baldwin, the salient point—if invariably also the most contentious—resides in the conjunction. Our concern is how he imagined America *and* beyond.

The Writer and the World

James Baldwin grew up unaccommodated in what he was later to call the American "house."[10] The immediate conditions of his life induced in him constant distrust, and he could take nothing for granted. The man he assumed to be his father he believed, as a young boy, to be a monster, "locked up in his terrors."[11] Perpetual poverty and fear dominated his upbringing. A trip downtown could end up in a nightmare entanglement with racist cops who were quite prepared, he reasoned, to inflict on him—child though he was—unspeakable violence. His burgeoning erotic desires, manifest in his attraction to men as well as to women, unsettled any last possibility of his attaining what prevailed as normalcy. His Harlem neighborhood, riven by unrestrained passions, seemed to present only defeat and destruction, feeding in him a terrible claustrophobia. "'Whose little boy are you?'" he was asked by the pimps and racketeers on Lenox Avenue, the same question posed to him by the pastor of his new church, offering—or so at first it appeared—salvation from the dangers outside.[12] Baldwin's entry into the social world was propelled by a series of identifications that were peculiarly charged and that he experienced as both irreconcilable and impossible. The threat of violence was always close by: not only of violence inflicted on his own self, but of a violence emanating from deep within him, directed out to others. As he himself implied, there is little doubt that his having to leave America in 1948 was due to a fear that he might be killed, or himself kill, an apprehension that should not be taken lightly. As Cheryl Wall suggests later in these pages, Baldwin's quarrel with America was "ultimately personal."[13]

Yet Baldwin also left America in order to be a writer, with Paris as his chosen destination. By doing so he determined to enter the world on his own terms. The very dislocations he'd experienced, the cause of such profound subjective distress for him in the United States, were to become, in his fiction and nonfiction, not so much "the theme" of his writing, in a conventional literary-critical sense, as its substance, the dislocations activating the impetus for him to write. In his 1961 "Introduction" to *Nobody Knows My Name* Baldwin emphasized the degree to which "the subject" of the "writer . . . is himself and the world," drawing on a phenomenological or existential idiom that was current in the Parisian intellectual environment that he had come to know well. "The questions which one asks oneself," he continued, "begin, at last, to illuminate the world, and become one's key to the experience of others."[14] Above all he was fearless in posing the "questions which one asks oneself," for, as he explained, "one can only face in others what one can face in oneself."[15] By turning inward he sought the means by which he could confront the multifarious antagonists ranged against him. The shifting relations between the self and the other he never conceived to be merely private transactions, only of subjective significance: the power of his writing derives from the fact that he consistently strove to imagine self and other in "the world," such that each was always "worldly."

These are terms that recur throughout Baldwin's writings. He thought of himself as entering into the world, and—unable to take anything for granted—he was peculiarly self-conscious of what this entailed. When he employed the notion of the world he understood it literally and figuratively, referring both to real geographies and, more elusively, to the properties of modernity itself. We'll return to this later.

Our principal focus in this volume is the interconnections between his imaginings of America and of the larger world beyond the United States.[16] In this reading his restless urge to relocate himself—across cities, nations, and continents—offers a privileged vantage point from which to understand how he came to conceptualize his own encounter between "himself and the world." In this respect his initial journeyings as a young man from Harlem to Greenwich Village and thence to Paris are formative.[17] Each move took him further away from the place of his birth. Each also brought him closer to recognition as a writer. As we've suggested, the two—how he imagined his life inside and outside America and how he imagined his life as a writer—are superimposed. He proved single-minded in creating a position for himself in American letters, as a writer inhabiting, in new ways, the English language: *this* America remained a constant reference point, providing for him a place of sorts.[18] The chapters that follow reflect on this interplay between place and writing, showing how Baldwin's various locations registered in his inner life and gave form to his writing, just as through his writing he internalized the dynamics of the larger world.[19]

Baldwin's desire for the modern world, for it to be his, was unyielding. The erotics were palpable: to be in the world was to open oneself to others. Indeed, in thinking through the question of race he repeatedly returned—particularly in the earlier writings—to the notion of love. Politically, this was the cause of great controversy, not least among those who found themselves on the violent frontiers of the color line facing the billy sticks, or the hoses, or the dogs, but also from those of more contemplative dispositions.[20] Baldwin constantly repeated the fact that he comprehended love, not as romance, in the Hollywood manner (enacted, say, by Doris Day or Gary Cooper), but as a complex set of relations encompassing both daring and growth, on the one hand, and a measure of darkness and danger on the other: "Love is a battle, love is a war; love is a growing up."[21] In *Giovanni's Room*, in *Another Country*, and less centrally in *The Fire Next Time*, he contrasted love in his meaning of the term to the more conventional notion of love as romance and (crucially for him) as innocence.[22] In *Giovanni's Room*, in particular, this contrast is encoded in terms of the opposition between Europe and America, in which the inhabitants of the latter are condemned to live a life of bad faith, crippled by their compulsion to act out the prevailing myths of the nation—and the prevailing myths of sexuality—to their eternal cost.[23] Elsewhere he acknowledged that he found something moving about the spectacle of Americans as a "lost people" who "don't yet know that the world is big and complex and dark and that you have to grow up and become yourself big and complex and dark in order to deal with it."[24]

Complexity and darkness certainly include homosexuality, obliquely present in Baldwin's autobiographical first novel and overtly so in *Giovanni's Room* and in *Another Country*, as well as forming part of the exemplary narrative of many of his essays—although, as Marlon Ross reminds us, the demarcation of Baldwin's writing into opposing categories of "black" and "gay" is misleading.[25] Baldwin himself argued that "*Giovanni's Room* is not really about homosexuality. It's the vehicle through which the book moves."[26] Growing up black and male in America always involved what he imagined, with some irony, to be his "dubious sexuality." It drove his powerful critique of American masculinity, its defensive and hypocritical machismo so redolent, he argued, of national, imperial, and racist—as well as personal—violence. The way in which he interrogated those "kaleidoscopic" terms—manhood, masculinity, male, man—making them always contingent, historically and culturally specific, grew from his conviction, summarized so well in the 1984 interview with Richard Goldstein, that "the sexual question and the racial question have always been entwined, you know. If Americans can mature on the level of racism, then they have to mature on the level of sexuality."[27] The "if" and the "can" here, suspended and doubtful for a people "who are terrified of feeling anything," are crucial, as was Baldwin's immediate qualification that for black people, the "sexual question came after the question of colour."[28] Baldwin was never, by temperament or political inclination, a "member," or a joiner. The postwar gay subcultures of New York and Paris did not appeal: they represented too often a frightening "underworld" and offered not companionship but a new kind of loneliness, and he remained "dubious" about the political utility of the later gay mobilization, or whether a "coalition" between black and gay movements were possible. Homosexuality was not an "identity," and who you slept with was ultimately for him "a private matter," not a campaign.[29]

Yet paradoxically, by going public on what was essentially private, Baldwin himself was a vanguard "opening the gates" for an affirmative and constantly mutating discourse and politics that was at odds, in many respects, with his own sensibility, but toward which he nevertheless felt a "special responsibility."[30] The "New Jerusalem" he still imagined in his "good fantasies" toward the end of his life represents a post-identity utopia—nearer perhaps to queer politics, but still not quite of it: "No one will have to call themselves gay."[31]

Yet Baldwin's resistance to the political dynamic of the gay movement—his emphasis on the privacy of sexual choice and the universality of the human need to love—contributes to the ways in which the question of sexuality was constitutive of, and absolutely entwined with, his thinking about race and writing. Of *Giovanni's Room*, and the decision to publish it, he said, "If I hadn't written that book I would probably have had to stop writing altogether. . . . The question of human affection, of integrity, in my case, the question trying to become a writer, are all linked with the question of sexuality."[32] In Baldwin's oeuvre these questions almost always take on a national and international dimension. *Giovanni's Room* is, among other things, a sustained exploration of the possibility of orchestrating these questions together. For there the question of human affection and integrity is explored through a radical reworking of Henry James's insistently reiterated fictional opposition between a dangerous, and endangered, American innocence in the moment of its confrontation with Europe.

America and its others; America and beyond: this was a dialectic that preoccupied Baldwin throughout his life, evolving into a complex imaginative geography that was peculiarly his.

Approaching his work in this way follows what is now a common perspective—geographical, spatial—in literary and cultural studies, looking beyond the framework of the singular nation-state. But as ever when it comes to Baldwin the received critical lexicon never quite seems to fit. All that makes him a fugitive figure slips out of sight and moves below the radar systems of theoretical categorization. The contending vocabularies employed to explain Baldwin's mobility—transnational, transatlantic, cosmopolitan, exile, expatriate—each tell us something. Whether any one of them catches the complexities of his situation, though, is another matter. When questioned about his reasons for leaving America, or for his extended stays in distant lands, he would invariably respond by insisting that uppermost in his mind was the question of survival, the elemental truth of which shouldn't be discounted. In some respects, by fleeing the United States he was repeating the experience of the previous generation, within his own family, who had fled the South for Harlem: "They had been driven north by the sheer impossibility of remaining in the South."[33] Yet in his own case he also alluded to his need to find a place, wherever it might be, where he could write, and throughout his adult life he was never able to assume where such a place was to be located or even if it existed. Often this was also a matter of improvisation, as his peripatetic life attests. Yet these are terms—"survival," "writing"—that might appear to vindicate the idea that his travels outside America represented nothing more than a personal, if always unfinished, escape attempt from the confines of his native land.

It might seem, indeed, as if his venturing into the larger world, beyond the shores of the Americas, was anything but worldly, absenting him from engagement in the crucible of the race politics of the United States, or from the urgent political issues of the countries in which he chose to live or to visit, and condemning him to a solipsistic relationship with his typewriter. This was an argument that was rehearsed by a number of civil rights and Black Power militants during the sixties and seventies who were doubtful about Baldwin's credentials as a black revolutionary, not least of which, in their view, was his homosexuality. And it is clear that there were occasions when Baldwin himself believed he needed to abandon his privilege of distance and return to the struggle. But if we follow this line of thought too strictly another dichotomy opens up, assuming that "real politics" is confined only to the frontline of the struggle.

Baldwin—"Jimmy"—never made a secret of the fact that he liked the good life. He was fond of eating and drinking well, held a deep commitment to the practices of what in our own day we might call "slow" sociability, evident in the long nocturnal conversations to which he was so partial, and was not one to shun the opportunity of mixing with the stars. There were great stretches of his life when he found it easier to live, day to day, outside the United States—in France, in Turkey—where he felt less immediately exposed to the forces of American society that menaced him. There were episodes too, especially in the years following the assassination of King, when illness, exhaustion, and despair took hold, imposing on him intermittent periods of isolation. On both counts he was open to censure by those active in the movement at home who wished more from him. Yet Baldwin was always alert to the connections that bound the self—himself—to the world. Writing and friendships were indeed part of his worldliness, making him who he was; but so too was his determination to act as witness to his age, forever finding himself "in the position of a kind of Jeremiah."[34] Location for Baldwin was never simply a question of geography, in its narrowly technical remit: it was allied in his own mind to a commitment to an active, ever-present moral-political responsibility. Generally for him, this ethic took precedence, conceptually, over the category of location. The crucial argument of his 1959 essay "The Discovery of What It Means to Be an American" turns on precisely this point. Reflecting on his departure from the United States, he comments:

> Once I was able to accept my role—as distinguished, I must say, from my "place"—in the extraordinary drama which is America, I was released from the illusion that I hated America.[35]

David Leeming, a longtime friend of Baldwin's and his most astute biographer, tells the following story, which also evokes this distinction between "place" and "role." Baldwin once asked a new acquaintance where she was when King was killed. She answered, too innocently by half, "Norman, Oklahoma," which elicited from Baldwin a prolonged, furious tirade.[36]

"Where were you?" was not a question that could be answered literally, on its own terms. It necessarily carried a larger ethical meaning. To ask "Where were you?" was to pose the question of where we all are *in the world* and to ask, consequentially, what responsibility each one of us assumes for the worlds we inhabit.[37]

Thus when Baldwin proposed that the subject of the writer was "himself and the world," his idea of the world—it's clear—carried varied, shifting resonances. Here we can identify three broad clusters of meaning.

It represented, first, the arena in which men could become properly modern social beings, recognized by others as complete selves, and were able actively to operate where history proved most pressing. In his early essays he imagined the barriers impeding participation in the social world—in history—most immediately in terms of race and hardly at all in terms of gender (the writer "himself") or sexuality. "I left America because I doubted my ability to survive the fury of the color problem here," he explained. "I wanted to prevent myself from becoming *merely* a Negro; or, even, merely a Negro writer."[38] Baldwin's determination to be in the world, and to be recognized as such, required of him unceasing struggle, both in comprehending his inner life and in seeking to unlock the social forces that worked to overdetermine his situation as a Negro. "What, in sum," he noted, "black men held in common was their ache to come into the world as men."[39] Or as he claimed elsewhere,

> to become a Negro man, let alone a Negro artist, one had to make oneself up as one went along. This had to be done in the not-at-all metaphorical teeth of the world's determination to destroy you. The world had prepared no place for you, and if the world had its way, no place would ever exist.[40]

When he described the essays that compose *Nobody Knows My Name*, which includes this passage, as "a very small part of a private logbook" it is largely this quest—making "oneself up as one went along"—that his book reconstructs, investigating the possibilities for the deracialization of his own self as the precondition for his being in the world.

In another register, second, the world signaled for Baldwin a deep desire to embrace a consciousness that lifted him—the modern being, the writer, Baldwin himself—out of his own region or nation, out of his own parish. Greenwich Village had served this purpose for him as a very young man, then Paris, then Istanbul. Yet as he discovered at the moment of his first arrival in Paris in 1948, America could never finally be banished from his mind. "Even the most incorrigible maverick," he observed, "has to be born somewhere. He may leave the group that produced him—he may be forced to—but nothing will efface his origins, the marks of which he carries everywhere."[41] From his "stony Corsican exile" or from "icy Sweden," the question of America—that "extremely controversial proper noun"—continued to "nibble" away at him.[42] The ambivalence ran deep. The geographical distance of Europe did indeed allow him to see his native land with new eyes. Yet this process of defamiliarization generated unexpected, paradoxical consequences, for it was in Paris, he realized, that "I found myself, willy-nilly, alchemized into an American."[43] Or as he has this in a beguiling, provocative formulation, it was only when he had left America that he had discovered himself "to be as American as any Texas G.I."[44] Even the linguistic displacement he experienced proved fruitful. The fact that he had "stepped out of the English language" allowed him to inhabit American English as he had not been able to before. This he described as "a very strange kind of odyssey," but one that he believed to have been formative in the evolution of his own writing.[45] If America remained within him, it did so as a consequence of his engagement with the world beyond. Most of all, the identification with America required also the capacity to see America through the eyes of others: "one must be willing," he wrote in 1962, "to ask one's self what the Indian thinks of this [American] morality, what the Cuban or Chinese thinks of it, what the Negro thinks of it."[46]

And third, as we've indicated, being in the world for Baldwin ultimately signified a moral imperative. To be in the world required repudiating innocence and learning to take responsibility for oneself and others.

These differing perceptions of the world and of what it represents appear in a range of configurations throughout Baldwin's work, the symbolic geographies he imagined moving back and forth to produce a kaleidoscopic pattern of changing elements. This spatial perspective, simultaneously national and transnational, provides one dimension for the explorations that follow. But we need also to think in terms of temporality.

Foreclosing the White World

"The world is white no longer, and it will never be white again."[47] These words, which close *Notes of a Native Son*, were first published in 1953, five years after Baldwin's arrival in Paris. The declarative, prophetic tone is significant. When he announced that "the world is white no longer," it was less an empirical observation than a statement of political intent. But it signified, as well, the historical perception that the world was on the point of a momentous transformation and that the end of the old racial order, if not present, was at least in sight. Recognition of this new history in the making was the consequence not only of the emergent Civil Rights Movement, seen exclusively through the optic of the United States. The conscious determination to destroy the white world in the postwar years was a global phenomenon, constitutive of the wider drive for decolonization. Baldwin himself recounted how, in Paris in the fifties, he was confronted by stories and images of the struggle for civil rights in the American South and told too of the unease and guilt he experienced as a result. This, after all, he believed to be *his* struggle, taking place in his own—American—"house." But though an ocean separated him from the battle to defeat segregation, his arrival in Europe had coincided with another decisive history: that of decolonization. And in France, in particular, where Baldwin made his base, colonial wars overseas impacted directly on the daily life of the metropole: as a black man in Paris he found these events proximate to him. When Baldwin anticipated the end of the white world, he had in mind not only the United States, nor even what he identified as "the American continent," but a history that was more profoundly global.[48]

Critical, in the first instance, is the intellectual history of decolonization. Baldwin traveled to Paris to be a writer, which, as we know, marked a peculiarly American, writerly sensibility. When he was living in Paris, at various times, he came across—among others—Philip Roth, Norman Mailer, Saul Bellow, and Truman Capote. But Richard Wright and Chester Himes were there too, along with many other black jazz musicians and singers, and it was in part because of Wright that Baldwin had made Paris his destination.[49] Yet neither Wright nor Baldwin could assume their vocation of writer with the same innocence as their white counterparts. Their situation as writers was, inevitably, overdetermined by their blackness. On the day of his arrival Baldwin's very first stop was at the café Les Deux Magots, to be greeted by Wright, who had just been lunching there with Jean-Paul Sartre. Thanks to Sartre's patronage Les Deux Magots had gained a mythic reputation as something akin to the headquarters of existentialism, which has given rise to a surfeit of anecdotes—who met whom, who fell out with whom, and so on—about Left Bank intellectuals. The significant point, however, is the prevalence of existentialism. Existentialism—"philosophy in the first person," in David Macey's words—provided a powerful political resource for elaborating the dispositions of black subjectivity, or more properly (the publication of Simone de Beauvoir's *The Second Sex* in 1949 notwithstanding), of black male subjectivity.[50] The ideas encapsulated in the negritude movement, in Fanon's musings in *Black Skin, White Masks*, in some variants of Pan-Africanism: all drew from the influences of phenomenological thought.[51] Baldwin's own invocations of the idea of the self in the world inhabited this same intellectual universe. Indeed, it has been argued that the black presence in Paris after the war gave existentialism itself, in its peculiarly Parisian manifestations, a new lease on life.[52] To Wright and to the other black expatriates from the United States it must have seemed as if, providentially, they were located not only at the center of things—Baldwin, for one, believed Paris to be "the intellectual capital of the Western world"—but also at a historical turning point.[53] When Baldwin had determined to travel to Paris in order that he should have his place in the world, he couldn't have realized how fortuitous a decision he had made.[54] Paris may or may not be understood to have been "the intellectual capital of the Western world." But in these years it did function as the forcing ground for anticolonial, antiracial thought without equal in the European metropole.[55]

We can't be certain of the details of Baldwin's engagements with the French postwar intellectual milieu. Nor should they be exaggerated: as he explained often enough, he remained an American, in his intellectual dispositions as much as in anything else, as he did as well in his determination to be recognized as an American writer.[56] However, there can be no doubt of the fact that he witnessed the debates on European decolonization close up and that they informed his historical consciousness of the world.

This is most evident from his long report on the First Negro Writers and Artists Congress, held at the Sorbonne in Paris in September 1956, which brought together anticolonial intellectuals from the French and British empires, on the one hand, and delegates from black organizations in the United States, resulting in what Alioune Diop declared the "second Bandung."[57] Confronted by, among others, the great luminaries of *Présence africaine*—Diop himself, Léopold Senghor, and Aimé Césaire—professing the virtues of negritude (in its many varieties), Baldwin was exercised by the question of whether the American Negro experience could be directly subsumed to a generalized category of blackness that had, for its deepest inspiration, the civilizations of ancient Africa. When Senghor, the most uncompromising of the *négritudiens*, attempted to reveal the essential African properties of Richard Wright's *Black Boy*, Baldwin was having none of it. Afrocentrism of this complexion was not for him.[58] He was persuaded more by Césaire's explicit denunciation of Europe, even though he found this "a very easy case to make," precisely because it left open the question of how the colonized were to imagine themselves in the future.

The anatomizing of the great injustice that is the irreducible fact of colonialism was yet not enough to give the victims of that injustice a new sense of themselves.

This Baldwin believed to be "the central question," which Césaire had dodged. In a characteristic response, he (Baldwin) chose to emphasize the ties that bound the colonized to the civilization of the colonizers—putting the weight of his argument on the conjunction between the two—just as he insisted that blacks in the United States were, "willy-nilly," American. For "whether they liked it or not," those colonized by the French, Baldwin continued, were "related to Europe" and "stained by European visions and standards." And more particularly he perceived Césaire himself to be, decisively and inescapably, the product of this colonial history:

> Césaire's speech had left out of account one of the great effects of the colonial experience: its creation, precisely, of men like himself. His real relation to the people who thronged about him now had been changed, by this experience, into something very different from what it once had been. What had made him so attractive now was the fact that he, without having ceased to be one of them, yet seemed to move with the European authority. He had penetrated into the heart of the great wilderness which was Europe and stolen the sacred fire. And this, which was the promise of their freedom, was also the assurance of his power.[59]

Whatever Baldwin's reservations about his arguments, this is a captivating depiction of Césaire as one of the historic generation of anticolonial intellectuals, who had purloined "the sacred fire" of learning from the colonizers and gone on to announce that this was so in the intellectual heartland of the old regime: at the Sorbonne.[60] Europe functions in this report of Baldwin's, as it did for Césaire, as a "wilderness," whose colonial authority was nearing its end.[61] At the same time the congress itself served as an arena in which his proposition made three years beforehand—"the world is white no longer, and it will never be white again"—was dramatically reasserted.

Indeed, the escalating politics of the struggle between white and black, in the closing days of the colonial nations and contemporaneously in the United States, created the means by which Baldwin, in his own telling, became conscious of his "role" as a participant in the struggle for America. This was how he discovered "what it means to be an American," and the colonial determinations, as he demonstrates, in part constituted this discovery:

> One day it begins to be borne in on the writer, and with great force, that he is living in Europe as an American. If he were living there as a European, he would be living on a different and far less attractive continent.
>
> This crucial day may be the day on which an Algerian taxi-driver tells him how it feels to be an Algerian in Paris. It may be the day on which he passes a café terrace and catches a glimpse of the tense, intelligent and troubled face of Albert Camus. Or it may be the day on which someone asks him to explain Little Rock and he begins to feel it would be simpler—and, corny as the words may sound, more honorable—to *go* to Little Rock than sit in Europe, on an American passport, trying to explain it.
>
> This is a personal day, a terrible day, the day to which his entire sojourn has been tending. It is the day he realizes that there are no untroubled countries in this fearfully troubled world; that if he has been preparing himself for anything in Europe, he has been preparing himself for—America. In short, the freedom that the American writer finds in Europe brings him, full circle, back to himself, with the responsibility for his development where it always was: in his own hands.[62]

In this rendition, in 1959, knowledge of the Algerian situation spurred Baldwin to reflect on his place in the world and, in so doing, to recognize anew his commitment to the events in his native land.

However, when he returned to these issues in *No Name in the Street*, in 1972, his perspective had changed. In 1959 he had suggested that Algeria, or colonial matters more generally, had worked as a catalyst to heighten his commitment to the Civil Rights Movement at home. In this later telling, with a sharper "Third Worldist" inflection, he indicated that during his time in Paris, twenty years before, colonial politics had in fact created in him a more powerful *identification* with the colonized throughout the world.[63] Baldwin didn't underestimate the relative privilege that derived from his own position as an American. Yet after the defeat the French suffered at Dien Bien Phu in May 1954, he directly witnessed the realities of colonial recidivism when the authorities sought vengeance for the catastrophe inflicted on them in Vietnam by turning on those dark-skinned peoples closest to home: the North African migrants living and working in France: "This is the way people react to the loss of empire . . . and I was to see this over and over again, not only in France."[64] In Paris he saw the street beatings and "the unconcerned faces of the French on the café terraces."[65] Returning after a stay in America he found familiar Arab cafés had been closed, and one of his favorite "low-life guides" had had his eyes put out: either, it seems, by the police or by his brothers due to the fact that they believed him to be an informer. Baldwin soon came to realize that all his old Algerian friends and acquaintances had disappeared. Rumors circulated of incarceration and torture and of murders too.[66] Algerians were being murdered "by my hosts"—the continuation, Baldwin argued, of a much longer colonial history in which he too was implicated.

> The fact that I had never seen the Algerian casbah was of no more relevance before this unanswerable panorama than the fact that the Algerians had never seen Harlem. The Algerian and I were both, alike, victims of this history, and I was still a part of Africa, even though I had been carried out of it nearly four hundred years before.

"The question of my identity," he continued, "had never before been so crucially allied with the reality—the doom—of the moral choice." In these circumstances "the moral choice" he confronted could only lead him to a single conclusion. The predicament of the Algerians "was somehow tied to mine, their battle was not theirs alone but was my battle also, and it began to be a matter of my honor not to attempt to avoid this loaded fact."[67]

The discrepancy between these two different narratives, in itself, is not an issue that need concern us. As Baldwin's views of the present changed, so his reflections on his past took on differing hues. He, of all people, was not one to seek the chimera of an immobile, singular self: particularly here, indirection supervenes. Yet a common perception of the global properties of the racial situation underlies both these tellings. When, from 1957, he actively involved himself in the Civil Rights Movement, he brought with him this larger sense of the world, in its literal as much as in its figurative meanings. From early on, for example, he came to believe that, whether consciously or not, black mobilization in the United States owed much to the struggle for African emancipation. Referring in 1960 to the emerging generation of militants, he noted that they had been "born at the very moment at which Europe's domination of Africa was ending," which itself had released new political energies across the Atlantic.[68] Indeed, he understood the radicalism of the students to have derived from their conviction that the entire racial order, across the globe, was on the point of transformation. This supposition is most fully spelled out in his 1961 political assessment of Martin Luther King. Here Baldwin, as ever, showed King a deep respect, but at the same time he sought to highlight the dilemmas that he faced. King, he argued, was stranded between the traditional forces of black reform—he named the National Association for the Advancement of Colored People (NAACP)—and those of the younger insurgents. While the former were incapable of grasping "what is happening in the world at large," the latter were instinctively more attuned to the fact that "the myth of white supremacy is exploding all over the world, from the Congo to New Orleans."[69] The sense of this profound historical change, both in America and beyond, gave to the students, Baldwin insisted, political insight and courage that was not shared by their elders. And King, he concluded, had yet to make his choice.

Baldwin was always alive to the complex interconnections that underwrote Europe and America. In his earliest formulations he believed that Europe offered the promise of overcoming "the alienation of the American from himself," as he himself had discovered in Paris. Yet this discovery, he maintained, was based on the realization that the self did not function as Americans, in their "confusion," thought it did. Of necessity the expatriate American learned the value of the world, of history.

> If the American found in Europe only confusion it would obviously be infinitely wiser for him to remain at home. Hidden, however, in the heart of the confusion he encounters here is that which he came so blindly seeking: the terms on which he is related to his country and to the world. This, which has so grandiose and general a ring, is, in fact, most personal—the American confusion seeming to be based on the very nearly unconscious assumption that it is possible to consider the person apart from all the forces which have produced him.[70]

By the time of *No Name in the Street*, his emphasis on American exceptionalism had diminished—as a number of the chapters that follow demonstrate—and he was more inclined to understand "the American crisis" as a manifestation of what he came to identify as the "global, historical crisis" in an entire racial order.[71] As in his strictures against the NAACP, the touchstone for his radicalism turned on the conviction that Americans involved in their domestic struggles needed to grasp the properly historical determinants that confronted them. In part, this necessitated thinking beyond the categories prescribed by an American parochialism. And in part, also, it meant conceiving of history not only as an external force, but as a process internalized deep in the self. "People are trapped in history," he had commented many years earlier, "and history is trapped in them."[72]

The Locations of James Baldwin

Baldwin's prose has an impressive mobility. It strives to disengage from the systems of falsehood—the national myth-making, the innocence, the disavowals, the bad faith—that he believed had been created by the American drive for civilization and then turns back on itself, sneaking up close to these very falsehoods in order to expose them or undermine them or, with knowing laughter, to ridicule their banalities. The prose itself is restless, as if even a momentary immobility would provide the opportunity for thought to stop and for the American "confusion" to insinuate itself and take control. This required of him that he simultaneously occupy different locations—different subject positions—standing both inside and outside the American "house." We have described something of this stance earlier, by exploring how the interconnections arose in his mind between the end of European colonialism and the struggle for U.S. civil rights. A parallel theme is addressed in a number of the chapters in this volume, which bring to light Baldwin's efforts to free himself from the orthodoxies of Cold War thought.[73] In his early writings, as we've suggested, the principal counterpoint by which he could imagine America was Europe, or even on occasion simply Paris, which served to signify the larger continent. But as his writing evolved, and his own travels became more extensive, this initial dualism began to unravel, and the counterpoints to America multiplied.

The substantive contributions to *America and Beyond* track this story, in its many variables. The new research into Baldwin's years in Istanbul, for example, evident in Magdalena Zaborowska's chapter here and in her longer study *James Baldwin's Turkish Decade*, clearly shows this process at work. In the latter part of 1961 Baldwin was in Israel, confronting a strange mix of ancestral biblical memory, on the one hand, and the contemporary political divide between Jew and Arab, on the other. Due to travel from Israel to Africa, at the last moment he changed his mind and took a flight to Istanbul, taking up a long-standing invitation from his old friend Engin

Cezzar. This was to be the first of a succession of visits. Although Turkey presented no political idyll, Baldwin discovered that in Istanbul the sexual and racial norms of the city didn't possess the gravity they held for him in the United States. A largely Islamic nation straddling Europe and Asia, Turkey called into question the very idea of Europe itself. It constituted for him something of a "third place"—neither America nor quite Europe—from which he could look, as if from the outside, on the civilizations that had formed him.[74]

Much the same could be said, although in a different register, about Baldwin's relations to Africa, which he first came to visit in the summer of 1962. Douglas Field, and from a different vantage Eleanor Traylor, both address this issue. As we've seen, Baldwin was characteristically unsentimental about the version of Afrocentrism embraced by Senghor at the First Negro Writers and Artists Congress in 1956. But politically, as we have also seen, he was certain that the struggle for African freedom had exerted a powerful influence on the new black radicalism in the United States. The "American Negro," he declared in 1961, "can no longer, nor will he ever again, be controlled by white America's image of him. This fact has everything to do with the rise of Africa in world affairs."[75] In the sixties he was a consistent advocate for African independence, and by the end of the decade he was as likely to be dwelling upon the shared predicament of blacks in the New World and in Africa as upon their differences.

But as Field demonstrates, recovering a poignant moment in Baldwin's life, this was an identification that could only become effective as a consequence of sustained intellectual labor. In the last year of his life Baldwin was questioned about an exhibition of African art that had just opened. He expressed an empathy for the artifacts he had seen, though he found it difficult to enlist an appropriate conceptual language in which this could be communicated. He could attest to the power of his "recognition," and to the significance of what he saw, but could say little more: "I'm not sure I can articulate it. I'm also very weary, weary, weary of trying to deal with this."[76] This incapacity to articulate Baldwin experienced as a kind of personal defeat. Although readier to concede the common predicament of blacks in the United States and blacks in Africa than he had been in the fifties, he nonetheless insisted that Africa could only ever become meaningful for African Americans through the work of intellectual transformation, particularly through a practice of translation.[77] Without this work of translation, the idea of Africa could only ever remain an abstraction, an axiom that lay at the root of his contention with Senghor in 1956.

In a complex, evolving palimpsest, Baldwin's experiences of one location folded into his visions of other locations, allowing delicate counterpoints of meaning to accumulate. "If I had not lived in France for so long," he once claimed, "I would have never found it necessary—or possible—to visit the American South."[78] And as Kevin Birmingham shows in his discussion of Baldwin's long preoccupation with the question of diasporic and ancestral memories, his conception of Africa came to be reworked as a consequence of his understanding of Israel, while both—Africa and Israel—occupy, half concealed, the subtext of *The Fire Next Time*, notwithstanding the American focus of his text.[79] Baldwin's skepticism about the virtues of a unilateral diasporic memory—embodied in different modes, as he saw it, in the philosophies of negritude, in Zionism, in the Nation of Islam—largely derived from these understandings of the contingencies of location.

In the early 1970s Baldwin was asked by the journal *Black Scholar* for his thoughts on black militancy. In a reply that probably elicited little enthusiasm on the part of his interlocutors, he responded with the observation that "it's a series of parentheses and it cannot be answered, you know."[80] "A series of parentheses": the phrase is characteristic of Baldwin's temperamental commitment to indirection, refusing not the goal of emancipation, but the means by which it was to be achieved. A little while earlier, when the *New York Post* upbraided him for spending much of his time in Istanbul, he replied—in a tone that may sound rather similar—that this was a matter of "preparation, not flight."[81] Baldwin was not one to be made anxious by the many detours he followed. "Preparation," though, signals a rather different phenomenon. It suggests that he conceived his travels, not simply in their own terms, but critically in relation to the place of his return. And for Baldwin the place of his return—as much as the point of his departure—always remained America.

Briallen Hopper's chapter on Baldwin's lifelong responses to *Uncle Tom's Cabin*, which he took to be *the* American story, gives a sharp sense of the compulsive force of this identification with his native land.[82] The "hysteria" of America inevitably pulled him in, even in the moments he fled. "The great wound" of his nation touched all its citizens.[83] Grief and desire were inextricably bound together. In St. Paul-de-Vence, in the final moments of his life, he asked that his friend David Leeming bring with him from America "Aunt Jemima pancake mix, Aunt Jemima syrup, Brer Rabbit molasses, and some jelly beans," a diet that didn't serve his digestive system well, causing him to utter the wry comment that "we can't escape our culture."[84] But for Baldwin it was not in this culture, nor in any other culture, that the salvation of the nation lay. It was, more properly, in politics: "The one thing that all Americans have in common is that they have no other identity apart from the identity which is being achieved on this continent. . . . The necessity of Americans to achieve an identity is a historical and a present personal fact and this is the connection between you and me."[85]

Ultimately "the connection between you and me" was a relation that yet had to be fashioned, and it was in that fashioning that he imagined the future of America. The conjunction is, again, symptomatic: between the self and the world; between you and me; between America and beyond.

Language and Form

It is in the end, of course, Baldwin's prose that we possess. Toni Morrison, in her eloquent tribute, identified his legacy as nothing less than a revolution in language, "spoken as well as written": he had "made American English honest—truly international." He had "decolonized" the language, "exposed its secrets and reshaped it until it was truly modern dialogic, representative, humane." More particularly, Morrison observes, in liberating the language from the hegemony of white America, he had "un-gated" English "for black people so that in . . . [his] . . . wake we could enter it, occupy it, restructure it." In Morrison's terms Baldwin's reshaping of "American English" cannot be separated from its ethical and political content.[86] In the view of Colm Tóibín, Baldwin was forthcoming about the syncretic sources of his prose style, characterizing it as Ray Charles and Miles Davis meeting Henry James or, offering a rather different take, "as in the list he provided in *Notes of a Native Son:* 'The King James Bible, the rhetoric of the store-front church, something ironic and violent and perpetually understated in Negro speech—and something of Dickens's love for bravura.'" Tóibín believes too that the styles of American novelists of the previous generation, especially Fitzgerald and Hemingway, are in the mix also, embedded in syntax and vocabulary, in spite of Baldwin's declared rejection of their influence.[87]

Tóibín's essay in this collection highlights these elements of Baldwin's style as they appear in the three early novels and in the short stories, the most enduring and the most highly crafted of his fictional oeuvre. Cheryl Wall traces them through the essay, the genre that Baldwin made his own and that is one of his most important gifts to future writers. Flexible and idiosyncratic, able to contain polemic, autobiography, observation, the essay has been, Wall suggests, an accommodating, liberating, and liberated genre for African Americans, allowing the "traditions of nineteenth-century oratory" and the "autobiographical impulse of the slave narrative" to find a new form.[88] Provocatively, but with an almost effortless ease, the essay in Baldwin's hands moves between time and place and between the autobiographical and the public/political event; it is his particular strength that the personal or private is always a route to, or exemplary of, a larger political point, while remaining absolutely idiosyncratic.

Baldwin's essays and his fiction are complementary and interpenetrating genres. The essays are, Wall points out, full of stories, and as Briallen Hopper shows in relation to that touchstone text for Baldwin, *Uncle Tom's Cabin*, certain figures and tropes move through and between them. Tóibín argues that "Baldwin understood the singular importance of the novel in America because he saw the dilemma his country faced as essentially an interior one," and fiction allowed him "a new freedom . . . to create characters as he pleased"—gay, white, black.[89] In the essay, as in his fiction, thoughts follow a reflective logic: metonymic, associative, they are structured through a rhetoric of feeling, for which "love," not as a "sentimental" emotion, but as a "battle," "a war," a difficult détente and uncertain peace, is a crucial element of what it is to be truly human—or as Baldwin often says, "a man," and always imperiled. "Innocence," often applied by Baldwin to America and Americans, is, as George Shulman says, always ironized as it was for Henry James, a dangerous condition for persons, races, or nations. Equally key and equally dangerous are the historic and present "disavowal" and "denial" of racism and of sexuality and of history itself, for these lead inexorably to violent projections on to oppressed others. History, for Baldwin, is not "merely or even principally" a reference "to the past." Rather, "the great force of history comes from the fact that we carry it within us, are unconsciously controlled by it in many ways, so history is literally *present* in all that we do."[90] Although he was no friend to psychoanalysis, the operations of the psyche are constitutive for Baldwin in thinking about what Jacqueline Rose, in her work on the oppressive operations of race in South Africa and in Israel, has called "states of fantasy."[91] These psychic tools of domination are defined and described in his political essays and dramatized in his fiction and plays. Affect is not, for Baldwin, at odds with reason—instead the feeling-self is taken seriously as indispensable to a proper, humane, and truthful rationality.

Baldwin had, at least initially, "never thought of" himself "as an essayist," but the capaciousness and freedom of the form itself gave him, as Wall indicates, "intellectual freedom—the freedom to work around, with, and through an idea." That work, Wall notes, takes longer, became "looser" and more digressive—as well as angrier and more despairing—as time went on. If *The Fire Next Time* issued a biblical warning to America, it also made a claim, with some hope, that it might be met and catastrophe averted. By *No Name in the Street*, in 1972, his tone was much more pessimistic, and as several of our contributors indicate, the cautious optimism for a regeneration of the whole American community, for the transformation of white Americans by themselves, comes to be eroded as his prophetic voice shifts from Jeremiah to Job. Yet even at his bleakest there is a kernel of hope born of pain and resistance. Wall argues that giving up the idea, too closely allied with Cold War philosophy, of what she calls "strategic American essentialism" led Baldwin toward a more mature and fully cosmopolitan understanding of America's predicament, while George Shulman argues that Baldwin's interpretation of America rested on the conviction that a "democratically authorized racial domination" constituted the nation's "regime of liberal nationalism." "Through him," Shulman writes, "we confront a modernity neither white nor secular, and we can thereby reimagine the meaning and making of a 'countermodernity,'" but to do so Baldwin insists that the "*unspeakable*" become audible and legible.[92]

In an article for the *New York Times* written in 1979, "If Black English Isn't a Language, Then Tell Me, What Is?"—a piece whose premise is the "brutal truth . . . that the bulk of the white people in American never had any interest in educating black people, except as this could serve white purposes"—Baldwin argues that "*a language comes into existence by means of brutal necessity, and the rules of the language are dictated by what the language must convey.*" We might say that Baldwin's use of language and literary form is also dictated by such brutalities, such necessity, but that it results in an expressive freedom that offers politically imaginative mapping—a cognitive and moral mapping of the conditions of a larger international freedom. It followed, for him, that American blacks are speaking a language and not a "dialect" and speaking fluently: they are "not inarticulate because we are not compelled to defend a morality that we know to be a lie."[93]

A year later, in the penultimate moment of his essay "Dark Days," he described a racially mixed class he was teaching when the question from a white student—"Why does the white hate the nigger?"—developed into "exchanges" that "were sharp and remarkably candid, but never fogged by an unadmitted fear or hostility. They were trying to become whole. They were trying to put themselves and their country back together." The conversation takes off between the students, with Baldwin only as a "benign adult presence," and it is a scene that strives toward a possible democratic future, a productive dialogue, but the conclusion, applicable "all over the world," brackets these possibilities: "Whatever it is that white Americans want, it is not freedom—neither for themselves nor for others."[94] The oscillation and conversation between this hopeful vignette and its bleak and damning dramatization might describe, in small, the dialectic of Baldwin's lifelong political and literary enterprise, as it runs through every genre he tackled.

NOTES

1. George Shulman discusses this aspect of Baldwin more fully in chapter 5 of this volume, "Baldwin, Prophecy, and Politics."
2. Bloch, *Strange Defeat*, 118.
3. Gaines, "Closing Plenary Panel," James Baldwin: Work, Life, Legacies, 28–30 June, 2007. What this may mean, and the complexities involved, are addressed by Robert Reid-Pharr in chapter 6 of this volume, "Rendezvous with Life."
4. McBride, "Introduction," 8–9.
5. Particularly King and Scott, *James Baldwin and Toni Morrison* (2006); Reid-Pharr, *Once You Go Black* (2007); Norman, *American Protest Essay* (2007); and Shulman, *American Prophecy* (2008).
6. And see the long response in the *New Yorker* to Zaborowska's monograph: Pierpoint, "Another Country."
7. "The Henry James of Harlem" in the *London Review of Books* (2001) and "James Baldwin and Barack Obama" in the *New York Review of Books* (2008).
8. Miller, *Re-Viewing James Baldwin*, argues for the creative importance of the later, relatively neglected works. Leeming, in "Foreword," cites *Blues for Mr Charlie* (1964) and "Going to Meet the Man" (1965) as the key, discomforting texts that first seriously began to undermine Baldwin's reputation. He might well have included Baldwin and Avedon, *Nothing Personal* (1964).
9. Decisive in this context is McBride, *James Baldwin Now*.
10. Part 1 of Baldwin, *Nobody Knows My Name*, is titled "Sitting in the House." The image is repeated throughout his writings.
11. Baldwin, "Notes of a Native Son," 75.
12. Baldwin, *Fire Next Time*, 32–33.
13. Wall, "Stranger at Home," in this volume.
14. Baldwin, "Introduction," 12–13. This is a formulation that—as Kevin Gaines argues later in this volume—echoes the title, and indeed the sentiments, of George Lamming's address at the 1956 First Negro Writers and Artists Congress, which Baldwin writes about later in *Nobody Knows My Name* (44–46) (Lamming, "Negro Writer and His World").
15. Baldwin, "Introduction,"13.
16. By America, Baldwin usually meant not only the United States but the white population of the United States. We have tended to follow this usage.

17. And formative in unexpected ways, as D. Quentin Miller demonstrates in relation to Baldwin's time in Paris. See "Separate and Unequal in Paris," chapter 8 of this volume.

18. And allowing others who followed to inhabit his "house." As Toni Morrison said of Baldwin, addressing him directly, "You gave me a language to dwell in" ("Life in His Language," 76).

19. For important recent discussions see Darsey, "Baldwin's Cosmopolitan Loneliness," M. Wright, "'Alas, Poor Richard,'" and Ferguson, "The Parvenu Baldwin," all in the section entitled "Baldwin and the Transatlantic" in McBride, *Baldwin Now;* and Zaborowska, *James Baldwin's Turkish Decade.*

20. Hannah Arendt, for one, was not persuaded. After the publication of *The Fire Next Time,* she informed Baldwin in a personal letter that "in politics, love is a stranger." Our own sense, however, is that she ascribed to Baldwin a sentimentalism that was far from accurate. See Campbell, *Talking at the Gates,* 162.

21. Baldwin, "In Search of a Majority," 113. Or as the closing words of Baldwin's story "The Outing" articulate this view: "After a moment Johnnie moved and put his head on David's shoulder. David put his arms around him. But now where they had been peace there was only panic and where there had been safety, danger, like a flower, opened" (54). Also see Shulman, "Baldwin, Prophecy, and Politics," in this volume.

22. And in terms of the themes of this volume, see Drowne, "'An Irrevocable Condition.'"

23. However, projections such as these were rarely constant in Baldwin's mind. Later in his writing life Baldwin could put what appears to be the contrary case. See *Devil Finds Work,* 509–10.

24. Baldwin, MacInnes, and Mossman, "Race, Hate, Sex and Colour," 60.

25. Ross, "White Fantasies of Desire."

26. Baldwin, "'Go the Way Your Blood Beats,'" 186.

27. Baldwin, "'Go the Way Your Blood Beats,'" 178.

28. Ibid., 180.

29. Ibid., 175, 181, 183.

30. Ibid., 175.

31. Ibid., 184.

32. Ibid., 176.

33. Baldwin, "Dark Days," 792.

34. Baldwin, "American Dream and the American Negro," 714.

35. Baldwin, "Discovery of What It Means to Be an American," 19.

36. Leeming, "Me and My House." The title that Leeming took for his talk was the original title of Baldwin's essay "Notes of a Native Son."

37. Darsey, in "Baldwin's Cosmopolitan Loneliness," argues in much the same manner, proposing that when we read Baldwin we always hold in mind the connections between *topos* and *ethos* (191).

38. Baldwin, "Discovery of What It Means to Be An American," 17.

39. Baldwin, "Princes and Powers," 35.

40. Baldwin, "Black Boy Looks at the White Boy," 183.

41. Baldwin, "Discovery of What It Means to Be an American," 22.

42. Baldwin, "Introduction," 12, 13; Baldwin, "Discovery of What It Means to Be an American," 17.

43. Baldwin, "Fly in the Buttermilk," 75.

44. Baldwin, "Discovery of What It Means to Be an American," 17. Baldwin provided many different riffs on this basic story. Earlier: "From the vantage point of Europe he [the American student in Paris] discovers his own country. And this is a discovery which not only brings to an end the alienation of the American from himself, but also makes clear to him, for the first time, the extent of his involvement in the life of Europe" ("Question of Identity," 116). And later: "I became an American in a foreign country because I was not anything else" (Baldwin and Mead, *Rap on Race*, 95).

45. Baldwin and Mead, *Rap on Race*, 47. He goes on to suggest that this "odyssey," in its various forms, underwrites more generally the emergence of black writing of his generation in the United States.

46. Cited in Norman, *American Protest Essay*, 91. Baldwin preceded this by claiming that the job of the writer was to "speak out about the world."

47. Baldwin, "Stranger in the Village," 149.

48. Ibid., 148. Baldwin, in this respect, was representative of a strand of black U.S. radicals who saw their own struggles in Atlantic terms: see von Eschen, *Race against Empire*.

49. Baldwin arrived in Paris in November 1948. It was earlier that year, in February, that Dizzy Gillespie made his historic tour of Europe, which included Paris. When in April 1952 Baldwin returned to New York, he discovered that sailing on the same boat was Gillespie, "with whom he spent hours at the bar talking" (Leeming, *James Baldwin*, 80).

50. Macey, "Fanon, Phenomenology, Race," 35. But for an incisive discussion of the contradictory legacies of existentialism, see Reid-Pharr, *Once You Go Black*.

51. For the prehistory see Edwards, *Practice of Diaspora*.

52. Gikandi, "Response."

53. Baldwin, "Princes and Powers," 24. For Wright in Europe see Gilroy, *Black Atlantic*. And just as French thought entered Baldwin's mind, so Baldwin became part of French intellectual life: see Bobia, *Critical Reception of James Baldwin in France*.

54. This story can be followed in Stovall, *Paris Noir*; and in Fabre, "Paris as a Moment."

55. The contrast to the postwar intellectual life of London, for example, is striking.

56. In retrospective accounts Baldwin was in the habit of distancing himself from the modishness of the Parisian existentialism of these years: "Alas, Poor Richard," 148; *No Name in the Street*, 44; *Devil Finds Work*, 506.

57. Cited by Baldwin, "Princes and Powers," 25. And see Kevin Gaines, "Exile and the Private Life," chapter 9 in this volume, and Kevin Birmingham, "'History's Ass Pocket," chapter 7 in this volume, both of which think through Baldwin's formal political experiences through the prism of private life.

58. In fact, Senghor's advocacy of Africa was untypical of many of those with whom he (Senghor) associated and presented something of a smoke screen, for

Francophone negritude and Anglophone Pan-Africanism were largely West Indian constructs, carrying the imprint of an imaginary, New World idea of Africa. Césaire, for example, came to negritude by way of the writings of the Harlem renaissance. Baldwin's connection to the Caribbean diaspora deserves a chapter in its own right. As he was growing up, the Caribbean elements in Harlem life were significant. More particularly, in regard to Baldwin's intellectual and political commitments, a key moment occurred in 1943, when he started frequenting the Calypso café on MacDougal Street in Greenwich Village, owned by the Trinidadian Connie Williams. One authority suggests that it was here that C. L. R. James "told Baldwin about Trotskyism" (Young, *World of C. L. R. James*, 172). In a 1969 talk at the West Indian Student's Centre in London, Baldwin reflected on the historical connections between the Caribbean and Harlem: see Horace Ové's film of the lecture, *Baldwin's Nigger* (1969), rereleased by the British Film Institute in 2005.

59. Baldwin, "Princes and Powers," 40–44. This report should be read alongside Richard Wright's important reflections on the end of the European colonial epoch: *Black Power* (1954), *The Color Curtain* (1956), and *White Man, Listen!* (1964), all recently republished in a single volume, *Black Power*. Wright spoke at the end of the Paris Congress, noting that it had marked "the beginning of the end of European domination" over the colonial world (cited in "Princes and Powers," 54).

60. This image provided the title for Horace Porter's 1989 study of Baldwin, *Stealing the Fire*.

61. See especially Césaire's *Discourse on Colonialism*, first published in 1955. In 1961 Baldwin stated that "it is the failure of the moral imagination of Europe which had created the forces now determined to overthrow it." He went on, "It was not dreamed, during the Second World War, that Churchill's ringing words to the English were overheard by English slaves—who, now, coming in their thousands to the mainland, menace the English sleep" ("Alas, Poor Richard," 169).

62. Baldwin, "Discovery of What It Means to Be an American," 21–22.

63. The movement of a political life separates these two accounts. Even so, it's worth reminding readers that the latter carries the imprint of Vietnam and to mention as well, as Baldwin himself does, that in the period between his writing these different versions he had the opportunity to visit the former French colonies of Guinea and Senegal and to see firsthand the consequences of colonial rule. We're drawing here from Baldwin, *No Name in the Street*, 23–29, 36–43.

64. Ibid., 25.

65. Ibid., 28.

66. Systematic murder of Algerians by the police did indeed take place, on a large scale, the most notorious occasion occurring shortly before Baldwin returned to Paris in the autumn of 1961. See House and MacMaster, *Paris 1961*. And for contemporaneous corroboration of Baldwin's perceptions, from an earlier moment, see Moscat and Péju, "Du colonialisme au racisme," published in *Les temps modernes* in 1952. In the six years between 1946 and 1952 some four hundred thousand North African migrants arrived in France.

67. Baldwin, *No Name in the Street*, 41. Nevertheless, it is important to grasp how many of these themes were anticipated in his 1960 story "This Morning, This Evening, So Soon."

68. Baldwin, "They Can't Turn Back," 637.

69. Baldwin, "Dangerous Road before Martin Luther King," 656–57. In July 1961, when he appeared on Studs Terkel's radio show in Chicago, he was at pains to spell out the interconnections between U.S. civil rights and the breakup of the old colonial world (Leeming, *James Baldwin*, 187).

70. Baldwin, "Question of Identity," 116, 115.

71. Baldwin, *No Name in the Street*, 196.

72. Baldwin, "Stranger in the Village," 138.

73. Most of all, see Vaughn Rasberry, "'Now Describing You,'" chapter 4 in this volume, which uncovers the connections between anticolonialism, civil rights, and the Cold War. See too Ferguson, "Parvenu Baldwin," and the influential studies by Borstelmann, *Cold War and the Color Line*, and Dudziak, *Cold War Civil Rights*.

74. In Zaborowska's monograph there is a wonderful snapshot, taken in 1965, showing Baldwin in a cheap café on the waterfront in Istanbul. He is sitting at a tiled counter, a slight, casually dressed figure, his face turned away from the camera, paying attention to the small basket of bread in front of him. Sitting nearby, and looking at him, is what appears to be an older man, wearing a traditional dark suit and cloth cap. Outside through the windows above the counter one can see the ferries plying the waters. Directly above Baldwin is a naked lightbulb. To its left is a large, formal, framed portrait of Kemal Atatürk, Turkey's great modern nation-maker, wearing the attire of an Edwardian statesman, the kind of portrait that still adorns many such bars and cafés. To the right, at a bizarre angle, is an equally formal, equally large portrait of J. F. Kennedy. Baldwin, the smaller figure, is placed between the two. The dynamic of the photograph derives from the fact that neither Baldwin nor his neighbor seems to notice the icons just above their heads: these are no more than abstractions, symptomatic of the "totems, taboos, crosses, blood sacrifices, steeples, mosques, races, armies, flags, nations" that he decried in *The Fire Next Time* as forces that "imprison" the human imagination. See Zaborowska, *James Baldwin's Turkish Decade*, 30; Baldwin, *Fire Next Time*, 79. It is significant that *The Fire Next Time*, which so evocatively recounts Baldwin's encounter with Islam in the United States, was largely drafted in Istanbul.

75. Baldwin, "East River Downtown," 72. He goes on to say that for the new generation of blacks in the United States, "the power of the white world to control their identities was crumbling as they were born; and by the time they were able to react to the world, Africa was on the stage of history" (73).

76. Field, "What Is Africa to Baldwin?" chapter 11 in this volume.

77. Baldwin pursues this idea most emphatically in Baldwin and Mead, *Rap on Race*.

78. Baldwin, "Fly in the Buttermilk," 75. See too Baldwin, "Discovery of What It Means to Be an American," 21–22.

79. Birmingham, "'History's Ass Pocket,'" chapter 7 in this volume.

80. Cited in Norman, *American Protest Essay*, 95.

81. Cited in Zaborowska, *Baldwin's Turkish Decade*, 25.

82. Hopper, "'Over and Over and Over Again,'" chapter 3 of this volume.

83. Baldwin and Mead, *Rap on Race*, 9.

84. Leeming, *James Baldwin*, 380.

85. Baldwin, "In Search of a Majority," 114.
86. Morrison, "Life in His Language," 76.
87. Tóibín, "Baldwin and 'the American Confusion,'" chapter 2 of this volume.
88. Wall, "Stranger at Home," chapter 1 in this volume.
89. Tóibín, "Baldwin and 'the American Confusion,'" in this volume.
90. Baldwin, "White Man's Guilt," 410.
91. Rose, *States of Fantasy.*
92. Wall, "Stranger at Home," chapter 1 in this volume; Shulman, "Baldwin, Prophecy, and Politics," chapter 5 in this volume.
93. Baldwin, "If Black English Isn't a Language, Then Tell Me, What Is?" 783, 782, emphasis in the original.
94. Baldwin, "Dark Days," 797–98.

BIBLIOGRAPHY

Baldwin, James. "The American Dream and the American Negro." In *Collected Essays.*
Baldwin, James. "The Black Boy Looks at the White Boy." In *Nobody Knows My Name.*
Baldwin, James. *Blues for Mr Charlie.* London: Corgi, 1972.
Baldwin, James. *Collected Essays.* Ed. Toni Morrison. New York: Library of America, 1998.
Baldwin, James. "The Dangerous Road before Martin Luther King." In *Collected Essays.*
Baldwin, James. "Dark Days." In *Collected Essays.*
Baldwin, James. *The Devil Finds Work.* In *Collected Essays.*
Baldwin, James. "The Discovery of What It Means to Be an American." In *Nobody Knows My Name.*
Baldwin, James. "East River Downtown: Postscript to a Letter from Harlem." In *Nobody Knows My Name.*
Baldwin, James. *The Fire Next Time.* Harmondsworth: Penguin, 1964.
Baldwin, James. "A Fly in the Buttermilk." In *Nobody Knows My Name.*
Baldwin, James. "Going to Meet the Man." In *Going to Meet the Man.*
Baldwin, James. *Going to Meet the Man.* London: Penguin, 1991.
Baldwin, James. "If Black English Isn't a Language, Then Tell Me, What Is?" In *Collected Essays.*
Baldwin, James. "In Search of a Majority." In *Nobody Knows My Name.*
Baldwin, James. "Introduction." In *Nobody Knows My Name.*
Baldwin, James. *Nobody Knows My Name: More Notes of a Native Son.* New York: Dell, n.d.
Baldwin, James. *No Name in the Street.* In *Collected Essays.*
Baldwin, James. "Notes of a Native Son." In *Notes of a Native Son.*
Baldwin, James. *Notes of a Native Son.* London: Corgi, 1969.
Baldwin, James. "The Outing." In *Going to Meet the Man.*
Baldwin, James. "Princes and Powers." In *Nobody Knows My Name.*

Baldwin, James. "A Question of Identity." In *Nobody Knows My Name.*
Baldwin, James. "Stranger in the Village." In *Notes of a Native Son.*
Baldwin, James. "They Can't Turn Back." In *Collected Essays.*
Baldwin, James. "This Morning, This Evening, So Soon." In *Going to Meet the Man.*
Baldwin, James. "White Man's Guilt." In *The Price of the Ticket: Collected Nonfiction, 1948–1985.* New York: St. Martin's, 1985.
Baldwin, James, and Richard Avedon. *Nothing Personal.* Harmondsworth: Penguin, 1964.
Baldwin, James, Colin MacInnes, and James Mossman. "Race, Hate, Sex and Colour." *Encounter,* July 25, 1965.
Baldwin, James, and Margaret Mead. *A Rap on Race.* London: Corgi, 1972.
Bloch, Marc. *Strange Defeat: A Statement of Evidence Written in 1940.* New York: Norton, 1999.
Bobia, Rosa. *The Critical Reception of James Baldwin in France.* New York: Peter Lang, 1997.
Borstelmann, Thomas. *The Cold War and the Color Line: American Race Relations in the Global Arena.* Cambridge: Harvard University Press, 2002.
Campbell, James. *Talking at the Gates: A Life of James Baldwin.* London: Faber and Faber, 1991.
Césaire, Aimé. *Discourse on Colonialism.* New York: Monthly Review Press, 1972.
Darsey, James. "Baldwin's Cosmopolitan Loneliness." In McBride, *James Baldwin Now.*
Drowne, Kathleen. "'An Irrevocable Condition': Constructions of Home and the Writing of Place in *Giovanni's Room.*" In McBride, *James Baldwin Now.*
Dudziak, Mary L. *Cold War Civil Rights: Race and the Image of American Democracy.* Princeton: Princeton University Press, 2000.
Edwards, Brent Hayes. *The Practice of Diaspora: Literature, Translation, and the Rise of Black Internationalism.* Cambridge: Harvard University Press, 2003.
Fabre, Michel. "Paris as a Moment in African Consciousness." In Werner Sollers and Maria Diedrich, eds., *Black Columbiad: Defining Moments in African American Literature and Culture.* Cambridge: Harvard University Press, 1994.
Ferguson, Roderick A. "The Parvenu Baldwin and the Other Side of Redemption: Modernity, Race, Sexuality and the Cold War." In McBride, *James Baldwin Now.*
Field, Douglas, ed. *Historical Guide to James Baldwin.* New York: Oxford University Press, 2009.
Gaines, Kevin. "Closing Plenary Panel." Paper presented at James Baldwin: Work, Life, Legacies. Queen Mary, University of London, June 2007.
Gikandi, Simon. "Response to Bill Schwarz." Paper presented at George Lamming and the Measure of Historical Time. Center for Afro-American and African Studies, University of Michigan, October 2002.
Gilroy, Paul. *The Black Atlantic: Modernity and Double Consciousness.* London: Verso, 1993.
Goldstein, Richard. "'Go the Way Your Blood Beats': An Interview with James Baldwin." In Troupe, *James Baldwin: The Legacy.*

House, Jim, and Neil MacMaster. *Paris 1961: Algerians, State Terror, and Memory.* Oxford: Oxford University Press, 2006.

King, Lovalerie, and Lynn Orilla Scott, eds. *James Baldwin and Toni Morrison: Comparative Critical and Theoretical Essays.* New York: Palgrave Macmillan, 2006.

Lamming, George. "The Negro Writer and His World." *Présence africaine*, nos. 8–10 (June–November 1956).

Leeming, David. "Foreword." In D. Quentin Miller, ed., *Re-Viewing James Baldwin: Things Not Seen.* Philadelphia: Temple University Press, 2000.

Leeming, David. *James Baldwin: A Biography.* London, Penguin, 1995.

Leeming, David. "Me and My House." Opening plenary presented at James Baldwin: In His Time/In Our Time. Suffolk University, March 2009.

Macey, David. "Fanon, Phenomenology, Race." In Peter Osborne and Stella Sandford, eds., *Philosophies of Race and Ethnicity.* London: Continuum, 2002.

McBride, Dwight A. "Introduction." In McBride, *James Baldwin Now.*

McBride, Dwight A., ed. *James Baldwin Now.* New York: New York University Press, 1999.

Miller, D. Quentin, ed. *Re-Viewing James Baldwin: Things Not Seen.* Philadelphia: Temple University Press, 2000.

Morrison, Toni. "Life in His Language." In Troupe, *James Baldwin: The Legacy.*

Moscat, Henri, and Marcel Péju. "Du colonialisme au racisme: Les Nord-africains dans le Métropole." *Les temps modernes* 8, no. 83 (1952).

Norman, Brian. *The American Protest Essay and National Belonging.* New York: State University of New York Press, 2007.

Pierpoint, Claudia Ruth. "Another Country: James Baldwin's Flight from America." *New Yorker*, February 9, 2009.

Porter, Horace A. *Stealing the Fire: The Art and Protest of James Baldwin.* Middleton: Wesleyan University Press, 1989.

Reid-Pharr, Robert. *Once You Go Black: Choice, Desire and the Black American Intellectual.* New York: New York University Press, 2007.

Rose, Jacqueline. *States of Fantasy.* Oxford: Clarendon Press, 1996.

Ross, Marlon B. "White Fantasies of Desire: Baldwin and the Racial Identities of Sexuality." In McBride, *James Baldwin Now.*

Shulman, George. *American Prophecy: Race and Redemption in American Political Culture.* Minneapolis: University of Minnesota Press, 2008.

Stovall, Tyler. *Paris Noir: African Americans in the City of Light.* Boston: Houghton Mifflin, 1996.

Tóibín, Colm. "The Henry James of Harlem: James Baldwin's Struggles." *London Review of Books*, September 24, 2001.

Tóibín, Colm. "James Baldwin and Barack Obama." *New York Review of Books*, October 23, 2008.

Troupe, Quincy, ed. *James Baldwin: The Legacy.* New York: Simon and Schuster, 1989.

Von Eschen, Penny M. *Race against Empire: Black Americans and Anticolonialism, 1937–1957.* Ithaca: Cornell University Press, 1997.

Wright, Michelle M. "'Alas, Poor Richard!' Transatlantic Baldwin, the Politics of Forgetting, and the Project of Modernity." In McBride, *James Baldwin Now.*

Wright, Richard. *Black Power. Three Books from Exile: "Black Power"; "The Color Curtain"; and "White Man, Listen!"* New York: Harper Perennial, 2008.
Young, James. *The World of C. L. R. James: The Unfragmented Vision.* Glasgow: Clydeside Press, 1999.
Zaborowska, Magdalena J. *James Baldwin's Turkish Decade: The Erotics of Exile.* Durham: Duke University Press, 2009.

PART ONE

What It Means to Be an American

ONE

Stranger at Home

James Baldwin on What It Means to Be an American

CHERYL A. WALL

> "It is a complex fate to be an American," Henry James observed, and the principal discovery an American writer makes in Europe is just how complex this fate is. America's history, her aspirations, her peculiar triumphs, her even more peculiar defeats, and her position in the world—yesterday and today—are all so stubbornly profound and stubbornly unique that the very word "America" remains a new, almost completely undefined and extremely controversial proper noun.
>
> —JAMES BALDWIN, "THE DISCOVERY OF WHAT IT MEANS TO BE AN AMERICAN"

> If I had-a my way, I'd tear this building down.
>
> —NEGRO SPIRITUAL

My title alludes of course to two of Baldwin's most famous essays, "Stranger in the Village" and "The Discovery of What It Means to Be an American." In the former, the last essay in *Notes of A Native Son* and one of his most eloquent meditations on identity, Baldwin reflects on a sojourn in a Swiss village where by virtue of phenotype and culture, he is a stranger. Against that white landscape, to the accompaniment of Bessie Smith's blues, he begins to re-create and embrace the life he had known as a child at home. Reflecting on his native land, however, he claims the status of citizen, not stranger. The second allusion is to "The Discovery of What It Means to Be an American," published in the *New York Times Book Review* in 1959 and the lead essay of his second volume, *Nobody Knows My Name.* Baldwin posed the question of what it means to be an American repeatedly across his career. During the 1950s, his answers frequently deploy a rhetorical approach that I call "strategic American exceptionalism." As the first epigraph confirms, despite the fact that he writes always to resist the "myth of America" to which Americans "cling so desperately,"[1] Baldwin's rhetoric could resonate with that of numerous pro-U.S. Cold War intellectuals.

By the time he wrote *No Name in the Street* (1972), Baldwin recognized the error, the futility of adopting this rhetorical strategy. In the aftermath of the assassinations and violence that deflated the dreams of the Civil Rights Movement, Baldwin battled against despair. He struggled to find a new language adequate to the situation. As he so often did, he turned to the repository of the past. Always conscious of the ways that people of the world were dominated by U.S. political and economic power, he records in his essays the process by which that consciousness grew keener as the events of the 1960s played out in Africa and Asia, as well as in the United States. In *No Name in the Street,* he maps some of the journeys he has taken and finds himself, more profoundly than ever before, a stranger at home.

Baldwin's career was launched on the cusp of the Cold War. Its politics necessarily shaped the reception of his work and doubtless the work itself. In and out of the academy, U.S. intellectuals were proposing ever grander versions of the uniqueness of the United States. Such ideas could be traced back to John Winthrop's "city on the hill," through Emerson and Whitman, to scholars Lewis Mumford and F. O. Matthiessen in the 1920s and 1930s. But during the 1950s scholars enshrined the tenet of American exceptionalism in journals, in academic monographs, and in the new discipline of American studies. As Michael Denning has written, "American studies which had taken shape in the early years of the Cold War, had become—despite the intentions of some of its intellectual founders—a part of what might be called 'the American ideology' of the age of three worlds: the deep sense of the exceptionalism of this 'people of plenty,' the unquestioned virtue of democracy and 'the American way of life,' and the sense that the world was entering an American century."[2] I do not quarrel with Denning's observation that in comparison to American studies, British cultural studies, which was a contemporary development, has been more influential, in part because it asked the question "What is culture?" rather than "What is an American?" I would insist, however, that for Baldwin the latter question was productive, not least because, as his characterization of America as "an extremely controversial proper noun" confirms, Baldwin's view of America always implied a critique. His texts of course contravene the representations of Americans as "people of plenty" and dispute the legitimacy of U.S. democracy. Always cosmopolitan, Baldwin answers the question in light of his experiences in a larger world. But he claims the uniqueness of his American identity consciously and with a particular purpose.

What I call Baldwin's strategic American exceptionalism is analogous to what Gayatri Spivak defines in another context as "a *strategic* use of positivist essentialism in a scrupulously visible political interest."[3] That is, like the scholars of subaltern studies who adopt strategic essentialism, Baldwin makes a purposeful and strategic use of American exceptionalism to advance the scrupulously visible political interest of African Americans, indeed, of Americans in general. He adopts this rhetoric partly in order to be heard, but also because it conforms to his belief in the democratic ideals set forth in the founding documents of the United States.

In the tradition of African American intellectuals from the early nineteenth century forward, Baldwin affirms the nation's democratic principles. From David Walker's *Appeal*, to Frederick Douglass in "What to the Slave Is the Fourth of July?", to Anna Julia Cooper's *A Voice from the South*, to Martin Luther King's "Letter from a Birmingham Jail," black activist intellectuals have used the oppression of African Americans to indict and shame a nation whose actions contradict its principles.

Yet while Baldwin extends this genealogy and affirms the democratic ideals enunciated in the letters of the republic, he repudiates in particular the myths and illusions of the American exceptionalism proposed by American studies scholars. In "Nobody Knows My Name," he asserts that the American dream has become the American illusion that material prosperity makes America the envy of the world.[4] He has no use for the myth of the American Adam, who in his innocence takes dominion over all he surveys. He rejects the long-standing dichotomy of American innocence and European experience, by arguing that the failure of his countrymen is the failure to acknowledge the burden of their own bloody history.[5] He mocks the myth of America as a classless society, when he contends that "it is easier to cut across social and occupational lines" in Europe.[6]

What is unique about the United States in Baldwin's view is the presence of black people and the challenge that their presence poses to Americans' sense of the nation and of themselves. This concern does not reflect a provincial point of view. Baldwin was always aware of the connections between Europe and the United States and noted that the principles of democracy of which Americans were so proud were in fact the legacy of European thinkers. The larger question that the American experience raises is whether such a thing as a multiracial democracy is possible. Though he writes in "Stranger in the Village" that "one of the things that distinguishes Americans from other people is that no other people has ever been so deeply involved in the lives of black men and vice versa," the implications were not for Americans alone. He ends the essay with one of his most prophetic declarations—"this world is white no longer, and it will never be white again"—a declaration that foretells not only the emergence of postcolonial nations but the emergence of a multiracial Europe.[7]

Baldwin's strategic American exceptionalism looks beyond the borders of the United States. In this regard, it contrasts sharply with that of Ralph Ellison, whose strategy was to examine American myths and symbols in order to identify the African American foundational presence in them. For Ellison the question was not "What does it mean to be an American?" but "What is American culture?" He argued that the heterogeneous culture of the United States was a forerunner of the political democracy that was yet to be achieved. The style of his essays appropriates the improvisational impulse of jazz, the art form that represented for him the highest achievement of American culture. His prose is often leavened with the vernacular. But Ellison's explorations are rarely personal. He does not often put himself on the line.

What sets Baldwin's critique further apart is that the political indictment of the failure of the United States to live out its own political creed is just his starting point; his argument with America is ultimately personal. In "Notes for a Hypothetical Novel," he contends:

> But to try and find out what Americans mean is almost impossible because there are so many things they do not want to face. And not only the Negro thing which is simply the most obvious and perhaps the simplest example, but on the level of private life which is after all where we have to get to in order to write about anything and also the level we have to get to in order to live, it seems to me that the myth, the illusion, that this is a free country, for example, is disastrous.[8]

The fixation on race prevents whites from confronting their individual fears; they hide behind the nation's myths. By virtue of their traumatic history, black Americans are immune to these myths. That history marks them as uniquely American nevertheless. As he elaborates in *The Fire Next Time*, however, they are vulnerable to the sway of the countermyths of black separatism that also block self-knowledge. At bottom, Baldwin was committed to defining what it means to be an American, but he was equally committed to figuring out what his personal responsibility as an American was.

Although Baldwin later revealed that he had been reluctant to publish his essays as a book, he was, from the 1955 publication of *Notes of a Native Son*, hailed as a master of the essay form.[9] For African American writers, the essay had long been a favorite, if critically undervalued, genre. Its compactness and potential for timeliness made it indispensable in times of political crisis—which were a virtual constant for black Americans. Drawing on traditions of nineteenth-century oratory and extending the autobiographical impulse of the slave narrative, black writers shaped the essay to serve their own purposes. Starting with Victoria Matthews's "The Value of Race Literature" in 1895 and continuing through the Harlem Renaissance and beyond, the essay became the medium in which debates over aesthetics were waged. Baldwin's writing distills the various elements of the African American essay: its political potency, its legacy of the pulpit and the podium, its utility for aesthetic debates, and the space it offers for personal recollection and philosophical reflection.

But unlike most black writers before him, Baldwin was as rigorous in judging his individual stance as a moral agent as he was the morality of the nation-state. He calculated the cost of white supremacy in starkly personal terms. Without the veil of fiction, few other black writers had been as willing to lay bare family secrets or the secrets of their own hearts, the self-hatred as well as the love. Baldwin's purpose was hardly to write advertisements for himself, though his example enabled his white peers, including Norman Mailer, to write more explicitly out of their personal experiences than American writers before them had done. Baldwin sought rather to explore the nexus between his individual experiences and social reality. The tour de force title essay "Notes of a Native Son" set the standard for his art, as it mapped the despair and rage of Harlem alongside the mental map of Baldwin's grief and rage over the death of his father.

In the introduction to *Nobody Knows My Name*, Baldwin describes the essays it contains as "a very small part of a private logbook. . . . The questions which one asks oneself begin, at last," he reflects, "to illuminate the world, and become one's key to the experience of others."[10] Provisional, speculative, and digressive, Baldwin's essays—like all essays—resist definition. As the few critics who consider the genre agree, the essay offers its creator intellectual freedom—the freedom to work around, with, and through an idea.[11] Baldwin takes full advantage of that freedom and in the process stretches the form. His early essays are tightly structured: they reach conclusions that while never predictable always seem both earned and apt. As he takes up more rancorous and more explicitly political questions, the style of the essays grows looser and more expansive. "Down at the Cross: Letter from a Region in My Mind," the longer essay of *The Fire Next Time*, runs to twenty thousand words. The two parts of *No Name in the Street* constitute a book. Yet despite their extended length, the sensibility that animates these writings is consistent with the earlier pieces. The larger the topic, the more the questions open out to other questions. The range of responses widens. Voices other than Baldwin's speak. But in part, because these essays always begin "with the questions one asks oneself," they retain the semblance of private truth-telling that accounts for so much of their power.

The hybridity of the essay makes it capacious enough to incorporate other genres. Letters, autobiography, and oratory feature in Baldwin's work. A fiction writer, Baldwin frequently interpolates stories in his essays. Some of his most memorable—the story of the purloined bedsheet and of the dinner at the home of Elijah Muhammad, for example—are told in essays. Such stories bump up against literary and political critique, memoir, and reportage. "In the essay," Theodor Adorno asserts, "discrete elements set off against one another come together to form a readable context; the essay erects no scaffolding and no structure. But the elements crystallize as a configuration through their motion. The constellation is a force field, just as every intellectual structure is necessarily transformed into a force field under the essay's gaze."[12] The intellectual structure of Americanness is a recurrent force field in Baldwin's essays.

Even at the level of the sentence Baldwin qualifies, complicates, and recalibrates his ideas. His periodic sentences allow him to draw ever finer distinctions between histories, experiences, and individuals. In "A Question of Identity," for example, he invokes the American past: "The truth about that past is not that it is too brief, or too superficial, but only that we, having turned our faces so resolutely away from it, have never demanded from it what it has to give."[13] Or, to take another example, as he writes of love in "Notes of a Native Son," "one is absolutely forced to make perpetual qualifications and one's own reactions are always canceling each other out."[14] These elegant sentences invite comparison to Henry James, a comparison Baldwin encouraged. The title *Notes of a Native Son* invokes the title of James's childhood memoir, *Notes of a Son and Brother*, as well as Richard Wright's novel. In *No Name in the Street*, Baldwin credits James with having taught him how to survive in Paris.[15] Beyond the transatlantic themes and survival lessons, however, the more important legacy that Baldwin inherits from James is the valorization of individual experience and the premium to be placed on interiority. Moreover, as a homosexual, Baldwin like James was acutely conscious of the ways that codes of masculinity stunted the development of American men's interior lives. His prose—with its layered elaborations of feelings as well as ideas—repudiates a conception of manhood as well as a conception of literary style, specifically that popularized in the 1940s by James Cain and Raymond Chandler as well as by Wright.[16]

Sussing out his influences in the "Introduction" to *Notes of a Native Son*, Baldwin omits James but identifies the "rhetoric of the store-front church, something ironic and violent and perpetually understated in Negro speech—and something of Dickens' love for bravura."[17] Baldwin's essays move across these discursive registers—the transcendent rhetoric of the pulpit, the biting irony of the blues, a complex pattern of figures that recalls James, bravura storytelling that is Dickensian—to produce a style so rich and distinctive that the Irish novelist Colm Tóibín deems Baldwin "the most eloquent man in the America of his time."[18]

"The Discovery of What It Means to Be an American" begins with a quotation from James. It concludes with the statement, "the interior life is a real life, and the intangible dreams of people have a tangible effect on the world,"[19] a statement that James would have endorsed. Baldwin shapes his expression of interiority with a prose style that looks back to the King James Bible, as well as to James. But his understanding of the "tangible" effects of dreams is both his inheritance, that is, the legacy of his racialized history in the United States—as expressed through the visionary rhetoric of African American sermons and the laconic ironies of the blues—and the birthright that is his by virtue of being human.[20]

For a brief moment in the early 1960s, Baldwin had reason to believe that African Americans were on the brink of claiming both their inheritance and their birthright. But the mountaintop experience of the Civil Rights Movement passed quickly. By the middle of the decade, Baldwin was distressed by conditions in America. Writing from Istanbul, he pleaded with his family and friends to send information about conflicts within the movement; he expressed deep concern about the welfare of his family and the repercussions on them of his activism. He also expressed the desire to conduct a lecture tour in the United States, but given the fractured state of the movement, Baldwin worried that he would be unable to find an organization to sponsor it. Nevertheless he considered it his duty to return to the struggle's front lines. He felt compelled to suggest new directions for the movement, especially in light of the state response to the increasing violence in the South and North. He believed that black urban communities in particular were virtually under a state of siege. The movement needed to clarify its goals; otherwise it might settle for the limited victories it was in the nation's interest to grant. Black people, no less than whites, needed to be reminded of what they were fighting for: not integration into a burning house, as he had written and rejected in *The Fire Next Time*, but a reconstructed nation in which its principles would be one with its actions.[21]

Almost a decade passed between the publication of *The Fire Next Time* (1963) and his next book of essays, *No Name in the Street* (1972), a book that, in its author's words, had been "much delayed by trials, assassinations, funerals, and despair."[22] Its two extended essays, "Take Me to the Water" and "To Be Baptized," are deeply autobiographical, structurally innovative, and intricately connected. They represent both a personal and a political crisis. Baldwin had given up serving his countrymen as Jeremiah and taken on the mantle of Job. He turned from the urgent importuning of those "relatively conscious whites and those relatively conscious blacks" to avert "the fire next time" and, like Job, offered a series of lamentations on the past and the present. His politics had changed; his prose had shifted to a minor key.

> The mind is a strange and terrible vehicle, moving according to rigorous rules of its own; and my own mind, after I had left Atlanta, began to move backward in time, to places, people, and events I thought I had forgotten. Sorrow drove it there, I think, sorrow, and a certain kind of bewilderment, triggered, perhaps, by something which happened to me in connection with Martin's funeral.[23]

The metaphor illuminates not only the author's mind but the genre of the essay. Its looping trajectory pays no heed to chronology or geography; it moves backward and forward in space as well as time. It follows a logic of its own that this passage suggests reflects rules that are no less rigorous for being undefined. It insists on its own autonomy. Its "elements crystallize as a configuration through their motion." The trigger for the interior journey in this case is an incident that transpired in private and seems to have only a tangential connection to the public events that are the essay's explicit concern. In the aftermath of the assassinations of Medgar, Malcolm, and Martin, Baldwin reflects on the national and international situation. But he does so through reconsidering his own individual past positions and actions. For the reader of Baldwin's earlier essays, "Take Me to the Water" revisits scenes from his growing up in Harlem, to his sojourns in Paris and the American South, to the lecture platforms of the Civil Rights Movement. But the tone has changed. As Baldwin puts it, "something has altered in me, something has gone away"; he seems to look back both in sorrow and in anger at the road he has traveled.[24]

If the trigger for this interior journey is a visit that Baldwin pays to an old friend and his family in the Bronx, the emblem of what he would elsewhere call "the price of the ticket" is a suit. In a bravura telling that shifts abruptly from dramatic exaggeration to understated irony, Baldwin describes how he told a newspaper columnist that he would never again wear the black suit that he wore to share the stage with Dr. King at Carnegie Hall, shortly before King's assassination, and wore again to King's funeral. After the column appears, the wife of a friend who had grown up with Baldwin and was "just his size" calls to say that if Baldwin cannot wear the suit, she hopes he will give it to her husband. Baldwin, the bicoastal celebrity, travels to the Bronx by limousine and begins en route to suffer pangs of guilt. Just as signs of celebrity are evoked throughout the first part of the essay, the adjective "guilty" now recurs five times in one paragraph. Entering the friend's apartment, Baldwin recognizes himself as a stranger in a home where he had once been kin. He condescends to those he has in fact left behind; with little justification he concludes that they have not changed in the intervening years. Acknowledging class divisions that he cannot overcome, he recognizes that his friend, a postal worker, needs a suit and cannot afford Baldwin's "elegant despair."

As it evokes moments in earlier essays, "Take Me to the Water" becomes a critique of its author, a series of judgments on Baldwin's judgments. On the defensive, Baldwin argues with his friend's stepdaughter over William Styron's *Confessions of Nat Turner*, which the girl condemns without having read.[25] His friend stands apart from this exchange, embarrassed. Baldwin's gloss on the moment ("I always think this is a terrible thing to happen to a man, especially in his own house, and I am always terribly humiliated for the man to whom it happens. Then, of course, you get angry at the man for allowing it to happen"[26]) echoes inexorably the moment in "Notes of a Native Son" in which the white schoolteacher's presence in the Baldwins' home confronts his father with "a wholly unprecedented and frightening situation."[27] Here Baldwin reenacts the role of the white schoolteacher as he embarrasses a father in front of his child. The situation continues to deteriorate as Baldwin hectors his friend, who supports the war in Vietnam, for his reactionary political beliefs. Baldwin's rage gets the better of him, and he utters expletives that rupture the prose as starkly as they do the scene. In this moment, Baldwin experiences a crisis of language as well as of empathy and kinship.

Tellingly, the expletive comes in response to the friend's attempt to tell Baldwin what "we," meaning Americans, are trying to do in Vietnam. Throughout his first three volumes of essays Baldwin had famously used this pronoun to claim his citizenship in the U.S. nation. As he once explained, he had done so to avoid assuming the stance of victim. He "shifted the point of view to 'we.' Who is the 'we'? I'm talking about we, the American people."[28] This usage had played a critical role in Baldwin's strategic American exceptionalism. It enabled him to claim a citizenship that had not been fully granted. Then, on the basis of that citizenship, he declared that because he "love[d] America more than any other country in the world, and exactly for that reason, [he] insisted on the right to criticize her perpetually."[29] He criticized out of love and a sense of belonging. Consequently, in "Take Me to the Water" he responds with fury to his friend's assertion of common cause sans critique. "What motherfucking *we*? You stand up, motherfucker, and I'll kick you in the ass!"[30] The reunion stumbles to an end.

On the surface Baldwin has cast himself forever out of the fold by his obscene language. Although his fiction can be deliciously profane, no precedent for this utterance exists in Baldwin's essays. Critics who dismiss *No Name in the Street* because of its anger point to passages like this one, as well as to sometimes withering attacks on America.[31] But it is not the specific words but the failure of language in general that is at issue here. Earlier in the essay, Baldwin worries needlessly that his friends, members of what was once his church family, would be appalled by his worldly habits. When he arrives, he finds that they have thoughtfully provided an ashtray and a bottle of whiskey. He describes himself to himself as "an aging, lonely, sexually dubious, politically outrageous, unspeakably erratic freak."[32] Then he quickly clears psychic space for himself by juxtaposing the multiple changes in his own identity to the psychological stasis that defines his friend. Baldwin angrily concludes, "nothing seemed to have touched this man."[33] Surely, nothing he says reaches his friend. Failing to communicate with him, he curses him.

This scene becomes the catalyst that enables Baldwin to reconsider his relation to the masses of black Americans from whom he feels alienated by reason of class, culture, politics, and sexual identity. In a manner characteristic of the essay, a private exchange becomes the ground that enables Baldwin to reconsider his relation to the larger society, in this case specifically his relation as a world-famous black writer to the masses of African Americans and as an African American to the dispossessed peoples of the world (beginning here with the Vietnamese), as well as to his white countrymen. As the rest of the essay loops backward and forward in time, the central question it asks is for whom the sacrifices of the sixties have been made. The bloody suit is finally the martyr's robe, the emblem of suffering and shame. It rightly belongs not to Baldwin or even to King, but to the many thousands gone. The essay struggles to hold at bay the despair that would overwhelm Baldwin were he forced even to consider the possibility that those sacrifices had been made in vain.

Baldwin's situation in *No Name in the Street* calls to mind W. E. B. Du Bois's meditation "Of Alexander Crummell" in *The Souls of Black Folk.* There Crummell, a nineteenth-century free black clergyman who traveled to Britain and Liberia advocating racial justice and eventually founded the American Negro Academy, becomes representative of all black intellectuals who are threatened with the temptations of hate, despair, and doubt. For Du Bois, the triumph of Crummell's life is that he transcended these temptations, temptations with which Du Bois, who places the essay on Crummell just after the elegy for his infant son, still wrestled. For Du Bois "the tragedy of the age" and of his homeland is that few white Americans had ever heard of Crummell. Baldwin occupies the inverse position. Many of his countrymen know his name, but few understand him or, more vexing, themselves. Rather than simply condemn their ignorance, Baldwin strives to identify failures of his own understanding. And, as he meditates on his own life, he struggles against the temptations of which Du Bois warned.

A transition that reflects on the passage of time and the nonlinearity of history introduces more autobiographical narratives in which Baldwin reflects on his ability and inability to read the situations he was in accurately. If, on the one hand, he anticipated the Algerian revolt based on his observations of Algerians in Paris, on the other hand, seeing Paris from the perspective of an American framework led him to misperceive the relative standing of Arabs and Africans in the metropole. In retrospect, he realizes that in fact the Arabs, who far outnumbered the darker-skinned Africans, were more feared and more exploited. He concedes that he "was also a member of the American colony, and we were, in general, slow to pick up on what was going on around us."[34] Even as his U.S. passport offers protection, his U.S. perspective distorts his vision. That vision restored, he draws an extended comparison between the rise of McCarthyism in the United States and anti-Arab racism in France during the 1950s.

Baldwin returns again and again in *No Name in the Street* to contemplate the relationship of African Americans to a transnational community of the dispossessed and their shared relationship to the West. In so doing, he gives up on strategic American exceptionalism; it has proved its ineffectiveness. Revising one of the most famous passages in "Stranger in the Village," he asserts that "the South African coal miner, or the African digging for roots in the bush, or the Algerian mason working in Paris, not only have no reason to bow down before Shakespeare, or Descartes, or Westminster Abbey, or the cathedral at Chartres: they have, once these monuments intrude on their attention, no honorable access to them." The Baldwin of the early essays was himself a pilgrim to the sacred sites of Western culture and a devoted student of its texts. Now, to bow down before these monuments is to accept "history's arrogant and unjust judgment of [the dispossessed]."[35] In "Stranger in the Village," by contrast, Baldwin had expressed the hope that what he, as an interloper, saw in the history of the West—its gargoyles—could awaken his white readers to the evil from which they benefit. No such hope survives in *No Name in the Street.*

At times Baldwin gives into despair. He has learned retrospectively that *Encounter*, the magazine that published his essay "Princes and Powers," was a CIA front. He wonders how else his idealism has been exploited and to what extent he has been "the Great Black Hope of the Great White Father."[36] Despite having articulated his positions in a fashion both scrupulously honest and meticulously precise, he recognizes that he has been used.

The possibilities of history are not foreclosed. As he recounts his travels through the U.S. South, where, he recalls, "though I was a stranger, I was home," Baldwin reintroduces readers to the still unsung heroes of the Civil Rights Movement. But his purpose is less to celebrate their valor than to suggest how difficult and how private the choice for nonviolence was and is. One anecdote he shares relates the experience of a black grocer in the South, a voting rights activist. After sitting night after night with his sons, armed and ready to protect his business, the man decides one day that this is no way to live. He gives up his arms—not because his enemies have put down theirs but in order to preserve his sense of who he is. Preserving that sense of oneself as a moral agent constitutes one challenge Baldwin lays down in *No Name in the Street.*

But he does not end there. The second part of the text, "To Be Baptized," moves across time and space with sometimes dizzying rapidity as it memorializes the dead and confronts the living. Baldwin recollects his friendship with Malcolm and the wariness that preceded it, the news of Malcolm's murder, the doomed effort to bring his story to film, Baldwin's distant relationship with King, the news of King's murder, Baldwin's years-long struggle to free his falsely accused friend Tony Maynard from prison, his meetings with Huey Newton and other members of the Black Panthers, and the broad opposition to the "racist war" in Vietnam. With each narrative the complexities of the current moment multiply. The stories intersect: news of King's death reaches Baldwin in Hollywood where he is talking to the actor Billy Dee Williams, his choice to play Malcolm on film. That memory triggers the memory of hearing the news of Evers's murder as Baldwin travels in Puerto Rico and of Malcolm's death as Baldwin and his sister dine in a London restaurant. The shifts of location reinforce the sense of dislocation, a personal dislocation that mirrors a national, indeed a global crisis.

Resolving that crisis requires not just a renewed sense of moral agency but a new set of "economic arrangements" that do not condemn the majority of the world's people to poverty. Resolving that crisis compels revised concepts of empathy and kinship that bind human beings regardless of race. In the meantime, black people respond to the present disarray as best they can. By 1972 blacks in the United States had begun calling themselves Afro-Americans, which Baldwin deems a "wedding . . . of two confusions, an arbitrary linking of two undefined and currently undefinable proper nouns"—Africa, because it is not yet free to define itself and America, which continues to pose "a profound and dangerous . . . mystery."[37] In the last paragraph of *No Name in the Street,* a volume that maps an ever-widening crisis, Baldwin turns back to the community from which he came. He reflects on what it means to be an Afro-American:

> To be an Afro-American, or an American black, is to be in the situation, intolerably exaggerated, of all those who have ever found themselves part of a civilization which they could in no wise honor-

> ably defend—which they were compelled, indeed, endlessly to attack and condemn—and who yet spoke out of the most passionate love, hoping to make the kingdom new, to make it honorable and worthy of life. . . . One would much rather be at home among one's compatriots than be mocked and detested by them. And there is a level on which the mockery of the people, even their hatred is moving because it is so blind: it is terrible to watch people cling to their captivity and insist on their own destruction. I think black people have always felt this about America and Americans, and have always seen, spinning above the thoughtless American head, the shape of the wrath to come.[38]

That Baldwin published these words evinces his continued resistance to despair and his determination to continue ringing that bell in the night that might yet save Americans from themselves. He continued even though the moral certitude of the movement was gone and even though Afro-Americans, tempted by the romanticized identities proffered by black nationalists, did not always take on the harder task of working through the complex and contradictory meanings of the terms on either side of the hyphen. Although he wavered, Baldwin never lost the faith that by getting the words right, pushing them until they revealed the complexities of ever more complex realities, insisting that we use language not to evade but to confront the toughest questions—both political and personal—*we*, that is not just Americans but humankind, just might manage to survive. In the meantime, as the wrath of history still threatens, we have no choice but to keep the faith: "hoping to make the kingdom new, to make it honorable and worthy of life."

NOTES

Baldwin, "Discovery of What It Means To Be An American," 137.

Baldwin used this lyric as his epigraph to "Take Me to the Water," the first essay in *No Name in the Street* (353).

1. Baldwin, "Discovery of What It Means to Be an American," 139.
2. Denning, "'Special American Conditions,'" 170.
3. Spivak, "Subaltern Studies," 214. Spivak later retracted the phrase because it had become "the union ticket for essentialism. As to what is meant by strategy, no one wondered about that." Consequently, she wrote, "as a phrase, I have given up on it." In borrowing her formulation, I want to argue that Baldwin was acutely aware of the strategy he deployed when he used the language of American excep-

tionalism in the 1950s and 1960s. But by the 1970s it was a concept he had given up on. See Denius and Jonsoon, "Interview with Gayatri Chakravorty Spivak, 35.

4. Baldwin, "Nobody Knows My Name," 197.

5. The allusion is to Lewis, *The American Adam* (first published 1955). Other foundational works of literary criticism in American studies include Chase, *The American Novel and Its Traditions* (first published in 1957), Charles Feidelson, *Symbolism in American Literature* (first published in 1953), and Leo Marx, *The Machine in the Garden* (first published in 1964).

6. Baldwin, "Discovery of What It Means to Be an American," 139.

7. Baldwin, "Stranger in the Village," 129.

8. Baldwin, "Notes for a Hypothetical Novel," 228–29.

9. In the preface to the 1984 edition of *Notes of a Native Son*, Baldwin explains that he was not enthusiastic when his high school friend Sol Stein, now a book editor, had suggested the book: "I had never thought of these essays as a possible book. Once they were behind me, I don't, in fact, think that I thought of them at all." In the same preface, he adds, "I had never thought of myself as an essayist: the idea had never entered my mind" (ix, xi).

10. Baldwin, introduction to *Nobody Knows My Name*, 136.

11. See, e.g., Hall, "Essay and Discovery," 73–91.

12. Adorno, "Essay as Form," 13.

13. Baldwin, "Question of Identity," 100.

14. Baldwin, "Notes of a Native Son," 83.

15. See Baldwin, *Collected Essays*, 377. Baldwin simplifies the truth here. As James Campbell points out, "Baldwin was well read by the time he quit New York, not only in English and American literature but in Russian and French as well—'Baldwin had read *everything*,' said Mary McCarthy—and his reading, which had drawn him towards France in the first place, also helped prepare him for his life there. He had read Balzac, for example, who taught him a lesson about the place of French institutions, from the universality of bureaucracy to the role of the concierge; from Flaubert he learned about the play of morality and hypocrisy, and the importance of conventional behavior; Hemingway advised him about food, drink, and waiters; Henry Miller revealed the secrets of sex in districts which, once only places of legend, now became his haunts: Montmartre, Montparnasse, St-Germain-des-Prés" (*Talking at the Gates*, 51).

16. In "Preservation of Innocence," the second essay that Baldwin published after moving to Paris, he wrote a defense of homosexuality that used the misogyny of Cain and Chandler's fiction to argue that the debasement of the homosexual indicated American culture's debasement of sexuality in general: see *Collected Essays*.

17. Baldwin, "Autobiographical Notes," 6.

18. Colm Tóibín, "James Baldwin: The Flesh and the Devil," 186. Tóibín argues that Baldwin used and adapted the tone of the great masters of English eloquence: Bacon, Sir Thomas Browne, Hazlitt, Emerson, and Henry James. Tóibín contends that this appropriation involved "a cast of mind that used qualification, the aside and the further sub-clauses to suggest that truth was brittle and easily undermined." I would suggest that these writers, all of whom are essayists, model ways of expressing a skepticism that was also part and parcel of African American

expressive culture. Baldwin appropriated elements of the style of the English essay, but he had in all probability already internalized the cast of mind. I agree with Tóibín that Baldwin's "prose played with the explicit and the implicit, the bald statement and the skeptical gloss. His style could be high and grave and reflect the glittering mind; his thought was embodied beautifully in his style, as though fresh language had led him to fresh thought" (188).

19. Baldwin, "Discovery of What It Means to Be an American," 142.

20. In the preface to the 1984 edition of *Notes of a Native Son*, Baldwin distinguishes inheritance from birthright. Marlon B. Ross analyzes the implications of this distinction in "White Fantasies of Desire." He reads the metaphor "rock of ages" that Baldwin uses to represent his racial inheritance to indicate "the ways in which the black writer relies on the uniqueness of African American experience as refuge, as a site of self-testing, as an offensive weapon of resistance, and as an obligatory charge to become a herald or witness on which the people can depend." But the inheritance is a mixed blessing. If on the one hand, it is a source of strength, on the other it is "a stumbling block, obstructing the way toward uninterrupted human desire by giving the individual a secure place to hide from the nakedness of desire (i.e. an identity)" (29). Although I agree with Ross that Baldwin in his fiction imagines "uninterrupted human desire" in ways that few of his peers even attempt, his essays retain a strong sense of the need for a communal belonging, whether in the nation, the race, or the fellowship of the like-minded.

21. Leeming, *James Baldwin*, 268–69, 273.

22. Baldwin, "Epilogue: Who Has Believed Our Report?" 475.

23. Baldwin, "Take Me to the Water," 358.

24. Ibid., 357. Eddie Glaude offers a complementary reading that analyzes *No Name* as a text that memorializes the losses of the sixties; he suggests that it models ways to ameliorate the current confusion and lack of direction in African American communities. This drifting, he contends, derives from the collective inability of black people to mourn the losses—both the individual martyrs and the dreams that remain deferred. "Memory," Glaude avers, "constitutes a constraint on hubris and enables passionately intelligent action." See Glaude, *In a Shade of Blue*, 15.

25. Styron's novel, which was written from the point of view of the black revolutionary, provoked a storm of controversy that culminated in the publication of *Confessions of Nat Turner: Ten Black Writers Respond.* Baldwin, who had encouraged Styron to write the novel while living as a guest in his home, stood by his friend. He wrote of Styron that "he has begun the common history—*ours*" (quoted in Styron, "Jimmy in the House," 46).

26. Baldwin, "Take Me to the Water," 362.

27. Baldwin, "Notes of a Native Son," 68.

28. Quoted in Baldwin and Stein, *Native Sons*, 10.

29. Baldwin, "Autobiographical Notes," 9.

30. Baldwin, "Take Me to the Water," 364.

31. A representative example of Baldwin's scathing judgment is "white Americans are probably the sickest and certainly the most dangerous people, of any color, to be found in the world today" (*No Name in the Street*, 386). Although the critical reception of this book remains mixed, biographer David Leeming deems *No Name*

in the Street "an original work," and he notes that most of the contemporary reviews were generally positive if not enthusiastic. Mel Watkins, in the *New York Times Book Review*, recognized in it "the old Baldwin ability to convey the national anguish and to see that anguish through his personal tragedy." The *Nation* and the *Saturday Review*, "while upset by Baldwin's new militancy and critical of his tendency to 'skim,' recognized the essential power of the work." According to Leeming, Baldwin found some of the reviews hurtful. As some whites considered him ungrateful given the success he had achieved, black nationalists were suspicious of his more militant tone. He confided to his brother that he was "trapped . . . between the 'white fantasy' and the 'black fantasy'" (see Leeming, *James Baldwin*, 316).

32. Baldwin, "Take Me to the Water," 363.

33. Ibid.

34. Baldwin, *No Name in the Street*, 375.

35. Ibid., 381.

36. Baldwin, "To Be Baptized," 410. Another source of despair and alienation was FBI surveillance. As James Campbell documents in "I Heard It through the Grapevine," the FBI kept Baldwin under "secret and continuous surveillance" for most of the 1960s. The agency tracked his movements across the globe, tricked friends and relatives into disclosing information, monitored his public appearances, and dug up dirt on his private life. Baldwin was convinced that his phones were tapped; Campbell found no proof of that. However, the file of more than a thousand pages identifies "James Arthur Baldwin [as] a person likely to pose a threat to the security of the United States."

37. Baldwin, "To Be Baptized," 472–73.

38. Ibid., 474.

BIBLIOGRAPHY

Adorno, Theodor. "The Essay as Form." In *Notes to Literature*, vol. 1. New York: Columbia University Press, 1991.

Baldwin, James. "Autobiographical Notes." In *Collected Essays*.

Baldwin, James. *Collected Essays*. Ed. Toni Morrison. New York: Library of America, 1998.

Baldwin, James. "The Discovery of What It Means To Be An American." In *Nobody Knows My Name: More Notes of a Native Son* (1961), in *Collected Essays*.

Baldwin, James. "Epilogue: Who Has Believed Our Report?" In *Collected Essays*.

Baldwin, James. *Nobody Knows My Name: More Notes of a Native Son*. In *Collected Essays*.

Baldwin, James. *No Name in the Street*. In *Collected Essays*.

Baldwin, James. "Notes of a Native Son." In *Collected Essays*.

Baldwin, James. *Notes of a Native Son*. Boston: Beacon Press, 1984.

Baldwin, James. "Notes for a Hypothetical Novel." In *Collected Essays*.

Baldwin, James. "A Question of Identity." In *Collected Essays*.

Baldwin, James. "Stranger in the Village." In *Collected Essays*.

Baldwin, James. "Take Me to the Water." In *No Name in the Street* (1972), in *Collected Essays*.

Baldwin, James. "To Be Baptized." In *No Name in the Street* (1972), in *Collected Essays.*

Baldwin, James, and Sol Stein. *Native Sons.* New York: One World/Ballantine Books, 2004.

Campbell, James. "I Heard It through the Grapevine." *Granta* 73 (2001).

Campbell, James. *Talking at the Gates: A Life of James Baldwin.* New York: Viking, 1991.

Chase, Richard. *The American Novel and Its Traditions.* Garden City, N.Y.: Doubleday, 1957.

Denius, Sara, and Stefan Jonsoon. "An Interview with Gayatri Chakravorty Spivak." *boundary* 2 20, no. 2 (1992).

Denning, Michael. "'The Special American Conditions': Marxism and American Studies." In *Culture in the Age of Three Worlds.* London: Verso, 2004.

Feidelson, Charles. *Symbolism in American Literature.* Chicago: Chicago University Press, 1953.

Glaude, Eddie. *In a Shade of Blue: Pragmatism and the Politics of Black America.* Chicago: University of Chicago Press, 2007.

Hall, Michael L. "The Essay and Discovery." In Alexander L. Butrym, ed., *Essays on the Essay: Redefining the Genre.* Athens: University of Georgia Press, 1989.

Leeming, David. *James Baldwin: A Biography.* New York: Henry Holt, 1994.

Lewis, R. W. B. *The American Adam: Innocence, Tragedy and Tradition in the Nineteenth Century.* Chicago: University of Chicago Press, 1955.

Marx, Leo. *The Machine in the Garden: Technology and the Pastoral Ideal in America.* New York: Oxford University Press, 1964.

McBride, Dwight A., ed. *James Baldwin Now.* New York: New York University Press, 1999.

Ross, Marlon B. "White Fantasies of Desire: Baldwin and the Racial Identities of Sexuality." In Dwight A. McBride, ed., *James Baldwin Now.* New York: New York University Press, 1999.

Spivak, Gayatri. "Subaltern Studies: Deconstructing Historiography." 1985. Reprinted in Donna Landry and Gerald MacLean, eds., *The Spivak Reader.* New York: Routledge, 1996.

Styron, William. "Jimmy in the House." In Quincy Troupe, ed., *James Baldwin: The Legacy.* New York: Simon and Schuster, 1989.

Tóibín, Colm. "James Baldwin: The Flesh and the Devil." In *Love in a Dark Time and Other Explorations of Gay Lives and Literature.* New York: Scribner, 2001.

TWO

Baldwin and "the American Confusion"

COLM TÓIBÍN

In December 1962 the *New York Times* asked some of the year's best-selling authors to write a piece describing "what they believe there is about their book or the climate of the times that has made [their book] so popular." In reply, Vance Packard, for example, explained that his book *The Pyramid Climbers* had been a best-seller, because, he believed, "there is a growing uneasiness among Americans about the terms of their existence, and many tell me that I often articulate their own apprehensions." Patrick Dennis, whose book *Genius* had also been a best-seller, wrote: "I can't imagine what it is that makes my books sell and any author who claims to know is a fool, or a liar or both." This did not deter Allen Drury, whose book *A Shade of Difference* was on the list. "I hope," he wrote, "those readers who like what I have to say like it because it is honest, well-expressed and pertinent to the world in which we live."

James Baldwin's *Another Country* had also been a best-seller, and Baldwin used the occasion to position himself ambiguously in two of the central pantheons of American beauty. "I don't mean to compare myself to a couple of artists I unreservedly admire," he wrote, "Miles Davis and Ray Charles—but I would like to think that some of the people who liked my book responded to it in a way similar to the way they respond when Miles and Ray are blowing. These artists in their very different ways, sing a kind of universal blues. . . . They are telling us something of what it is like to be alive. It is not self-pity which one hears in them but compassion. . . . I think I really helplessly model myself on jazz musicians and try to write the way they sound. . . . I am aiming at what Henry James called 'perception at the pitch of passion.'"

Baldwin was claiming for his prose style and the structure of his novels something of the soaring, melancholy beauty of Davis and Charles; he was suggesting that the rhythms of his own diction took their bearings from the solitary pain, the uncompromising glamour that these two American musicians offered the world. But just in case anyone reading him wanted thus to place him as a primitive, a writer who did not plan his work but merely let it soar, a writer not steeped in a writerly tradition, Baldwin needed to invoke as well the high priest of American refinement, an author known not for his passion, however pitched, but for the rigor of his controlling imagination.

Baldwin the best-seller in 1962 wanted to have it both ways. This need was first of all a way of unloosening him from any easy categories, but it was also central to his procedures as an artist that he carried in his temperament a sense of James's interest in consciousness as something glittering and also as something hidden and secretive, a concern with language as both mask and pure revelation. But Baldwin also had a fascination with eloquence itself, the soaring phrase, the rhythm pushed hard, the sharp and glorious ring of a sentence. The list of what had made him such an interesting stylist would be long. Over the years he would vary its ingredients. Sometimes, he would do so to distract the reader from his own artistry and sophistication; other times, he would do so because he liked the list for its sound and variation, as in the list he provided in *Notes of a Native Son:* "The King James Bible, the rhetoric of the store-front church, something ironic and violent and perpetually understated in Negro speech—and something of Dickens's love for bravura."

But the style itself did not come simply; it could not be easily defined because it varied and shifted. It had real bravura moments, like a set of famous riffs, or an encore, such as this passage in part 1 of *Another Country* when Rufus and Vivaldo arrive at Benno's Bar in the Village:

> The bar was terribly crowded. Advertising men were there, drinking double shots of bourbon or vodka, on the rocks; college boys were there, their wet fingers slippery on the beer bottles; lone men stood near the doors or in the corners watching the drifting women. The college boys, gleaming with ignorance and mad with chastity, made terrified efforts to attract the feminine attention, but succeeded only in attracting each other. Some of the men were buying drinks for some of the women—who wandered incessantly from the juke box

> to the bar—and they faced each other over smiles which were pitched, with an eerie precision, between longing and contempt. Black-and-white couples were together here—closer together now than they would be later, when they got home. These several histories were camouflaged in the jargon which, wave upon wave, rolled through the bar; were locked in a silence like the silence of glaciers. Only the juke box spoke, grinding out each evening, all evening long, syncopated synthetic laments for love.

It is easy to sense the rhythms of jazz, but also of the prose writers of an earlier generation in this passage, the Fitzgerald of *The Great Gatsby*, the Hemingway of *The Sun Also Rises*. Baldwin was not afraid of repetition ("some of the men were buying drinks for some of the women"), or setting up patterns of beat and sound (note the constant use of "were"), or using punctuation with care and control (note the comma before "when they got home"; note the semicolon after "rolled through the bar"), and then striking home with a phrase or an observation utterly surprising, and full of delight with itself (note "gleaming with ignorance and mad with chastity" or "an eerie precision, between longing and contempt").

While Baldwin was at times in full possession of this bravura tone, he was also able to write quiet and effective and emotionally charged sentences. The sixty-two words in the opening paragraph of *Go Tell It on the Mountain* have only one word—the first—with more than three syllables and forty-three words with only one syllable.

> Everyone had always said that John would be a preacher when he grew up, just like his father. It had been said so often that John, without ever thinking about it, had come to believe it himself. Not until the morning of his fourteenth birthday did he really begin to think about it, and by then it was already too late.

This style seems closer to Hemingway than to jazz or James; it suggests that Baldwin was as comfortable with the tradition he inherited from a generation of writers, most of whom were at the height of their fame as he was starting to write. No young writers ever wish to give too much credit to the writers who could have been their father. They prefer to pay homage to grandfathers or to painters or musicians or ballet dancers or acrobats. It is one way of killing your father, to pretend that he made no difference to you while watching his cadences like a hawk.

So, too, in Baldwin's short stories this plain opening style had not an ounce of James or of jazz. "The Rockpile" opens: "Across the street from their house, in an empty lot between two houses, stood the rockpile." "The Outing" opens: "Each summer the church gave an outing." "Sonny's Blues" opens: "I read about it in the paper, in the subway, on my way to work."

Between the publication of *Go Tell It on the Mountain* in 1954 and the volume of stories *Going to Meet the Man* in 1965, Baldwin wrote a piece for the *New York Times* that set about openly killing some of his literary fathers. In January 1962, he wrote:

> Since World War II, certain names in recent American literature—Hemingway, Fitzgerald, Dos Passos, Faulkner—have acquired such weight and become so sacrosanct that they have been used as touchstones to reveal the understandable, but lamentable, inadequacy of the younger literary artists. . . . Let one of us, the younger, attempt to create a restless, unhappy, free-wheeling heroine and we are immediately informed that Hemingway or Fitzgerald did the same thing better—infinitely better.

Having made clear, in grudging tone, his immense respect for these writers, Baldwin proceeded to demolish them.

> It is useful . . . to remember in the case of Hemingway that his reputation began to be unassailable at the very instant that his work began that decline from which it never recovered—at about the time of *For Whom the Bell Tolls.* Hindsight allows us to say that this boyish and romantic and inflated book marks Hemingway's abdication from the efforts to understand the many-sided evil that is in the world. This is exactly the same thing as saying that he somehow gave up the effort to become a great novelist.

Having also demolished Faulkner ("such indefensibly muddy work as 'Intruder in the Dust' or 'Requiem for a Nun' ") and "the later development" of Dos Passos ("if one can call it that") and Fitzgerald ("there is no longer anything to say about Fitzgerald"), Baldwin considered the matter of America itself as a realm of failed imaginations.

> The previously mentioned giants have at least one thing in common: their simplicity. . . . It is the American way of looking on the

world as a place to be corrected, and in which innocence is inexplicably lost. It is this almost inexpressible pain which lends such force to some of the early Hemingway stories—including "The Killers"—and to the marvelous fishing sequence in "The Sun Also Rises"; and it is also the reason that Hemingway's heroines seem so peculiarly sexless and manufactured.

Baldwin, in his attempt to establish a context for his own work, now invoked the spirit of Henry James by taking the unusual step of claiming James as a novelist who dealt with the matter of failed masculinity in America. In *The Ambassadors*, Baldwin wrote,

> What is the moral dilemma of Lambert Strether if not that, at the midnight hour, he realizes that he has, somehow, failed his manhood: that the "masculine sensibility" as James puts it, has failed in him? . . . Strether's triumph is that he is able to realize this, even though he knows it is too late for him to act on it. And it is James' perception of this peculiar impossibility which makes him, until today, the greatest of our novelists. For the question which he raised, ricocheting it, so to speak, off the backs of his heroines, is the question which so torments us now. The question is this: How is an American to become a man? And this is precisely the same thing as asking: How is America to become a nation? By contrast with him, the giants who came to the fore between the two world wars merely lamented the necessity.

Baldwin understood the singular importance of the novel in America because he saw the dilemma his country faced as essentially an interior one, a poison which began in the individual spirit and only made its way then into politics. His political writing remains as raw and vivid as his fiction because he believed that social reform could not occur through legislation alone but through a reimagining of the private realm. Thus, for Baldwin, an examination of the individual soul as dramatized in fiction had immense power. It was, in the end, he saw, a matter of love, and he was not afraid to use the word. In his *New York Times* article of January 1962 he wrote:

> The loneliness of those cities described in Dos Passos is greater now than it has ever been before; and these cities are more dangerous now than they were before, and their citizens are yet more unloved.

> And those panaceas and formulas which have so spectacularly failed Dos Passos have also failed this country, and the world. The trouble is deeper than we wish to think: the trouble is in us. And we will never remake those cities, or conquer our cruel and unbearable human isolation—we will never establish human communities—until we stare our ghastly failure in the face.

Before he began to publish fiction, Baldwin was a reviewer with attitude, a writer with a high sense of aesthetic grandeur, an Edmund Wilson with real poison in his pen. In the *New Leader* in December 1947, for example, the twenty-three-year-old Baldwin employed a triple negative to take a swipe at Erskine Caldwell's *The Sure Hand of God:* "Certainly there is nothing in the book which would not justify the suspicion that Mr Caldwell was concerned with nothing more momentous than getting rid of some of the paper he had lying about the house, resurrecting several of the tired types on which he first made his reputation, and (incidentally) making a few dollars on the deal." Earlier that same year, he took on Maxim Gorky: "Gorky, not in the habit of describing intermediate colors, even when he suspected their existence, has in *Mother*, written a Russian battle hymn which history has so summarily dated that we are almost unwilling to credit it with any reality." Gorky, he went on, "was the foremost exponent of the maxim that 'art is the weapon of the working class.' He is also, probably, the major example of the invalidity of such a doctrine. (It is rather like saying that art is the weapon of the American housewife.)"

Moving from Russia with careful, youthful deliberation and delight, Baldwin in August 1948 did something close to many serious novelists' hearts. He took on a popular writer much praised for his terse style and pace, in this case poor James M. Cain, author of *The Postman Always Rings Twice.* Baldwin considered Cain's body of work: "Not only did he have nothing to say," he wrote, "but he drooled, so to speak, as he said it. . . . He writes with the stolid, humorless assurance of the American self-made man. Rather a great deal has been written concerning his breathless staccato 'pace,' his terse, corner-of-the-mouth 'style,' his significance as a recorder of the seamier side of American life. This is nonsense: Mr Cain writes fantasies and fantasies of the most unendurably mawkish and sentimental sort."

In January 1949 in an essay in *Commentary*, Baldwin formulated what would become his characteristic battle cry, which would so puzzle and irritate white liberals and reformers in the 1960s when they found they had reason to listen to him—the problem in America, he believed, lay in each individual American soul, black as much as white; and the black population was not seeking equality with a white world that had so significantly failed to understand itself, let alone those whom it had oppressed. "In a very real sense," he wrote in that essay, "the Negro problem has become anachronistic; we ourselves are the only problem, it is our hearts that we must search. It is neither a politic nor a popular thing to say, but a black man facing a white man becomes at once contemptuous and resentful when he finds himself looked upon as a moral problem for that white man's conscience."

In March 1950 Baldwin published a short story in *Commentary* called "Death of a Prophet," which he did not collect in *Going to Meet the Man*. It was, as far as I can make out, his second piece of published fiction. The first—also published in *Commentary*, in October 1948—called "Previous Condition," was included in *Going to Meet the Man* and contained a few of the elements that went into *Another Country*. It is easy to see why Baldwin did not want to publish "Death of a Prophet" in a collection, as it too obviously contained the seeds of *Go Tell It on the Mountain*, being the story of a boy in Harlem whose father was a preacher. The subject of a father and his son, Baldwin knew, was an interesting one. In 1967, in a review in the *New York Review of Books*, he wrote: "The father-son relationship is one of the most crucial and dangerous on earth, and to pretend that it can be otherwise really amounts to an exceedingly dangerous heresy."

Although the story of the father and son told in "Death of a Prophet" and *Go Tell It on the Mountain* was, to a large extent, his own story, recounted also in some autobiographical essays, Baldwin understood that the tension between the generations of men was a quintessential American story. It was, he believed, not only what set America apart, but what disfigured his country—the shame that so many men felt at their father, the lack of pride sons in a society moving onward and upward felt at their fathers. Thus his work in his fiction, and even in a novel like *Another Country*, notable for the absence of fathers, dealt with a most public and pressing matter in the most private and personal way. In an essay in 1964 Baldwin formulated the theory of this:

> And what happens to a person, however odd this may sound, also happens to a nation. . . . The Italian immigrant arriving from Italy, for example, or the sons of parents who were born in Sicily, makes a great point of not speaking Italian because he's going to become an

> American. And he can't bear his parents because they are backward. This may seem a trivial matter. But it is of the utmost importance when a father is despised by his son, and this is one of the facts of American life, and this is what we are really referring to, in oblique and terrible fashion, when we talk about upward mobility.

The writing in "Death of a Prophet" is high-toned, almost overwrought at times, but pitched with zeal and serious ambition and great tenderness. The story is what Baldwin himself called in a review in the *New Leader* in September 1947 "a study of human helplessness"; it sees the character of Johnnie, whose father is dying, and who has become a stranger in his father's eyes, not "in relation to oppression," as Baldwin put it in another piece on Gorky in 1947, but in relation to the character's own fear and inadequacy. Baldwin, even as he began, and despite his deep awareness of the relationship between the political and the personal, was determined that his characters should not be confined by a narrow political agenda; he sought to ensure that the behavior and the failure of his characters should be seen first as particular and private and then only as part of some general malaise that took its bearings from the Fall of Man as much as the creation of slavery, and emphatically not from a predetermined role as black men oppressed by bad laws. He also wanted to follow the example of Robert Louis Stevenson, whose novels and stories he reviewed in January 1948; he wanted to write, as Baldwin put it, "superbly well" and know that this would be, as with Stevenson, "the most enduring delight."

Baldwin wished to create and live as an American and as a man, and had much to say about the state of his nation and about its masculinity. (In April 1966 he wrote: "Much of the American confusion, if not most of it, is a direct result of the American effort to avoid dealing with the Negro as a man.") He was helped by his insistence that he did not belong to anyone's margin and his ability in the same moment to take full possession of the margin when it suited his purpose. He relished the ambiguity of his position and was skilled at covering his tracks.

When it came to the matter of boxing, for example, a subject that would thrill many of his heterosexual colleagues, he claimed to know nothing. Instead, using the full force of his homosexuality, he wrote beautifully about Floyd Patterson and his fight with Sonny Liston in 1963, studying the state of the two men's souls and the intricacies of their aura with an erotic intensity. Of Patterson, he wrote:

> And I think part of the resentment he arouses is due to the fact that he brings to what is thought of—quite erroneously—as a simple activity a terrible note of complexity. This is his personal style, a style which strongly suggests that most un-American of attributes, privacy, the will to privacy; and my own guess is that he is still relentlessly, painfully shy—he still lives gallantly with his scars, but not all of them have healed—and while he has found a way to master this, he has found no way to hide it; as, for example, another miraculously tough and tender man, Miles Davis, has managed to do.

Of Liston, Baldwin wrote:

> He reminded me of big, black men I have known who acquired the reputation of being tough in order to conceal the fact that they weren't hard. . . . Anyway, I liked him, liked him very much. He sat opposite me at the table, sideways, head down, waiting for the blow: for Liston knows, as only the inarticulately suffering can, just how inarticulate he is. But let me clarify that: I say suffering because it seems to me that he has suffered a great deal. It is in his face, in the silence of that face, and in the curiously distant light in his eyes—a light which rarely signals because there have been so few answering signals, . . . I said, "I can't ask you any questions because everything's been asked. Perhaps I'm only here, really, to say that I wish you well." . . . I'm glad I said it because he looked at me then, really for the first time, and he talked to me for a little while.

But in those same years he also spoke and wrote as though he were a founding father, in an unassailable position in his country, one of its central voices. In the *New York Times* in 1959 he wrote: "I think that there is something suspicious about the way we cling to the concept of race, on both sides of the obsolescent racial fence. White men, when they have not entirely succumbed to their panic, wallow in their guilt, and call themselves, usually 'liberals.' Black men, when they have not drowned in their bitterness, wallow in their rage, and call themselves, usually 'militant.' Both camps have managed to evade the really hideous complexity of our situation on the social and personal level." In the same year, in reply to a question about whether the fifties as a decade "makes special demands on you as a writer," he adopted one of his best tones, lofty and idealistic and filled with candor, while remaining sharp and direct and challenging: "But finally for me the difficulty is to remain in touch with the private life. The private life, his own and that of others, is the writer's subject—his key and ours to his achievement." Henry James would have been proud of him.

(The pride worked both ways. In *Playboy* in 1964 Baldwin managed to commandeer James as a member of his tribe, as someone who did not, as the vast majority of Americans did, spend their lives "in flight from death." He compared a passage from a letter James wrote to a friend who had lost her husband—"Sorrow wears and uses us but we wear and use it too, and it is blind. Whereas we, after a manner, see"—with these lines from Bessie Smith:

> Good mornin' blues.
> Blues, how do you do?
> I'm doin' all right.
> Good mornin'.
> How are you?

Once more James would have been proud, although it should be added that in his lifetime or in the years after his death he and his followers were not ever fully aware that what he was really doing was singing the blues.)

In 1959 also, in a paper called "Mass Culture and the Creative Artist" given to a symposium, Baldwin concluded: "We are in the middle of an immense metamorphosis here, a metamorphosis which will, it is devoutly to be hoped, rob us of our myths and give us our history, which will destroy our attitudes and give us back our personalities. The mass culture, in the meantime, can only reflect our chaos: and perhaps we had better remember that this chaos contains life—and a great transforming energy." He was, in these years, moving himself carefully to the center of the debate, refusing a role, offered to him always, as spokesman for a minority, to be listened to only when that minority grew restive or dangerous or newsworthy.

During the 1960s, the voice Baldwin used in his journalism grew less ambiguous, however, more strident, especially when he was addressing a black audience. In a speech he gave to the Student Co-ordinating Committee in November 1963, after the Kennedy assassination, for example, he began:

> Part of the price that Americans have paid for delusion, part of what we have done to ourselves, was given to us in Dallas, Texas. This happened in a civilized nation, the country which is the moral leader

> of the free world, when some lunatic blew off the President's head. Now, I want to suggest something, and I don't want to sound rude, but we all know that it has been many generations and it hasn't stopped yet that black men's heads have been blown off—and nobody cared. Because, as I said before, it wasn't happening to a person, it was happening to a "nigger."

Two years later, in an angry essay about black history, he saw no possibility of change, merely excuses for change.

> In the meantime ladies and gentlemen, after a brief intermission—time out for one or two committee reports, time out for an antipoverty pep talk, time out to make a Vietnamese child an orphan and then lovingly raise him to love all our works, time out for a White House conference, time out to brief and augment the police forces, time out to buy some Negroes, jail some, club some, and kill some—after a brief intermission, ladies and gentlemen, the show begins again in the auction room. And you will hear the same old piano, playing the blues.

At other times, he seemed to be amusing himself by preaching to the white population, insisting that whites, in fact, were the group most in need of freedom from tyranny. In 1961, he wrote: "There is a great captive Negro population here, which is well publicized, and what is not known at all, is that there is a great captive white population here too. No one has pointed out yet with any force that if I am not a man here, you are not a man here. You cannot lynch me and keep me in ghettos without becoming something monstrous yourselves." In *Playboy* in January 1964, he wrote: "What I'm much more concerned about is what white Americans have done to themselves; what has been done to me is irrelevant because there is nothing more you can do to me. But, in doing it, you've done something to yourself. In evading my humanity, you have done something to your own humanity."

In an essay called "The White Problem," also published in 1964, he sneered at the icons of white America, insisting that the difference between white and black in America was close to the difference between foolishness and seriousness, childhood and maturity:

> In this country, for a dangerously long time, there have been two levels of experience. One, to put it cruelly, but, I think, quite truth-

> fully, can be summed up in the images of Doris Day and Gary Cooper: two of the most grotesque appeals to innocence the world has ever seen. And the other, subterranean, indispensable, and denied, can be summed up in the tone and face of Ray Charles. And there never has been in this country any genuine confrontation between these two levels of experience.

In another essay from 1964, "Color and American Civilization," he had more fun at the expense of the neuroses suffered by his white brothers and sisters:

> The white man's unadmitted—and apparently, to him, unspeakable—private fears and longings are projected onto the Negro. The only way he can be released from the Negro's tyrannical power over him is to consent, in effect, to become black himself, to become part of that suffering and dancing country that he now watches wistfully from the heights of his lonely power and, armed with spiritual traveler's checks, visits surreptitiously after dark. . . . I cannot accept that proposition that the four-hundred-year travail of the American Negro should result merely in his attainment of the present level of the American civilization. I am far from convinced that being released from the African witch doctor was worthwhile if I am now . . . expected to become dependent on the American psychiatrist. It is a bargain I refuse.

Five years later, writing in the *New York Times*, he was at his most eloquent, insisting once more that the black population's burden in the United States could not be changed by legislation, but by something more far-reaching in its implications—the total conversion of the white population, whose moral degeneration and distance from themselves he judged to be abject. "I will state flatly," he wrote,

> that the bulk of this country's white population impresses me, and has so impressed me for a very long time, as being beyond any conceivable hope of moral rehabilitation. They have been white, if I may so put it, too long; they have been married to the lie of white supremacy too long; the effect on their personalities, their lives, their grasp of reality, has been as devastating as the lava which so

> memorably immobilized the citizens of Pompeii. They are unable to conceive that their version of reality, which they want me to accept, is an insult to my history and a parody of theirs, and an intolerable violation of myself.

In his fiction, Baldwin sought a new freedom, a freedom to create characters as he pleased. His black characters did not have to be filled with stoical virtue to be destroyed by white forces. His novel *Giovanni's Room* did not even have any black characters at all. Nor did his gay characters have their destiny worked out for them by history; he made them too interesting for that. In his journalism he sought to rewrite history first before paying attention to politics. In an address to Harlem teachers in October 1963, he said:

> What passes for identity in America is a series of myths about one's heroic ancestors. It's astounding to me, for example, that so many people really appear to believe that the country was founded by a band of heroes who wanted to be free. That happens not to be true. What happened was that some people left Europe because they couldn't stay there any longer and had to go some place else to make it. That's all. They were hungry, they were poor, they were convicts. Those who were making it in England, for example, did not get on the *Mayflower*. That's how the country was settled.

By 1979, his version of American history had become more alarmed. In an article for the *Los Angeles Times*, he wrote:

> A very brutal thing must be said: The intentions of this melancholic country as concerns black people—and anyone who doubts me can ask any Indian—have always been genocidal. They needed us for labor and for sport. Now they can't get rid of us. We cannot be exiled and we cannot be accommodated. Something's got to give. The machinery of this country operates day in and day out, hour by hour, to keep the nigger in his place.

In that article he called the Civil Rights Movement "the latest slave rebellion." Five years later in an article for *Essence*, he continued to muse on the idea of American history and genocide:

> America became white—the people who, as they claim "settled" the country became white—because of the necessity of denying the Black presence, and justifying the Black subjugation. No community can be based on such a principle—or, in other words, no community can be established on so genocidal a lie. White men—from Norway, for example, where they were *Norwegians*—became white by slaughtering the cattle, poisoning the wells, torching the houses, massacring Native Americans, raping Black women.

Reading his speeches and his journalism, it is, most of the time, easy to imagine, twenty years after his death, how he would respond to contemporary events. Hardly anything that has happened since 1987 would have surprised him. In 1979 he wrote: "If they couldn't deal with my father, how are they going to deal with the people in the streets of Tehran? I could have told them, if they had asked." It would be easy to put Baghdad or Basra in that sentence now. In 1964 he wrote: "People who do not know who they are privately, accept, as we have accepted for nearly fifteen years, the fantastic disaster which we call American politics and which we call American foreign policy, and the incoherence of the one is an exact reflection of the incoherence of the other." It would be merely necessary now to change the dates. He would have not been surprised by the counting of votes in Florida; he would not have been shocked by Abu Ghraib; he would not have been shocked by New Orleans. He would have known each time what to say. On 9/11, however, it is harder to be sure of his response, except that the soaring pity he was capable of could have been matched by the calm eloquent wisdom that was, most of the time, his hallmark. But it is hard also not to remember what he told William Styron in 1960 when Styron and his friends asked him what was going to happen now. "Jimmy's face would become a mask of imperturbable certitude," Styron wrote. "'Baby,' he would say softly and glare back with vast glowering eyes, 'yes, baby, I mean *burn*. We will *burn your cities down*.'"

Reading his speeches and journalism now, there seems only one fresh hell that has happened in his country that he did not foresee and that would have shocked him deeply. And this is the vast and merciless increase in the prison population, especially of young black males. He saw the context for it, however, and made his own position very clear in an article in *Playboy* in 1964:

> The failure on our part to accept the reality of pain, or anguish, of ambiguity, of death, has turned us into a very peculiar and mon-

> strous people. It means, for one thing, and it's very serious, that people who have had no experience have no compassion. People who have had no experience suppose that if a man is a thief, he is a thief; but, in fact, that isn't the most important thing about him. The most important thing about him is that he is a man and, furthermore, that if he's a thief or a murderer or whatever he is, *you* could also be and you would know this, anyone would know this who had really dared to live.

He did not see the full implications of this, and so in the same year he wrote something that seems naive now, perhaps the only truly naive observation he ever made: "There is a limit to the number of people any government can put in prison, and a rigid limit indeed to the practicality of such a course." And fifteen years later, in the *Los Angeles Times*, he ended his article on a note of pure optimism: "But black people hold the trump. When you try to slaughter people, you create a people with nothing to lose. And if I have nothing to lose, what are you going to do to me? In truth, we have one thing to lose—our children. Yet we have never lost them, and there is no reason for us to do it now. We hold the trump. I say it: Patience and shuffle the cards."

The cards were shuffled all right; and the idea that there was a limit to the number of people any government can put in prison became a joker; the game included the possibility of "three strikes and you are out" with all the mindlessness, mercilessness, and lack of compassion that that implied. At the end of 2005, there were close to 2.2 million prisoners in federal, state or local jails in the United States. Three thousand one hundred forty-five black men out of every 100,000 lived as sentenced prisoners, compared to 471 white male sentenced prisoners per 100,000 white males; this compares to an estimated 3,000 out of every 100,000 members of the population of Russia who were in jail during Stalin's reign. As of 2006, 7 million people in the United States were behind bars, on probation, or on parole. The United States has 5 percent of the world's population and 25 percent of its prisoners, 737 per 100,000 compared to 100 in Australia and 59 in Norway and 37 in Japan and 29 in Iceland and India. England and Wales, with roughly the same crime rate as the United States, have 149 per 100,000 in prison. A report from the Justice Department estimated that 12 percent of American black men in their twenties and early thirties are in jail now, compared to 1.6 percent of white males of the same age group. The general prison numbers in the United States have doubled since 1990.

In his address to Harlem schoolteachers in 1963, Baldwin set the context for crime among young black men. He wrote about every street boy's relationship to the law.

> If he is really cunning, really ruthless, really strong—and many of us are—he becomes a kind of criminal. He becomes a kind of criminal because that's the only way he can live. Harlem and every ghetto in this city—every ghetto in this country—is full of people who live outside the law. They wouldn't dream of calling a policeman. . . . They have turned away from the country forever and totally. They live by their wits and really long to see the day when the entire structure comes down.

It seems sad, almost strange, reading his work now, even when its tone was calm and ambiguous and measured, but especially as he grew angry and strident, to realize that, in the twenty years after James Baldwin's death, brand-new structures made of concrete have gone up all over America with laws to match, and in those buildings much of the beauty he wrote about, and many of the dreams his friends had, lie incarcerated. Baldwin's legacy is to help us understand how something has happened that even he could not have imagined.

THREE

"Over and Over and Over Again"

James Baldwin, *Uncle Tom's Cabin,* and the Afterlife of an American Story

BRIALLEN HOPPER

> "You are full of nightmares," Harriet tells me. . . .
>
> I watch her face. I know that it is quite impossible for her to be as untroubled as she seems. . . . Harriet . . . has reacted against all the advanced doctrines to which she has been exposed by becoming steadily and beautifully old-fashioned. . . .
>
> Whenever I become upset, Harriet becomes very cheerful and composed.
>
> —JAMES BALDWIN, "THIS MORNING, THIS EVENING, SO SOON" (1960)

When it comes to James Baldwin and *Uncle Tom's Cabin*, everybody knows "Everybody's Protest Novel." Published in 1949, when Baldwin was only twenty-four, the essay is an impassioned denunciation of Harriet Beecher Stowe's novel and the literary and political traditions it represents. In it, Baldwin accuses both Stowe and Richard Wright of oversimplifying the complexity of black experience. In consequence, Baldwin claims, *Uncle Tom's Cabin* and *Native Son* are bad novels that fail both aesthetically and politically. "Bigger is Uncle Tom's descendant, flesh of his flesh," he writes, "so exactly opposite a portrait that, when the books are placed together, it seems that the contemporary Negro novelist and the dead New England woman are locked together in a deadly, timeless battle." In Baldwin's version of literary history, Stowe and Wright are caught in a relationship that is at once intimate, erotic, and murderous: "Within this web of lust and fury, black and white can only thrust and counter-thrust. . . . The thrust, the counter-thrust, the longing making heavier that cloud which blinds and suffocates them both, so that they go down into the pit together."[1]

As Michael Nowlin has observed, Baldwin's claim that flawed aesthetics result in flawed politics was hardly revolutionary and in fact amounted to Trillingesque orthodoxy.[2] What *was* revolutionary, however, was Baldwin's decision to apply these political standards to the hitherto untouchable classics of racial protest fiction. When Baldwin said *Uncle Tom's Cabin* was a poorly written novel, he was expressing the critical consensus. When he said it was a politically pernicious novel, he was expressing something new and shocking. Perhaps most shocking of all was his decision to damn Stowe and Wright together. In *Uncle Tom's Children* (1938), *Native Son* (1940), and "How Bigger Was Born" (1940), Wright had explicitly sought to distance himself from Stowe and the sentimental reform tradition she symbolized. But in Baldwin's revisionist genealogy of American protest, Wright and his characters become incestuous descendants of Stowe, suffocating in her eternal maternal embrace.

"Everybody's Protest Novel" established Baldwin as a writer to be reckoned with. The essay is a rhetorical tour de force. A pamphlet on the evils of pamphleteering, the essay catalogs acts of violence as a protest against the cataloging of violence and employs metaphors of witch burnings and miscegenation to make an argument against sensationalism. The essay is eminently quotable and ubiquitously cited, and it continues to haunt critical engagements with Baldwin, Wright, and Stowe, as well as with sentimentality and protest fiction generally. This is especially true of critical engagements with *Uncle Tom's Cabin.* Hortense Spillers, Eric Sundquist, Kenneth Warren, Richard Yarborough, and others have used "Everybody's Protest Novel" as a touchstone in their discussions of Stowe.[3] A recent and extreme example of the ubiquity of the essay in Stowe criticism is Henry Louis Gates's new introduction to *The Annotated Uncle Tom's Cabin:* Gates's introduction is twenty pages long, and the Baldwin of "Everybody's Protest Novel" is referenced on sixteen of these pages.[4]

But despite the indisputable power and importance of "Everybody's Protest Novel," it is only one of Baldwin's many engagements with *Uncle Tom's Cabin.* "Everybody's Protest Novel" is a single snapshot taken during one moment of a lifelong relationship. As Baldwin wrote in 1975 in *The Devil Finds Work,* "I read *Uncle Tom's Cabin* over and over and over again—

this is the first book I can remember having read," and in his writing he read it over and over and over again as well.[5] In their discussions of Baldwin's relationship to *Uncle Tom's Cabin*, however, few critics have read beyond 1949.[6] In this essay, I fill in some of the blank pages in the Baldwin-Stowe album with a series of literary snapshots taken over the course of Baldwin's career. In roughly chronological order, I narrate the reappearances of *Uncle Tom's Cabin* in Baldwin's essays, fiction, and pedagogy and trace in these citations a commemorative practice that allows Baldwin repeatedly to reimagine the family tree of American literary history. I argue that through remembering Stowe, Baldwin is able to retell his own origin-story as an artist, to find sources for his creative work, and to make meaning out of the miscegenated histories of American cultural production and reproduction across the generations. In other words, I read Baldwin's returns to Stowe as a series of photographs in a family album, each giving its insight into his fraught artistic ancestry and legacy.

My argument both extends and revises the common Oedipal reading of "Everybody's Protest Novel," an essay that is often thought of in familial and Freudian terms as a moment of symbolic patricide in Baldwin's relationship with his one-time mentor Richard Wright. Of course, Baldwin went on to mitigate this violent assessment of Wright in "Alas, Poor Richard" (1961) and elsewhere, writing Wright back into his family tree. As I will show, Baldwin produced similarly complicated and multiple accounts of his literary kinship to Stowe. In attending to these varied histories, I tell a story that extends Baldwin's literary family drama both to, but also beyond, matricide.

From the very beginning, in Baldwin, Stowe is there. In fact, Baldwin chose to commence his literary career by introducing himself as a child of Stowe and Dickens. In the first paragraph of the "Autobiographical Notes" that preface his first two books, *Go Tell It on the Mountain* (1953) and *Notes of a Native Son* (1955), Baldwin writes that, as a child, "I read *Uncle Tom's Cabin* and *A Tale of Two Cities* over and over and over again; in this way, in fact, I read just about everything I could get my hands on—except the Bible, probably because it was the only book I was encouraged to read."[7] As an origin-story that also functions as a kind of authenticating document, Baldwin's "Autobiographical Notes" initially establishes a lineage that is at once engaging, respectable, and problematic. As common cultural touchstones, Dickens and Stowe connect Baldwin with many of his potential readers, and both authors also symbolize a nineteenth-century novelistic heft and social seriousness that signal Baldwin's own literary ambitions. But *Uncle Tom's Cabin* in particular also evokes a range of less authenticating resonances: it is associated with an aesthetically discredited women's sentimental tradition and with the specter of the racial "problem novelist" as a one-hit wonder.

One page later Baldwin is already silently revising this problematic literary genealogy. When he lists his literary influences, the only two written texts he cites are the King James Bible and Dickens.[8] Baldwin's much-read *Uncle Tom's Cabin* has been replaced by his supposedly not-read Bible; Stowe's place as literary parent has been usurped by God. This substitution nicely sets up a legitimating provenance for *Go Tell It on the Mountain* and *Notes of a Native Son*, while attempting to solve with silence the problems posed by Stowe. Baldwin's "forgetting" of *Uncle Tom's Cabin* here is an efficacious erasure. Unlike Dickens and the Bible, Baldwin implies, Stowe is more a point of origin than an influence. As Baldwin grew into the Bible, he grew out of Stowe. She is relegated to the world of childhood reading, to a prior age of immaturity. Stowe's appearance and disappearance in his "Autobiographical Notes" allow Baldwin to establish himself as a young man who has put childish reading and writing behind him. His carefully managed allusion to *Uncle Tom's Cabin* is a bildungsroman in a nutshell.

But Baldwin's story of his own maturation through Stowe's erasure requires repeated retelling, mostly because Stowe won't stay erased. In the original edition of *Notes of a Native Son*, the excised *Uncle Tom's Cabin* returns almost immediately. Here the "Autobiographical Notes" is immediately followed by "Everybody's Protest Novel," in which the novel reappears only to be violently dispatched, and then by "Many Thousands Gone," in which Baldwin declares:

> Aunt Jemima and Uncle Tom are dead, their places taken by a group of amazingly well-adjusted young men and women, almost as dark, but ferociously literate, well-dressed and scrubbed, who are never laughed at, who are not likely ever to set foot in a cotton or tobacco field or in any but the most modern of kitchens.[9]

In *Notes of a Native Son*, whether reincarnated as Bigger Thomas or a mythic stereotype, Uncle Tom must die to make room for the next generation. But even when dead, Tom remains necessary. Throughout his essays of the 1950s, Baldwin cannot tell the story of his "ferociously literate" generation's relationship to its forbears except through allusions to Stowe or to her most famous character.

However, the story doesn't always stay the same. Baldwin's 1956 essay "The Crusade of Indignation," a review of J. C. Furnas's *Goodbye to Uncle Tom*, gives him yet another opportunity to revisit his unfinished business with *Uncle Tom's Cabin*, but here the power dynamic has changed. No longer fighting for the right to his literary voice, Baldwin is now an acclaimed novelist, and he can afford to be more generous. The particular cultural history Baldwin wants to tell has changed as well: he is tracing the ancestry of the white American liberal, not the black American artist. Thus in "The Crusade of Indignation," Baldwin's first concern is no longer that *Uncle Tom's Cabin* denies blacks humanity, but that it denies whites political and cultural sophistication. He is proportionately less concerned about the existential threat posed by the novel's medieval morality and theological terror and more concerned by the intellectual threat posed by its lack of accurate knowledge and rigorous analysis. Baldwin sees Stowe's legacy not in lynch mobs, but in the "ordinary [white] American of goodwill" and his or her everyday engagements with black culture—in, for example, whites' undertheorized experiences of "some Billie Holiday records, perhaps a trip or two through Harlem, perhaps one or two Negro colleagues, or a Negro college friend."[10] *Uncle Tom's Cabin* is most troubling, Baldwin observes, "when one reflects, above all, how it flatters the popular mind, positively discouraging that mind from any tendency to think the matter through for itself."[11] Stowe's worst flaw is that "she knew nothing"; "perhaps if she had known more . . . she would have had a more realistic, more responsible view." For the first time, Baldwin can afford to damn Stowe not with curses or silence, but with faint praise, observing that she "was able to have such a tremendous effect because she was a mildly gifted woman who mirrored the assumptions of her time—and place—so perfectly."[12]

Even more successfully than in "Everybody's Protest Novel," Baldwin's citation of Stowe in "The Crusade of Indignation" performs his literary maturity. In calmly putting Stowe in her place—in describing her as a "shoddy" and "mildly gifted" novelist instead of a "terrible" one—Baldwin has left behind the most extreme forms of the anxiety of influence. And by establishing Stowe as the common matriarch of both black artists and white Billie Holiday fans, Baldwin expands the scope of his cultural critique as well. No longer focusing his commentary on the problems of the problem novelist, the Negro artist, or even white liberal politics, Baldwin uses Stowe to engage with broader and subtler questions about whites' relationship to and appropriation of black culture.

As Baldwin was grappling with the legacy of *Uncle Tom's Cabin* in his essays, he was working it out in his fiction as well. All of Baldwin's early novels begin with a citation of *Uncle Tom's Cabin,* and all can be read as revisions of *Uncle Tom's Cabin.* After beginning with the "Autobiographical Notes," *Go Tell It on the Mountain* returns to Stowe's novel in its tropes and its form. Baldwin's reliance on epiphanies in *Go Tell It on the Mountain* owes as much to Stowe as it does to Joyce, and John Grimes's conversion experience is a close rewriting of Tom's death. And both *Uncle Tom's Cabin* and *Go Tell It on the Mountain* share an unusual narrative structure: each novel tells multiple generations of black migration narratives across space and time and then winds up all the scattered strands of plot at the end by representing one black man's confrontation with death, his visions of glory, and his religious transfiguration. In Baldwin's important revision, however, John, unlike Tom, lives.

Baldwin's fiction of the later 1950s and early 1960s also takes *Uncle Tom's Cabin* as its point of origin and departure. The title of *Giovanni's Room* (1956) is a play on the title of *Uncle Tom's Cabin,* and in this novel Baldwin, like Stowe, is interested in exploring the complex connections between masculinity and domesticity. Most especially in his representation of Giovanni's death, Baldwin both recalls and calls into question Stowe's investment in the sentiment and spectacle of male martyrdom. Baldwin's pattern of beginning his fiction with allusions to *Uncle Tom's Cabin* is perhaps most explicit in *Another Country* (1962), in which Rufus's white girlfriend Leona is repeatedly referred to as "Little Eva" in the opening pages. In *Another Country,* Baldwin again moves from explicitly referencing *Uncle Tom's Cabin* in the beginning to implicitly rewriting it throughout. As in *Uncle Tom's Cabin,* the Eva figure in *Another Country* is Southern and innocent and doomed, and as in *Uncle Tom's Cabin,* the black man who loves her is helpless to save her and is doomed to an early death as well. In Baldwin's version, which both gives to and takes away from Stowe's, the pair are given expressive sexuality but denied the possibility of redemption.

The most haunting allusion to Stowe in Baldwin's fiction is in the short story "This Morning, This Evening, So Soon" (1960), which is collected in *Going to Meet the Man* (1965). The story's portrait of a marriage between a white woman named Harriet and the narrator, a black singer, inescapably invites an allegorical reading, especially in the opening paragraphs from which my epigraph is taken:

> "You are full of nightmares," Harriet tells me. . . .
>
> I watch her face. I know that it is quite impossible for her to be as untroubled as she seems. . . . Harriet . . . has reacted against all the advanced doctrines to which she has been exposed by becoming steadily and beautifully old-fashioned. . . .
>
> Whenever I become upset, Harriet becomes very cheerful and composed.[13]

Over and over in this story, the narrator finds himself watching his wife's face and seeing his reverse reflection there. As he says later, "Her eyes seek mine in the mirror."[14] "It is astonishing the lengths to which a person, or a people, will go in order to avoid a truthful mirror," he observes, but he and Harriet always seek the other's reflection.[15] In the mirrored symmetry of their anger and composure, the long marriage between Harriet and the narrator finds its form. Unlike the willfully and culpably innocent Harriet of "Everybody's Protest Novel," this Harriet, though perhaps also willfully innocent, is not a known quantity to be repudiated and damned. The narrator says, unnecessarily, "I wonder what she is really thinking."[16] She is a daily enigma and a constant companion.

"Harriet repeats, 'Nightmares, nightmares,'" the narrator says: and Harriet may need the narrator's nightmares, and he may need her composure.[17] His repeated nightmares might signify a marriage based on the compulsions of traumatic recurrence and (to allegorize) a compulsive citationality in Baldwin's writing based on the traumas of literary history. But the story offers other images of their relationship as well:

> I fall back with her on the bed, and she smiles down into my face. . . . And for a moment we are silent, alone in our room, which we have shared for so long. The slight rise and fall of Harriet's breathing creates an intermittent pressure against my chest.[18]

Like the eternal thrust and counterthrust of Stowe and Wright, this is an image of the "intermittent pressure" of interracial intimacy and its relation to historical time. The "so long" reverberates elsewhere in Baldwin's work. Writing in *The Fire Next Time* (1963) about sharing the "house" of the American continent with white people, Baldwin exclaims, "One has been perishing here so long!"[19] But in this image of the couple on the bed, "so long" evokes duration, not desperation. It is an image not of mutually assured annihilation, but of mutual endurance. And though the pressure

Harriet puts on the narrator's chest may evoke the suffocation of Stowe and Wright's embrace, Harriet's breathing also signifies the intermittent pressure of Stowe's repeated inspiration.

For many reasons, "This Morning, This Evening, So Soon" marks a turning point, and perhaps the high point, in Baldwin's genealogical use of Stowe. Not only does it reimagine the terms of the relationship between Stowe and the black artist figure; it also, for the first time, uses Stowe to imagine the black artist as a father and not just a son (or an uncle). The narrator of "This Morning, This Evening" is an anxious and loving father. He yells at and chats with his young son, and worries and watches over him, and he obsesses over the arbitrary and inevitable qualities of his family history. The narrator wonders what this history would have been like if he hadn't ended up with Harriet:

> Perhaps . . . I would have found another woman and had another son. But that other woman, that other son are in the limbo of vanished possibilities. I might also have become something else. . . . But no, I am what I have become and this woman beside me is my wife, and I love her. All the sons I might have had mean nothing, since I *have* a son.[20]

In this passage, the narrator first imagines an alternative to the family story he finds himself in before choosing to recommit himself to it. In claiming possession of this family, the narrator is confirmed in his own sense of identity. And by settling on this story, he can claim a connection to future generations, as well as to past and present ones; he can begin to imagine his own legacy.

In "This Morning, This Evening," the narrator's daily practice of marriage with Harriet is not an end in itself, but a means to a future. Though the story begins with a conversation between the narrator and Harriet, and continues by narrating their past and present life as a couple, it ends with the narrator and his son alone together and about to begin a long journey. In an image simultaneously evoking imprisonment, movement, and ascent, the narrator and his son step into an elevator: "I open the cage and we step inside. . . . I press the button and the cage, holding my son and me, goes up."[21]

My penultimate snapshot of Baldwin and Stowe is arguably another picture of (among other things) anxious parenting. Taken when Baldwin was teaching at Bowling Green State University in the late 1960s and early

1970s, the snapshot confirms the centrality of *Uncle Tom's Cabin* to Baldwin's sense of his literary history and legacy, and the urgency of his attempt to communicate this history to the next generation. Ernest A. Champion, a professor at Bowling Green State at the time, gives an account of Baldwin's classes in his book *Mr. Baldwin, I Presume* (1995). Champion begins with a description of the syllabus:

> Baldwin instructed us that he would want the following books to be read for the course: 1. *Uncle Tom's Cabin* by Harriet Beecher Stowe, 2. *Native Son* by Richard Wright, 3. *Things Fall Apart* by Chinua Achebe, and 4. His own novel *Go Tell It on the Mountain*.[22]

During the height of the Black Power Movement, and two decades after he first wrote about Stowe and Wright, Baldwin's insistence on the importance of *Uncle Tom's Cabin* remains as strong as ever. *Uncle Tom's Cabin* is a strange text to assign in a contemporary literature or creative writing course, and particularly so at this historical moment, when (partly thanks to Baldwin) Stowe's critical capital was at its lowest point. But despite the inclusion of Achebe, in essentials the syllabus simply retells Baldwin's autobiographical literary genealogies of the 1940s and '50s. In its grand generational movements from Stowe to Wright to Baldwin, the syllabus seems to repeat yet again the familiar matrilineal and mongrel family story. The 1950s are over, and Baldwin's is no longer the newest novel on the list, but (perhaps in an expression of his desire to forge a closer connection between himself and the new generation—to create a link between the fourth novel on the list and the fifth, whatever it may be) Baldwin has silently altered dates in his history to preserve its ending: though *Go Tell It on the Mountain* appeared six years before *Things Fall Apart*, Baldwin lists it last.

Champion's account of Baldwin and Stowe in the classroom together at Bowling Green is both poignant and troubling:

> When Baldwin arrived and began teaching the course, it became clear to us why he had chosen those four books. He led the students into a discussion of *Uncle Tom's Cabin* and in the process was trying to elicit from them the missing element in the novel which Baldwin wanted them to find out for themselves. He began emphasizing what he saw as some of the problems in the novel, granting of course the reasons for its immense popularity at the time it was published. He kept prodding them into a realization of what he termed "the in-

> nocence of the American mind," the kind of innocence, he said, [that] was a menace to him and his people. . . . When Baldwin gave his first assignment to the students, his intentions in choosing *Uncle Tom's Cabin* as a text became clearer. He asked the students to try and tell the story from Uncle Tom's point of view. He wanted them to see if a black man, after all, had a mind of his own, whether he had any feelings that were even remotely connected to his own humanity, quite apart from the humanity of those who lived in the big white house. He said he wanted the students to probe one of the central issues of the whole problem of Negroes in the United States, the problem of human sexuality and in particular the paralyzing fear of white men about the sexual prowess of Negro men. Did Uncle Tom live in a world of complete sexual suppression, did he even have sexual fantasies that would at least make him somewhat human and give some insight into the condition of black people during slavery? That was the reason Baldwin juxtaposed Richard Wright's *Native Son* with *Uncle Tom's Cabin*, because Richard Wright uses Bigger Thomas to play the very role in which the white imagination, the "brainwashed white imagination," wanted to believe.[23]

Champion's narration highlights the anxiously controlling nature of Baldwin's teaching: Baldwin "led" the students, he "tried to elicit" specific things from them, he "kept prodding them," his intentions were clear. Baldwin urgently needs his students to read *Uncle Tom's Cabin*, and he needs them to read it in the same way that he is always reading it. Baldwin is trying to pass on his own literary history to the next generation. And in requiring the students to relate to *Uncle Tom* as he does, he is also trying to universalize this personal history.

Baldwin teaches an American literary history beginning with Stowe because he believes this genealogy is still generative. What is more: he teaches it because he cannot imagine American literary production and reproduction outside this genealogy. If Baldwin believes that the first text his students should read is *Uncle Tom's Cabin*, this is because he believes the only way for students to learn to write is for them to attempt to rewrite *Uncle Tom's Cabin*. For Baldwin, every story—his own story, the story of American literature, the stories of his own novels, the stories of the novels his students may one day write—*every* American story, past, present, and future, begins with *Uncle Tom's Cabin*.

Baldwin's lifelong practice of continual and compulsive return to his

Stovian literary roots reappears to an extreme extent in my final snapshot, which is from *The Devil Finds Work*. Written in 1975, *The Devil Finds Work* is Baldwin's book about movies, and thus *Uncle Tom's Cabin* needn't have made an appearance in it at all, since Baldwin knew it only as a novel. But *Uncle Tom's Cabin* is mentioned repeatedly in the first chapter, initially in a series of what seem to be non sequiturs. In one instance, Baldwin has just finished a paragraph about going to the movies as a child. He begins the next paragraph with the words "I read *Uncle Tom's Cabin* over and over and over again—this is the first book I can remember having read—and then I read *A Tale of Two Cities*—over and over and over again."[24] Baldwin then goes on to describe seeing the film version of *A Tale of Two Cities*, without discussing *Uncle Tom's Cabin* at all. Later, in a paragraph about a movie called *The Prisoner of Shark Island*, he inserts the following sentence: "I know that I read everything I could get my hands on, including movie advertisements, and *Uncle Tom's Cabin* had had a tremendous impact on me, and I certainly reacted to the brutal conjunction of the words, *prisoner*, *shark*, and *island*."[25] He goes on to write about the film without further reference to Stowe.

The third time Baldwin returns to *Uncle Tom's Cabin*, however, traces of his underlying logic can be discerned. Baldwin is describing his wonder at seeing the biblical verse "I am the resurrection and the life" at the end of the movie of *A Tale of Two Cities*. He writes:

> I had no idea what *Two Cities* was really about, any more than I knew what *Uncle Tom's Cabin* was really about, which is why I had read them both so obsessively: they had something to tell me. It was this particular child's way of circling around the question of what it meant to be a nigger.[26]

Here again, at last, nearly thirty years later, are all the literary ancestors from Baldwin's first family tree—the Bible, Dickens, Stowe. And here as well, fittingly, is a promise of eternal life, a promise that prefaces a model of reading as an eternal return. Whether *Uncle Tom's* repeated return is figured as a resurrection, or as a lifetime of circling back around, it is always at the heart of the question.

Baldwin has again restored *Uncle Tom's Cabin* to its centrality in his literary genealogy. But before long, in a familiar move, he circles around the novel again a few pages later, incorporating it into yet another family story. This last part of the story of Baldwin and Stowe ends, as it began in 1949, with an image of *Uncle Tom's Cabin* as the catalyst that allows Baldwin to enact a coming-of age ritual and declare his literary independence. Baldwin writes:

> I had read *Uncle Tom's Cabin* compulsively, the book in one hand, the newest baby on my hipbone. . . . My mother got scared. She hid the book. The last time she hid it, she hid it on the highest shelf above the bathtub. I was somewhere around seven or eight. God knows how I did it, but I somehow climbed up and dragged the book down. Then, my mother, as she herself puts it, "didn't hide it anymore," and, indeed, from that moment, though in fear and trembling, began to let me go.[27]

Baldwin clearly learned his pedagogical style from his mother, who taught him to seek out the hidden *Uncle Tom's Cabin* over and over and over again. Years later, in a repetition and revision of his mother's anxious parenting, Baldwin will worry over his students' distance from the novel's hidden knowledge. But now, in this moment of origin, reading Stowe allows Baldwin to free himself from his literal ancestry by adopting a literary one.

Uncle Tom's Cabin in one hand, the newest baby on his hipbone: holding on to the embodied past and future of America, Baldwin begins his literary life.

This extended version of the Stowe-Baldwin genealogy supplements our other, simpler stories of American literary kinship and allows us to imagine an unfamiliar literary history. In uncovering a hidden pattern in Baldwin's reading and writing over the course of his life, the story of Baldwin and *Uncle Tom's Cabin* illuminates the troubling but generative legacy of the nineteenth-century sentimental reform tradition in twentieth-century African American literature.

This story matters because Stowe's legacy troubles us still. I conclude my discussion of Baldwin, Stowe, and literary genealogy by turning to Henry Louis Gates's recent introduction to *Uncle Tom's Cabin*, which I read as a modern-day rewriting of "Everybody's Protest Novel" and a thought-provoking offshoot of this literary family tree. As a critic long fascinated by canon formation and, more recently, by his own literal genetic inheritance, Gates shows most clearly how the Stowe-Baldwin genealogy I have traced continues to be both compelling and generative for American literary historians. Indeed, Gates's introduction reads like an extended act of signifying on "Everybody's Protest Novel," in which Gates is ventriloquizing the young Baldwin, and Baldwin is standing in for Richard Wright or Stowe. Like the Baldwin of "Everybody's Protest Novel," Gates uses a discussion of *Uncle Tom's Cabin* as an occasion to criticize an older black male author, and he criticizes Baldwin in ways uncannily similar to those that Baldwin used to criticize Stowe and Wright. Echoing Baldwin's dismissal of *Uncle Tom's Cabin* as "a very bad novel,"[28] Gates describes Baldwin's novels as "didactic, often heavy-handed,"[29] and "carelessly crafted."[30] He quotes extended passages from Baldwin's novels without analyzing them, treating them as irrefutable proof of the novels' self-evident problems, just as Baldwin quotes Stowe, and he criticizes Baldwin for being blind to Stowe's sexuality, just as Baldwin criticizes Stowe for failing to see Tom's sexuality. Though Gates doesn't condemn Baldwin by calling him "sentimental," as Baldwin labeled Stowe, he uses the term "melodramatic" to achieve much the same purpose. He even gives an extended definition of melodrama that parallels Baldwin's famous definition of sentimentality. "Sentimentality, the excessive parading of excessive and spurious emotion," writes Baldwin about Stowe, "is the mark of dishonesty, the inability to feel; the wet eyes of the sentimentalist betray his aversion to experience, his fear of life, his arid heart."[31]

"Melodrama," writes Gates about Baldwin,

> is a form of drama rendered over the top. Its use implies a writer's deepest mistrust of the instincts or intelligence of the reader. Melodramatic eruptions often flag a writer's incapacity or unwillingness to show or to dramatize.[32]

Like "Everybody's Protest Novel," Gates's introduction commits the very same rhetorical crimes that it condemns. Gates concludes his introduction with a tableau as melodramatic as anything he finds in Baldwin's novels. "When Baldwin looked in the mirror of his literary antecedents," he writes, "what he saw, to his horror, was Harriet Beecher Stowe in blackface. Although it pains me to say it, James Baldwin, in many ways, is Harriet Beecher Stowe's most legitimate twentieth-century heir."[33]

For Gates, when Baldwin sees Stowe in the mirror it is a moment of sheer horror. For Baldwin, the mirror moment is many other things: instructive; liberating; useful; necessary. As Baldwin glances obliquely at the mirror of *Uncle Tom's Cabin* over and over and over again in his novels and essays, he is trying to catch Harriet's eye. He sees in the mirror not a shameful mask of burnt cork, but an enigmatic and familiar face known to him through long intimacy and family resemblance. Gates experiences Baldwin's "legitimate" literary inheritance from Stowe as purely painful, but Baldwin, intimately familiar with the pain of illegitimate descent, chooses to claim and reclaim this mixed literary inheritance and to tell and retell its history. More than matricide, more than love and theft, the story of Baldwin and Stowe is the story of Baldwin's constant search for a future in his literary past.

NOTES

1. Baldwin, *Collected Essays*, 18.
2. Nowlin, "Ralph Ellison, James Baldwin," 119.
3. See Spillers, "Changing the Letter"; Sundquist, introduction to *New Essays on* Uncle Tom's Cabin; Warren, "Afterlife of *Uncle Tom's Cabin*"; Yarborough, "Strategies of Black Characterization."
4. Gates, "Introduction," cites "Everybody's Protest Novel" directly seven times (xi, xiii, xv, xviii, xix, xxii, and xxvi), and his nine additional references to Baldwin (xii, xvii, xx, xxv, xxvii, xxviii, xxix, and xxx) presume that Baldwin's stance toward Stowe remained unchanged from "Everybody's Protest Novel" onward.
5. Baldwin, *Collected Essays*, 483.
6. A notable exception is Horace A. Porter, who writes, "*Uncle Tom's Cabin* is, in effect, the hidden mother text conspiring to work itself out in [Baldwin's] life" (*Stealing the Fire*, 56). Porter devotes an entire chapter to Stowe in his book. But even Porter mainly focuses on "Everybody's Protest Novel," with some additional discussion of Baldwin's positive representation of Christianity and martyrdom in *The Fire Next Time*. Porter is inclined to give *Uncle Tom's Cabin* the credit for Baldwin's Christian preoccupations and symbolism in this novel, though Baldwin's childhood in the church doubtless has much to do with this as well.
7. Baldwin, *Collected Essays*, 5.
8. Ibid., 6.
9. Ibid., 21.
10. Ibid., 610.
11. Ibid.
12. Ibid., 612.
13. Baldwin, *Early Novels and Stories*, 865.
14. Ibid., 868.
15. Ibid., 871.
16. Ibid., 868.
17. Ibid.
18. Ibid., 869.
19. Baldwin, *Collected Essays*, 330. I am grateful to Gregory Londe for this reference.
20. Baldwin, *Early Novels and Stories*, 869.

21. Ibid., 907.
22. Champion, *Mr. Baldwin, I Presume*, 38.
23. Ibid., 38–39.
24. Baldwin, *Collected Essays*, 483.
25. Ibid., 484.
26. Ibid., 485.
27. Ibid., 488.
28. Ibid., 11.
29. Gates and Robbins, *The Annotated Uncle Tom's Cabin*, xxvi.
30. Ibid., xxviii.
31. Baldwin, *Collected Essays*, 12.
32. Gates, "Introduction," xxvii.
33. Ibid., xxx.

BIBLIOGRAPHY

Baldwin, James. *Collected Essays*. Ed. Toni Morrison. New York: Library of America, 1998.

Baldwin, James. *Early Novels and Stories*. Ed. Toni Morrison. New York: Library of America, 1998.

Champion, Ernest A. *Mr. Baldwin, I Presume—James Baldwin—Chinua Achebe: A Meeting of the Minds*. Lanham, Md.: University Press of America, 1995.

Gates, Henry Louis, Jr. "Introduction." In Harriet Beecher Stowe, *The Annotated Uncle Tom's Cabin*, 1852, ed. Henry Louis Gates Jr. and Hollis Robbins. New York: Norton, 2007.

Leeming, David. *James Baldwin: A Biography*. New York: Knopf, 1994.

Nowlin, Michael. "Ralph Ellison, James Baldwin, and the Liberal Imagination." *Arizona Quarterly* 60, no. 2 (2004).

Porter, Horace. *Stealing the Fire: The Art and Protest of James Baldwin*. Middletown, Conn.: Wesleyan University Press, 1989.

Spillers, Hortense. *Black, White, and in Color: Essays on American Literature and Culture*. Chicago: University of Chicago Press, 2003.

Spillers, Hortense. "Changing the Letter: The Yokes, the Jokes of Discourse, or, Mrs. Stowe, Mr. Reed." In Hortense Spillers, ed., *Black, White, and in Color: Essays on American Literature and Culture*. Chicago: University of Chicago Press, 2003.

Sundquist, Eric, ed. *New Essays on* Uncle Tom's Cabin. New York: Cambridge University Press, 1986.

Warren, Kenneth. "The Afterlife of *Uncle Tom's Cabin*." In Cindy Weinstein, ed., *The Cambridge Companion to Harriet Beecher Stowe*. Cambridge: Cambridge University Press, 2004.

Yarborough, Richard. "Strategies of Black Characterization in *Uncle Tom's Cabin* and the Early Afro-American Novel." In Eric Sundquist, ed., *New Essays on* Uncle Tom's Cabin. Cambridge: Cambridge University Press, 1986.

FOUR

"Now Describing You"

James Baldwin and Cold War Liberalism

VAUGHN RASBERRY

In 1950, W. E. B. Du Bois's literary journal *Phylon* devoted a special issue to the situation of the "Negro Writer." Overwhelmingly, contributors noted how black writers appeared to be approaching artistic maturity and finally shedding what Alain Locke described as the "adolescence" and "lingering immaturity" of the Negro Renaissance of the 1920s and '30s. Several titles in the issue echo this judgment: Charles H. Nichols Jr. describes the 1940s as "a Decade of Growth"; N. P. Tillman reads postwar black literary production as an entrance into the "Threshold of Maturity"; Thomas D. Jarrett heralds the "Negro Novelist's Coming of Age" as a graduation "Toward Unfettered Creativity." Commentators observed that the increasing number of literary texts ostensibly uncommitted to racial protest or naturalistic representation furnished further proof of the coming of age of the black novelist. "The most heartening thing for me," writes Langston Hughes in *Phylon*, "is to see Negroes writing works in the general American field, rather than dwelling on Negro themes solely. . . . I have been pleased to see [Willard] Motley, [Frank] Yerby, [Ann] Petry, and Dorothy West presenting in their various ways non-Negro subjects. . . . Until this particular period there have not been so many Negroes writing of characters not drawn from their own race."[1] In the next several years, James Baldwin would publish the novels *Giovanni's Room* (1956) and *Another Country* (1962), joining a distinguished group of black writers who had inaugurated a new genre or at least rehabilitated a marginal one: the so-called novel of white life.

Widely seen as literary evidence of black political progress, the proliferation of this and other experimental genres at midcentury suggested to many commentators the prospect for an unprecedented realm of freedom now open to African American writers. Critics argued that the slow but irreversible decline of Jim Crow segregation by midcentury had liberated African American writers from the racial protest genre, empowering them to pursue modes of "universal" expression that resonated with the national experience "as a whole."

Yet is this notion—that black writers and artists at midcentury sought to transcend racial particularism in favor of a nonracial universalism or "broader" national narrative—a viable way of understanding the shift in postwar African American aesthetics? Discussing a recent retrospective on the work of black artist Jacob Lawrence, Nikhil Pal Singh observes how the museum catalog highlights his mid-1950s series, "Struggle . . . From the History of the American People," as a work in which Lawrence "went beyond African American history to deal with the American experience as a whole." Such a description, he writes, "is characteristic in the history of black arts and letters." "It suggests that universal expression or representation in art or social thought necessarily transcends what is an implicitly narrow racial or minority experience."[2]

Similarly critical of the idea of racial transcendence as the prerequisite for universality, this chapter delineates Baldwin's navigation of the cultural and political milieu of the Cold War in order to suggest an alternative reading and historical logic of a period that, to echo Hughes, *did* produce an extraordinary quantity of black-authored narratives about white subjectivities. But in contrast to accounts that read these narratives as an index of black artistic maturation or as a capitulation to what Thomas Schaub calls the "liberal narrative"[3] of the Cold War, this chapter will argue that Baldwin's intellectual energies in this period embody the anticolonial zeitgeist encapsulated in his observation: "We who have been described so often are now describing [you]."[4] Reconstructing his Cold War milieu—which encompasses the global anticolonial and Civil Rights movements, the onset of centrist liberalism, and the calamities of the Second World War—reveals Baldwin as not only a singular voice on "America" or the "Negro problem," but an indispensable analyst of what Alain Badiou, with mock solemnity, calls the "totalitarian century," the apocalyptic site of ghastly twentieth-century events that can be thought principally in terms of organized state crime. As Badiou puts it, and as Baldwin was all too aware, "[The twentieth] century is an accursed century." "The principal parameters for thinking it," writes Badiou, "are the extermination camps, the gas chambers, massacres, tortures and organized state crime. . . . The union of this real with state crime has a name: this century is the totalitarian century."[5] Updating Arendt's controversial (and, despite its Eurocentric bias, underappreciated) linkage of fin-de-siècle imperialism in Africa with the origins of totalitarianism in Europe, Badiou revises the periodization of the twentieth century: "[The] blessed period before the war is also that of the apogee of colonial conquest, of Europe's stranglehold over the entirety of the earth, or very nearly. And therefore that elsewhere, far away but also very close to everyone's conscience, in the midst of every family, servitude and massacre are already present. Well before the war of 1914, there is Africa, delivered over to what some rare witnesses and artists will call an upright conquering savagery."[6] It is this revision of the twentieth century—a refusal to disentangle the Great War from imperialism, or totalitarianism from Jim Crow—that closely approximates the thrust of Baldwin's work at midcentury and that will serve as a historical framework for this chapter.

I

Discussing a photographic record of West Indian emigrants arriving in British cities in the 1950s, Bill Schwarz notes how these images "evoke a sense of hardships in the past overcome and hardships just around the corner yet to confront." Taken together, these photographs "serve to fix the collective memory of the momentous transformation of postwar migration." Yet "their very familiarity," Schwarz continues, "works to conceal other angles of vision. We become so habituated to the logic of the camera-eye that we are led to forget that the vision we are bequeathed is uncompromisingly one-way. . . . There are in the public domain no reverse-shots, in which—from gangplank or from railway station platform—we see, through the eyes of the emigrant, the huddles of journalists and onlookers, police and social workers, white faces all."[7]

Indeed, no such "reverse-shots" exist in the public domain, but Baldwin's analyses of liberalism and subalternity constitute an effort to reverse or dismantle this rigorously one-directional gaze as well as to tease out the historical and political stakes of its maintenance. And though commentators rarely regard Baldwin as an anticolonial theorist, his work functions to dissolve this "logic of the camera-eye" in a manner analogous to Fanon's or

Césaire's investigations of European consciousness, or James's and Wright's transatlantic investigations. Often embedded in a spiritual discourse, Baldwin's essays relentlessly disrupt liberalism's construction of the Negro as an object of sympathy and sociology's fixation on the Negro as an object of knowledge. As Baldwin addresses his nephew in *The Fire Next Time:* "Try to imagine how you would feel if you woke up one morning to find the sun shining and all the stars aflame."

> You would be frightened because it is out of the order of nature. Any upheaval in the universe is terrifying because it so profoundly attacks one's sense of one's own reality. Well, the black man has functioned in the white man's world as a fixed star, as an immoveable pillar: and as he moves out of his place, heaven and earth are shaken to their foundations.[8]

This passage advances a profound, if oblique, response to the question posed recently by scholars of modern genocide, who have wondered "why there was no genocide aimed at the blacks in the United States, and why African Americans were nevertheless more concerned than most whites at the Nazi persecution of the Jews."[9] This question is not a purely academic one: both Du Bois and Marcus Garvey posed the same question ("Shall the Negro be exterminated?") earlier in the century. In hindsight, the historical reliance of American capital on the labor extracted by black bodies rendered the specter of genocide highly improbable; yet the onset of emancipation and the attendant volatility of Jim Crow would, as Garvey and Du Bois worried, seem to have opened the possibility of mass extermination anew. Baldwin's imaginary scenario suggests why such an extermination did not transpire, *could* not have transpired. For Baldwin, the economic motives at the heart of the interracial affair that defines American identity have transformed into an irreversible form of desire, the disruption of which quakes with the force of "an upheaval in the universe." Unlike the European political movements whose memory successive regimes sought to efface, the forms of desire generated by colonial or interracial contact resist erasure. Foregrounding the impossibility of disentangling black and white identities, Baldwin's work operates to dislodge the Negro from his Atlantean role, his position in the white imagination as "fixed pillar" and "immoveable star."

Yet Baldwin does directly address the specter of genocide in the Second World War, which transformed the race problem in the United States in ways that black Americans and other colonized subjects immediately grasped. As Horace Cayton and St. Clair Drake conclude in *Black Metropolis* (1945), their landmark study of the emergent black middle-class Bronzeville neighborhood of Chicago, the "[Second World] War changed the course of race relations and brought America face to face with the contradictions in our culture in a manner and to an extent which made it impossible for either Negroes or whites to evade them longer."[10] Because National Socialism had demonstrated to the world the consequences of the intersection of scientific racism, fascist ideology, and mechanized warfare, the contradictions of American racial democracy could no longer be avoided or repressed. "For the crime of their ancestry," Baldwin observes in *The Fire Next Time*, "millions of people in the heart of Europe—God's citadel—were sent to a death so calculated, so hideous, and so prolonged that no age before this enlightened one had been able to imagine it, much less achieve and record it." The only event more frightening, according to Baldwin, than the calculated destruction of Europe's Jewry was the world's indifference to it; and this indifference explains much of black Americans' keen investment in the course of the Second World War. "I could not but feel," writes Baldwin,

> in those sorrowful years, that this human indifference, concerning which I knew so much already, would be my portion on the day that the United States decided to murder its Negroes systematically instead of little by little and catch-as-catch-can. I was, of course, authoritatively assured that what had happened to the Jews in Germany could not happen to the Negroes in America, but I thought, bleakly, that the German Jews had probably believed similar counselors, and, again, I could not share the white man's vision of himself for the very good reason that white men in America do not behave toward black men the way they behave toward each other.[11]

The language of enlightenment, calculation, and human indifference in the face of inhumanity recalls the argument, first advanced by Weber and amplified by Horkheimer and Adorno, that modern instrumental reason contains its own seeds of barbarism.

More recently, Zygmunt Bauman, drawing on Weber's theory of rationalization, reprises this argument in *Modernity and the Holocaust.* Bauman challenges standard interpretations of the Holocaust "as something that happened to the Jews" or as "the culmination point of European-Christian antisemitism."

> In so far as it is defined as, so to speak, the continuation of anti-Semitism through other means, the Holocaust appears to be a "one item set," a one-off episode, which perhaps sheds some light on the *pathology* of the society in which it occurred, but hardly adds anything to our understanding of this society's *normal* state. Still less does it call for any significant revision of the orthodox understanding of the historical tendency of modernity, of the civilizing process, of the constitutive topics of sociological inquiry.[12]

If the Holocaust is interpreted and codified as an aberration from modernity and its civilizing processes, then the latter are consequently exonerated. Yet modernity and its civilizing processes are precisely what Bauman wants to call into question. Likewise Baldwin, who observes in this same passage that the

> Tunisians were quite right in 1956—and it was a very significant moment in Western (and African) history—when they countered the French justification for remaining in North Africa with the question "Are the *French* ready for self-government?" Again, the terms "civilized" and "Christian" begin to have a very strange ring, particularly in the ears of those who have been judged to be neither civilized nor Christian, when a Christian nation surrenders to a foul and violent orgy, as Germany did during the Third Reich.[13]

Analogous to Baldwin's rejection of the sociology of race, Bauman indicts sociology's methods—its compilation of statistics and data, correlation of variables, deployment of charts and graphs—as incapable of grasping the historical truth of the Second World War.[14]

Baldwin's sojourns in Europe enabled a subtlety of analysis forbidden him in the suffocating context of U.S. racial terror. Whereas, for instance, "Notes of a Native Son" (1955) describes his adolescent confrontation with segregation in the language of hatred, rage, and violence that confirms his umbilical connection with Richard Wright—"There is not a Negro alive who does not have this rage in his blood," writes Baldwin, before recounting his "murderous" desire to choke a white waitress[15]—his ruminations in "Stranger in the Village" (1953) reveal a more penetrating diagnosis.

"From all available evidence," the essay begins, "no black man had ever set foot in this tiny Swiss village before I came." After describing a local custom in which the villagers "buy" African natives for the purpose of symbolically converting them to Christianity (the money is apparently sent to missionaries in Africa), Baldwin meditates on the first colonial encounters between whites and African villagers. Comparing this imaginary scenario with his experience among the Swiss, Baldwin notes that astonishment and curiosity would mark these improbable encounters on both sides. "But there is a great difference," he continues, "between being the first white man to be seen by Africans and being the first black man to be seen by whites."

> The white man takes the astonishment as a tribute, for he arrives to conquer and to convert the natives, whose inferiority in relation to himself is not even to be questioned; whereas I, without a thought of conquest, find myself among a people whose culture controls me, has even, in a sense, created me, people who have cost me more in anguish and rage than they will ever know, who yet do not even know of my existence. The astonishment with which I might have greeted them, should they have stumbled into my African village a few hundred years ago, might have rejoiced their hearts. But the astonishment with which they greet me today can only poison mine.

Like the account of his own Jim Crow experience in "Notes of a Native Son," this essay ventilates Baldwin's "anguish and rage," but these emotions are counterbalanced by the pathos of a historical situation that frustrates liberal solutions or assignments of blame. Pathos accrues in his recognition that the Swiss villagers—quite unlike his Jim Crow antagonists—are inheritors of a colonialist past they hardly recognize. Blissfully unaware of and yet oddly constituted by the heritage of European colonialism, his villagers are not easily incriminated.

Fond of Joyce's notion of history as nightmare—to which he adds that it "may be the nightmare from which no one *can* awaken"—Baldwin's melancholic admission that Western culture controls and has created him should arrest critics who see in his work a facile celebration of individuality and an absorption of other modes of Western normativity. Which is not to suggest that a fierce individualism does not permeate Baldwin's writing. Acknowledging the persistent individualist strain coursing through "Stranger in the Village," Lawrie Balfour argues that "his praise of human singularity is linked to an account of the painfulness of exclusion and to the denial of humanity that is at its root." (This sense of exclusion, she adds, pervades Baldwin's titles: "Stranger in the Village," *Nobody Knows My Name*, *No Name in the Street*.) "In lieu of elaborate arguments for recognition or respect," Balfour comments, Baldwin "provides a phenomenology of exclusion, a phenomenology, moreover, of the experience of excluding as well as that of being excluded. He shows how anonymity harms and how the enforcement of others' anonymity reassures."[16] Black alienation, in other words, is the price of the ticket for white consolidation. Yet this phenomenology of exclusion might contain the prospect for both black regeneration and the dissolution of whiteness. As Toni Morrison sensitively notes, Baldwin's ruminations also illustrated how one "could go as a stranger in the village and transform the distances between people into intimacy with the whole world."[17]

How do these reflections on racial alterity in a Swiss village relate to Baldwin's more enduring subject—the plight of blacks in urban modernity? Interestingly, his conception of cultural inheritance constitutes a thread connecting his experience of alterity in the Swiss village with alienation in the urban metropolis. For Baldwin, and later for Toni Morrison, the question of cultural inheritance is crucial for understanding subaltern experience as well as broader questions of power and its exclusions. "I say that the culture of these people controls me—but they can scarcely be held responsible for European culture," Baldwin writes. Paradoxically, inheritance is what perpetuates power but absolves its progeny from the sins of the fathers: the modern world is the legacy and the entitlement of the contemporary "West," even as its beneficiaries can disclaim responsibility for its past crimes. "America comes out of Europe, but these people have never seen America, nor have most of them seen more Europe than the hamlet at the foot of their mountain. Yet they move with an authority which I shall never have; and they regard me, quite rightly, not only as a stranger in their village but as a suspect latecomer, bearing no credentials, to everything they have—however unconsciously—*inherited*" (emphasis added). Given the prominence of theories of cultural hybridity in recent decades, few would endorse without reservation this idea of culture (and its implicit concession to an "integral Western civilization"), but the questions it raises are more provocative than its tacit acceptance of cultural integrity is problematic.

> For this village, even if it were incomparably more remote and incredibly more primitive, is the West, the West onto which I have

> been so strangely grafted. These people cannot be, from the point of view of power, strangers anywhere in the world; they have made the modern world, in effect, even if they do not know it. The most illiterate among them is related, in a way that I am not, to Dante, Shakespeare, Michelangelo, Aeschylus, Da Vinci, Rembrandt, and Racine; the cathedral at Chartres says something to them which it cannot say to me, as indeed would New York's Empire State Building, should anyone here ever see it. Out of their hymns and dances come Beethoven and Bach. Go back a few centuries and they are in their full glory—but I am in Africa, watching the conquerors arrive.[18]

Like most of his black contemporaries in the West, Baldwin can be accused of a "Eurocentric" historical perspective—of confining to modernity his view of power and cultural inheritance. Go back a few centuries, participants at the First Negro Writers and Artists Congress convened in Paris in 1956 were essentially arguing, and yes, Europe's renaissance was under way, while Africans were indeed "watching the conquerors arrive." But go back a few *millennia*, they countered, and the situation was quite the reverse.

Baldwin and his colleagues in the Atlantic world had little use for the millennial historical view contemplated by negritude writers and also by many of the representatives assembled at Bandung in 1955. Though such an approach enabled the retrieval and reconstruction of African and Asian societies, it was less useful for engaging with the modern liberal democracies that were Baldwin's intellectual target. Albert Murray was perhaps the earliest commentator to highlight Baldwin's probing of the consequences of "living in an over-mechanized civilization" dominated by instrumental reason, the drive toward efficiency, and a scientific rationalism that demoted questions about, say, spirituality or the irrational ("man's complexity," in Murray's and Baldwin's phrasing).[19] Certainly this view of modernity is familiar, if not clichéd, but it is worth asking whether Baldwin complicates the common assumptions on which such debates about modernity are typically conducted. Whether one envisages urban modernity from the point of view of modernist despair or in the ebullient, exhilarating terms employed in Marshall Berman's celebrated *All That Is Solid Melts into Air*, both these antitheses fail to capture the insights Baldwin's unique position yields.[20] As Toni Morrison illustrates, Baldwin's stress on "mechanization" and alienation differs crucially from his European and Euro-American predecessors—a difference that, as her sketch of Baldwin's reaction to the Chartres cathedral in France suggests, extends beyond the historical scope of modernity as such. Whereas Henry Adams had "come to Chartres . . . for the cathedral that fills our ideal," Baldwin was "terrified by the slippery bottomless well to be found in the crypt down which heretics were hurled to death, and by the obscene, inescapable gargoyles strutting out of the stone." According to Morrison, "When James Baldwin looked at Chartres,"

> He was doing more than reflecting on the schizophrenia of Western civilization. He was responding to what are universally believed to be the best and the most magnificent features of pre-industrial life from the singular position of a Black writer. [His observation] brings up the question of how a dispossessed people, a people without orthodox power, views the cities that it inhabits but does not have a claim to. . . . If Baldwin could respond in that manner to Chartres, how much more despairing we would expect him to be in his view of twentieth-century post-industrial urban America.

The notion that black Americans cannot lay "claim to" the cities they have built and inhabit is a controversial one, not least because it appears underwritten by a problematic notion of cultural integrity, if not essentialism, in its sense of the achievements of Western civilization; but such a risky measure might clear a space for what is distinctive in Baldwin's interpretation of the course of Western societies and of the subaltern's place within them.[21] Conceding that American literature has always deplored the city, Morrison argues that whether black writers profess to love or despise urban life, appear empowered or malnourished by it, "the emotion cannot be compared to Sandburg's or Fitzgerald's or Henry James's, simply because its sources are not the same. . . . For Black people are generally viewed as patients, victims, wards, or pathologies in urban settings, not as participants."[22] White or modernist urban alienation, then, no matter how apocalyptically this tradition depicts the modern metropolis, does not usher from a presumptive sense of disempowerment and incarceration. For Morrison, Baldwin's life and work exemplify this predicament.

The black American's sense of disinheritance and alienation comes into clearer focus in the 1950 essay "Encounter on the Seine: Black Meets Brown." Unlike the American Negro, Baldwin writes, the African colonial subject has "not so very many miles away, a homeland to which his relationship, no less than his responsibility, is overwhelmingly clear: His country must be given—or it must seize—its freedom."

> The African before him has endured privation, injustice, medieval cruelty; but the African has not yet endured the utter alienation of himself from his people and his past. His mother did not sing "Sometimes I Feel Like a Motherless Child," and he has not, all his life long, ached for acceptance in a culture which pronounced straight hair and white skin the only acceptable beauty.[23]

Ever the modernist, Richard Wright accepted this sense of homelessness ("I'm a rootless man, but I'm neither psychologically distraught nor in any wise particularly disturbed by it," he wrote in 1957)[24] as a condition endemic to modern society and conducive, ironically, to forging a diasporic identity.[25] As his penetrating report of the First Negro Writers and Artists Congress suggests, Baldwin was less comfortable with such a diasporic project or the negative identification—one based on shared histories of subjugation—on which it relied. Confronting the African in Paris might reaffirm the black American's alienation, but it also clarifies the trajectory of his political consciousness, which for Baldwin arcs toward an embattled integration rather than repatriation or revolution.

II

Another Country (1962), perhaps Baldwin's most ambitious novel, dramatizes the politically charged atmosphere of integration against the backdrop of a decaying postindustrial metropolis. The novel consists of three books, the first of which, "Easy Rider," narrates the malaise and fall from grace of its protagonist, Rufus Scott. A quintessential Baldwinian hero, Rufus is a jazz drummer from Harlem inhabiting the bohemian music scene of Greenwich Village. He associates with an interracial crowd, and his closest friend, Vivaldo Moore, is a white hipster and aspiring novelist. His mother and younger sister, Ida, idolize Rufus and expect that his talent and musicianship—which they associate with degenerate whites and nightclub culture—will nonetheless eventually pay dividends for the family.

The novel opens with an exhausted, homeless, and destitute Rufus, who has been sleeping all day in a movie theater for want of anywhere else to go. If, as Jacqueline Stewart has argued recently, African American cinematic production and spectatorship at the turn of the century symbolize black migration to urban modernity, this opening scene suggests the exhaustion, perversion even, of mass hope promised by the Northern metropolis.[26]

When Rufus decides to visit, shamefacedly, his friend Vivaldo, he comprehends at last the meaning of a Bessie Smith recording, "Backwater Blues":

> *There's thousands of people*, Bessie now sang, *ain't got no place to go*, and for the first time Rufus began to hear, in the severely understated monotony of this blues, something which spoke to his troubled mind. . . . Now that Rufus himself has no place to go— *'cause my house fell down and I can't live there no mo'*, sang Bessie—he heard the line and the tone of the singer, and he wondered how others had moved beyond the emptiness and horror which faced him now.[27]

The song's lyrics and Rufus's reaction to them suggest both the genre's renowned mix of interiority and the communal resources of black vernacular culture (the "blues sensibility"), as well as the menacing, socially destabilizing image of mass displacement—the image of thousands of people who have nowhere to go.

What precipitates Rufus's reversal of fortunes, during which time he had severed contact with his friends and family and occasionally "peddled [his] ass"? The narrative—which does not unfold in a linear fashion, but traverses time and space—re-creates Rufus's introduction to Leona, a poor white "Southern jezebel" with whom he commences a relationship. Immediately, Rufus knows that his sister Ida will disapprove. Described as beautiful and "very, very dark," Ida inspires in Rufus the thought that "ages and ages ago, Ida had not been merely the descendant of slaves. . . . It could be seen that she had once been a monarch."[28] The narrative ironically juxtaposes the regal Ida, whose color alone projects an aura of promiscuity among whites, with the actually promiscuous Leona, whose whiteness alone guarantees a measure of respect but whose attraction to blacks renders her suspect. Taking up with Leona, Rufus expects "trouble with the landlord, with the neighbors, with all the adolescents in the Village" and his parents, but he is only really concerned about Ida: "She had always expected a great deal from Rufus, and she was very race conscious. She would say, You'd never even have looked at that girl, Rufus, if she'd been black. But you'll pick up any white trash just because she's white. What's the matter—you ashamed of being black?"[29]

The interplay of racial shame and interracial desire long predates Baldwin's treatment of this theme in *Another Country*, but the historical reality of desegregation infuses these scenes with an unprecedented social urgency. African American fiction, at least since Paul Laurence Dunbar's *Sport of the Gods* (1902), features no shortage of narratives presaging hardship, racial oppression, and dissolution of the black family in the Northern metropolis. But the tragedy of Baldwin's novel relies less on the eulogizing of the cohesive black family than on the tension between the impossibility and the inevitability of integration. As elsewhere in Baldwin's oeuvre, the novel stresses the entwined fate of blacks and whites: "At Fifty-ninth Street many came on board and many rushed across the platform to the waiting local. Many white people and many black people, chained together in time and in space, and by history, and all of them in a hurry. In a hurry to get away from each other, he thought, but we ain't never going to make it. We been fucked for fair."[30] Condensing the critical themes of the novel—the burden of history, the future of integration, the ineluctability of interracial desire, the claustrophobia of the postindustrial metropolis—this passage furnishes concrete imagery for the famous question Baldwin posed in *The Fire Next Time:* "Do I really *want* to be integrated into a burning house?"

"Since you have no other, yes," F. W. Dupee replied in his review of *The Fire Next Time*. "And the better-disposed firemen will welcome your assistance." Though intended as tough-minded yet comforting wisdom, Dupee's response contains an unintentionally revealing presentation of the implied political stakes involved in integration. His concession that blacks possess no other house, and a burning one at that—a rebuttal not only to the idea of repatriation but also, it seems, to the romantic notion of autonomous black communities operating outside of mainstream American society—confirms black displacement and alienation rather than challenges it. And his extension of Baldwin's fire metaphor (the "better-disposed firemen") maintains whites in power and relegates blacks to the role of "assistants." Indeed, if the "better-disposed firemen" are white liberals, as it appears they must be, the metaphor contains yet another irony, for Baldwin was, of course, suspicious above all of well-intentioned liberals.[31]

Baldwin's dialectical approach to integration perplexed many of his contemporaries on both the liberal and the black nationalist sides of the ideological chasm. Liberals like Dupee chastised Baldwin for what appears to be pessimism, if not defeatism, regarding the horizon of integration and racial equality, whereas black nationalists accused Baldwin of a secret sycophancy of those same white liberals.[32] The interpretive divide between liberals and black nationalists would appear to be unbridgeable. Yet these polarities—manifested in the notion of the necessity and impossibility of integration—are connected in dialectical tension in Baldwin's work rather than irreconcilable. Working in the tradition of internal critique, Baldwin attempts the most searing critique of the terms and trajectory of integration while accepting its immanence as a historical movement. This approach enables him to challenge official narratives of racial progress and restore a sense of historicity to landmark legal decisions and political events that inspired historical amnesia among many observers, black and white. Seen as an enormous act of goodwill among whites and cause for national buoyancy, the watershed *Brown v. Board of Education* desegregation decision of 1954, Baldwin rewrites in terms of political necessity (and "necessity means concessions made in order to stay on top"). "White Americans congratulate themselves on the 1954 Supreme Court decision outlawing segregation in the schools," Baldwin writes in *The Fire Next Time*. "They suppose, in spite of the mountain of evidence that has since accumulated to the contrary, that this was proof of a change of heart—or, as they like to say, progress."

> Perhaps. It all depends on how one reads the word "progress." Most of the Negroes I know do not believe that this immense concession would ever have been made if it had not been for the competition of the Cold War, and the fact that Africa was clearly liberating herself and therefore had, for political reasons, to be wooed by the descendants of her former masters. Had it been a matter of love or justice, the 1954 decision would surely have occurred sooner; were it not for the realities of power in this difficult era, it might very well not have occurred yet.[33]

Baldwin's emphasis on the dynamics of the Cold War, desegregation, and decolonization is prescient. Revising the conventional view that this conflict originates exclusively in European developments and unfurls in the Third World via proxy wars and (neo)colonialist interventions, historians in recent decades have stressed the global, and specifically non-Western, sources of the Cold War.[34] The consolidation of power in the United States—specifically its strategic foreign policy interests in its spheres of influence—required a radical revision of the national *image* if not a full enfranchisement of its black citizens, who are inscribed in a historicist gesture of (inter)racial progress. Assuming, then, integration as a historical given, *The Fire Next Time* and *Another Country* sought to isolate and critically examine those crevices of historical experience that militate against what Nikhil Singh and other critics have identified as the interracial, nationally consolidated vision projected in early Cold War propaganda and eventually replicated in King's civil rights imagery.

III

No less than his rejection of the protest fiction model, Baldwin's unwillingness to concede that integration represented progress rankled his detractors across the ideological spectrum. Leftist critics held, perhaps ironically, that Baldwin had succumbed to the centrist drift pervading the postwar landscape. "The kind of criticism Baldwin wrote," Irving Howe intones,

> was very fashionable in America during the post-war years. Mimicking the Freudian corrosion of motives and bristling with dialectical agility, this criticism approached all ideal claims, especially those made by radical and naturalist writers, with a weary skepticism. . . . What Baldwin was saying here was part of the outlook so many American intellectuals took over during the years of a postwar liberalism not very different from conservatism.[35]

Howe envisaged Baldwin's acquiescence in the "post-war Zeitgeist" as simultaneously a capitulation to the so-called new or centrist liberalism—one characterized by transcendental or religious considerations of unsavory human motivations, by a renewed emphasis on spirituality and notions of "good and evil," and by doubts about the ideologies of human progress and perfectibility—emerging in the wake of the Second World War. But Baldwin's concern with the spiritual health of western societies can scarcely be seen as symptomatic of a cultural trend toward nonsecula· idioms in postwar America; this concern marks Baldwin's biography and aesthetic imagination from the very start.

More recently, however, Baldwin has emerged as one of liberalism's most pungent and prestigious critics, a reputation that might be gauged by his participation in the roundtable discussion "Liberalism and the Negro," organized by the journal *Commentary* in 1964. In addition to Baldwin, participants included sociologist of race relations Nathan Glazer; then–left wing philosopher Sidney Hook; and Gunnar Myrdal, author of *An American Dilemma*. Norman Podhoretz, editor of *Commentary* and the discussion moderator, began the roundtable with a distinction between two competing schools of thought within liberalism vis-à-vis the "Negro problem." On the one side, Podhoretz says, liberals envision the gradual absorption of blacks into mainstream society; on the other side, many liberals and radicals were beginning to demand preferential treatment for blacks as a social group. The first approach emphasizes the rights of individuals, the second stresses the priority of groups, and both presume the eradication of racist attitudes and discrimination. Baldwin, however, appears to reject both approaches and, apparently, any liberal paradigm.

Clearly, as the discussion proceeds, Baldwin's staunch refusal incurred the frustration, if not the ire, of his interlocutors. He repeatedly invokes what we might call a racial realpolitik—political concessions, that is, made on behalf of racial progress designed to further larger geopolitical goals—that liberals only begrudgingly acknowledge and refuse to consider in evaluations of the political present. At several points in the conversation, the participants pin Baldwin in a corner, demanding that he at least concede that the nation as a whole has progressed in the domain of race relations: that the material conditions of blacks had improved substantially and that the attitudes of whites toward blacks had also advanced.

Yet he concedes neither of these points. Astutely, Baldwin notes that as the nation's economy and acquisition of wealth soared at midcentury—the consequence of intensified mass production, technological acceleration, and comparatively minor human and capital losses in the United States during the Second World War—the material conditions of blacks rose accordingly. "As far as I can tell," Baldwin says, "the progress that has been made in the last twenty years has not been mainly due to the application of ethical principles but to the fact that the country has been extremely prosperous. When the economic level of the country as a whole rose, obviously the Negro level rose more or less proportionately with it."[36] Accompanying the robust American economy and expansion of the middle class after the war, the U.S. effort to consolidate its global hegemony depended on addressing the problem of civil rights for black Americans. It became increasingly untenable for U.S. diplomats and state officials to extol the virtues of American-style democracy and freedom when blacks were routinely lynched and the nation subscribed to Jim Crow segregation.

What precludes the sort of communicative ethics the conference hoped for, according to Baldwin, was a malfunction in language. Indeed, it becomes apparent in the course of the roundtable that Baldwin and his liberal counterparts are not speaking the same language. "What strikes me here," Baldwin observes, "is that you are an American talking about American society, and I am an American talking about American society—both of us are very concerned with it—and yet your version of American society is really very difficult for me to recognize." Later in the roundtable, during the question-and-answer session, the black psychology professor Kenneth Clark defends Baldwin with the observation that "so far as the Negro is concerned, the ethical aspect of American liberalism or the American Creed is primarily verbal. There is a peculiar kind of ambivalence in American liberalism, a persistent verbal liberalism that is never capable of overcoming an equally persistent illiberalism of action."[37]

In "The Crusade of Indignation," Baldwin writes that "the concepts contained in words like 'freedom,' 'justice,' 'democracy' are not common concepts; on the contrary they are rare. People are not born knowing what these are. It takes enormous and, above all, individual effort to arrive at the respect for other people these words imply."[38] Can liberalism employ a vocabulary that, by the onset of the Cold War, had become exhausted, to the extent that critical terms invoked in the public sphere had come to signify their opposites? The very notion of a Cold War, Ann Douglas observes, "implies a war that is not really a war, a war that cannot involve open conflict for those participating in it, a war that makes no gesture toward victory or defeat, much less peace." Revising traditional war aims of victory or defeat, and therefore containing an ominous prospect of perpetuity, the Cold War "spawned a host of equally oxymoronic phrases like 'dual hegemony,' 'limited nuclear war,' 'peace-keeping missiles,' and 'win the peace.'"[39] (The Soviet Union, we might also add, spawned its own equally bizarre language disorder.)

Like the Axis powers had done during the war, the Soviet Union and China seized the opportunity to proliferate images of lynching around the globe—images and narratives that resonated with oppressed and colonized people in Africa, Latin America, and Asia.[40] Mary Dudziak shows how a 1958 event—the sentencing to death of a black man from Alabama accused of stealing less than two dollars—spread in a media wildfire across Africa, Asia, and the Soviet Union, adding fuel to their own political agendas and crippling U.S. claims of legitimacy.[41] The oppression of black Americans, then, played a decisive role in the Communist effort to recruit the Third World as allies against the United States' brand of liberal democracy. Though Stalinist brutalities were routinely invoked in U.S. Cold War propaganda to indict Communist regimes worldwide, the atrocities of liberal democracies in Western Europe and the United States were subjected to historical erasure or regarded as temporary setbacks on the road to racial conciliation. The necessary relation between communism and repression was self-evident; liberal democracy's record of oppression, on the other hand, was pure contingency, an aberration from its forward march of progress. So long indifferent to Jim Crow, American officials now realized the impact of lynching and segregation in the international arena and how these racial practices amounted, from their perspective, to a slew of global public relations guffaws.

Consequently, as Dudziak suggests, by the late 1940s U.S. officials began "telling stories about race and democracy" to counteract the effects of Soviet propaganda. With the nation as collective protagonist, these narratives depict America emerging from its dark racial past while proceeding toward a new interracial horizon. "The Negro in American Life," an influential pamphlet published by the U.S. Information Agency in 1950, conceded that, in "answer to the ever growing demand for cheap labor," whites enslaved Africans en masse, and "from there began in the United States a theory of racial inferiority which became a key tenet in support of slavery and, later, of economic and social discrimination." It is against this historical backdrop, the pamphlet suggested, "that the progress which the Negro has made and the steps still needed for the full solution of his problems must be measured."[42] Of course, stories like "The Negro in American Life" contained more than a little rhetorical prestidigitation: as the progress of the Negro at midcentury was measured against an abject slave past, rather than against the normative socioeconomic status of whites, these narratives could not fail to impress foreign observers (often their intended audience) as indicative of a "serious" national commitment to the Negro problem. And gauging present progress against the abject slave past had the added rhetorical advantage of affecting honesty about race relations—by appearing to confess the nation's sins, while simultaneously obscuring the question of equality with whites. Baldwin understood *this* dubious narrative as structuring the Cold War discourse on race, even, or perhaps especially, among his liberal colleagues.

In retrospect, it is difficult to avoid the cynical and disquieting conclusion that postwar racial progress was neither the product of progressive racial attitudes nor even the outcome of the heroic struggle of civil rights protestors and anticolonial radicals, as much as a series of concessions by the federal government that ultimately served to secure its dominance over the Communist bloc. Indefatigably, Baldwin sought to articulate this historical state of affairs, connecting Cold War civil rights to the ghastly events of the totalitarian century. Disappointing, opaque even, though this message was to many of Baldwin's contemporaries, it is urgent for the present, as we continue to take stock of the postwar era and to witness comparable formations on the horizon.

NOTES

1. Hughes, "Some Practical Observations."

2. Singh wonders whether "this is an adequate way to understand the relationship of black struggles for equality to the constitution of national democratic norms and foundations" and if "the relationship [is] really one of racial particularity to a national universality." See Singh, *Black Is a Country*, 15–17.

3. Schaub, *American Fiction in the Cold War*, 6–7.

4. Quoted in O'Dell, "Foundations of Racism in American Life," 535.

5. Badiou, *Century*, 2. Badiou's quote must be understood, however, within its proper philosophical context, which is a critique of the discourse of "totalitarianism," insofar as this essentially cold war discourse functions to sustain the hegemony of what he calls "the liberal century": the "triumph of capitalism and the global market," "parliamentarianism," and "miniscule ideas," ibid., 2–3.

6. Badiou continues: "After two or three centuries of the deportation of human meat for the purpose of slavery, conquest managed to turn Africa into the horrific obverse of European, capitalist, democratic splendor. And this continues to our very day. In the dark fury of the thirties, in the indifference to death, there is something that certainly originates in the Great War and the trenches, but also something that comes—as a sort of infernal return—from the colonies, from the way that the differences within humanity were envisaged down there" (ibid., 7–8). For Arendt's account of the relation between totalitarianism in Europe and the Scramble for Africa, see *Origins of Totalitarianism*, 185–221.

7. Schwarz, *West Indian Intellectuals in Britain*, 1.

8. Baldwin, *Fire Next Time*, 336.

9. See Gellately and Kiernan, *Specter of Genocide*, 10.

10. Drake and Cayton, *Black Metropolis*, 760.

11. Baldwin, *Fire Next Time*, 52–53.

12. Bauman, *Modernity and the Holocaust*, 1–2.

13. Baldwin, *Fire Next Time*, 51–52. Or as the Austrian novelist Joseph Roth put it in 1937: "Why then do the European states claim for themselves the right to spread civilization and manners to different continents? Why not to Europe itself?" (quoted in Mazower, *Dark Continent*, ix).

14. Bauman goes as far as to suggest that allegiance to these rationalized methods functions as an adjunct to the modern civilizing process. Baldwin would likely agree with Bauman's conclusion that "*the Holocaust has more to say about the state of sociology than sociology in its present shape is able to add to our knowledge of the Holocaust*" (*Modernity and the Holocaust*, 3) (emphasis original) December 1, 2010.

15. In "Notes of a Native Son," Baldwin describes his introduction to Jim Crow while working as a teenager in a defense plant in New Jersey. Accompanied by a white friend, Baldwin was refused service in a number of restaurants until he finally exploded at a white waitress: "'We don't serve Negroes here.' She did not

say it with the blunt, derisive hostility to which I had grown so accustomed, but, rather, with a note of apology in her voice, and fear. This made me colder and more murderous than ever. I felt I had to do something with my hands. I wanted her to come close enough for me to get her neck between my hands" (134).

16. Balfour, *Evidence of Things Not Said*, 25.

17. Morrison, "James Baldwin: His Voice Remembered," 92.

18. Baldwin, "Stranger in the Village," 83.

19. Murray, *Omni-Americans*, 143.

20. Of course, Berman tempers his ebullience, pace Marx, with a critique of capitalist modernity's perpetual dissolutions.

21. On the question of essentialism in Morrison's oeuvre, see McBride, "Speaking the Unspeakable."

22. Morrison, "City Limits, Village Values," 37.

23. Baldwin, "Encounter on the Seine: Black Meets Brown," 39.

24. Wright, *Three Books from Exile*, 647.

25. Kevin Gaines credits Wright with dismantling the diaspora-homeland binary that "powerfully underwrites nationalist and essentialist understanding of blackness" and replacing that defective model with a dialectical vision of diaspora understood "as the product of slavery, dispersion, and oppression, and simultaneously, as the necessary condition for black modernity and the forging of an anti-imperialist critique of Western culture" ("Revisiting Richard Wright in Ghana," 75).

26. See Stewart, *Migrating to the Movies.*

27. Baldwin, *Another Country*, 49.

28. Ibid., 7.

29. Ibid., 28.

30. "The Crusade of Indignation," 156.

31. For a recent update of Baldwin's suspicion of midcentury liberalism—and vigorous critique of black neoconservatism—see Baker, *Betrayal.*

32. See Cleaver, "Notes on a Native Son," 67; Dupee, "James Baldwin and the 'Man.'"

33. Baldwin, *Fire Next Time*, 87.

34. See Kent and Young, *International Relations since 1945*, and Westad, *Global Cold War.*

35. Howe, "Black Boys and Native Sons."

36. Baldwin et al., "Liberalism and the Negro," 31.

37. Ibid., 39.

38. Baldwin, "The Crusade of Indignation," 156.

39. Douglas, "Periodizing the American Century," 76.

40. See Borstelmann, *Cold War and the Color Line.*

41. Dudziak, *Cold War Civil Rights.*

42. Ibid., 47–55.

BIBLIOGRAPHY

Arendt, Hannah. *The Origins of Totalitarianism.* New York: Harcourt, 1951.

Badiou, Alain. *The Century.* Cambridge: Polity Press, 2007.

Baker, Houston A. *Betrayal: How Black Intellectuals Have Abandoned the Ideals of the Civil Rights Era.* New York: Columbia University Press, 2008.

Baldwin, James. *Another Country.* New York: Vintage International, 2005.

Baldwin, James. "The Crusade of Indignation." In *Price of the Ticket.*

Baldwin, James. "Encounter on the Seine: Black Meets Brown." In *Price of the Ticket.*

Baldwin, James. *The Fire Next Time.* In *Price of the Ticket.*

Baldwin, James. "Notes of a Native Son." In *Price of the Ticket.*

Baldwin, James. *The Price of the Ticket: Collected Nonfiction, 1948–1985.* New York: St. Martin's, 1985.

Baldwin, James. "Stranger in the Village." In *Price of the Ticket.*

Baldwin, James, Nathan Glazer, Sidney Hook, Gunnar Myrdal, and Norman Podhorertz. "Liberalism and the Negro: A Roundtable Discussion." *Commentary* 37, no. 3 (1964).

Balfour, Lawrie. *Evidence of Things Not Said: James Baldwin and the Promise of American Democracy.* Ithaca: Cornell University Press, 2001.

Bauman, Zygmunt. *Modernity and the Holocaust.* Ithaca: Cornell University Press.

Berman, Marshall. *All That Is Solid Melts into Air: The Experience of Modernity.* New York: Penguin Books, 1982.

Borstelmann, Thomas. *The Cold War and the Color Line: American Race Relations in the Global Arena.* Cambridge: Harvard University Press, 2001.

Cleaver, Eldridge. "Notes on a Native Son." In Keneth Kinnamon, ed., *James Baldwin: A Collection of Critical Essays.* Englewood Cliffs, N.J.: Prentice-Hall, 1974.

Douglas, Ann. "Periodizing the American Century: Modernism, Postmodernism, and Postcolonialism in the Cold War Context." *Modernism/Modernity* 5, no. 3 (1998).

Drake, St. Claire, and Horace R. Cayton. *Black Metropolis: A Study of Negro Life in a Northern City.* Chicago: University of Chicago Press, 1993.

Dudziak, Mary L. *Cold War Civil Rights: Race and the Image of American Democracy.* Princeton: Princeton University Press, 2000.

Dupee, F. W. "James Baldwin and the 'Man.'" *New York Review of Books* 1 (February 1963).

Gaines, Kevin. "Revisiting Richard Wright in Ghana: Black Radicalism and the Dialectics of Diaspora." *Social Text* 67 (2001).

Gellately, Robert, and Ben Kiernan, eds. *The Specter of Genocide: Mass Murder in Historical Perspective.* Cambridge: Cambridge University Press, 2003.

Howe, Irving. "Black Boys and Native Sons." *Dissent* (Autumn 1963).

Hughes, Langston. "Some Practical Observations: A Colloquy." *Phylon* 4 (1950).

Kent, John, and John Young. *International Relations since 1945: A Global History.* Oxford: Oxford University Press, 2004.

Mazower, Mark. *Dark Continent: Europe's Twentieth Century.* London: Allen Lane, 1998.

McBride, Dwight A. "Speaking the Unspeakable: On Toni Morrison, African American Intellectuals and the Uses of Essentialist Rhetoric." In Nancy J. Peterson, ed., *Toni Morrison: Critical and Theoretical Approaches.* Baltimore: Johns Hopkins University Press, 1997.

Morrison, Toni. "City Limits, Village Values: Concepts of the Neighborhood in Black Fiction." In Michael C. Jaye and Chalmers Watts, eds., *Literature and the Urban Experience: Essays on the City and Literature.* New Brunswick: Rutgers University Press, 1981.

Morrison, Toni. "James Baldwin: His Voice Remembered; Life in His Words." In Carolyn C. Denard, ed., *What Moves at the Margins: Selected Nonfiction.* Jackson: University Press of Mississippi, 2008.

Murray, Albert. *The Omni-Americans: New Perspectives on Black Experience and American Culture.* New York: Outerbridge and Dienstfrey, 1970.

O'Dell, J. H. "Foundations of Racism in American Life." *Freedomways* 4 (1964).

Schaub, Thomas Hill. *American Fiction in the Cold War.* Madison: University of Wisconsin Press, 1991.

Schwarz, Bill, ed. *West Indian Intellectuals in Britain.* Manchester: Manchester University Press, 2003.

Singh, Nikhil Pal. *Black Is a Country: Race and the Unfinished Struggle for Democracy.* Cambridge: Harvard University Press, 2005.

Stewart, Jacqueline Najuma. *Migrating to the Movies: Cinema and Black Urban Modernity.* Berkeley: University of California Press, 2005.

Westad, Odd Arne. *The Global Cold War: Third World Interventions and the Making of Our Times.* Cambridge: Cambridge University Press, 2006.

Wright, Richard. *Three Books from Exile: "Black Power";" The Color Curtain"; and "White Man, Listen!"* New York: HarperCollins, 2008.

FIVE

Baldwin, Prophecy, and Politics

GEORGE SHULMAN

Although James Baldwin's essays depict the relationship of white supremacy to the formation of American society and the shaping of national identity, prevailing forms of liberal and Marxist political thought, as well as most versions of so-called democratic theory, do not recognize him as a political thinker or even as contributing to the understanding of politics. Their resounding silence about race, and his exclusion from their canons, bespeak the very conditions he analyzes as a political and moral catastrophe. These conditions are, in short, ongoing racial domination at the foundation of American life, and its disavowal by those it enfranchises. On the one hand, Baldwin analyzes the price of this silence in American life, and by extension in our theoretical practice: what is occluded and obscured, about life and politics, when thinkers ignore race? On the other hand, what kind of theorizing, or critical practice, is required or called forth by the issue of race, in what thinkers must say and how they must say it? In both regards, Baldwin shows how attention to the issue of race transforms prevailing views of (how to theorize) politics.

Surely, Baldwin would have white readers "see" race, which is invisible to them. But what does this mean? Partly, seeing race means grasping the related meanings of whiteness and blackness—the impossible purity and unmarked authority of one and the unspeakable horror of embodiment and vulnerability invested in the other—as a symbolic code, discursive system, and collective imaginary shaping every aspect of life in the United States. Partly, seeing race means grasping how this discursive system is woven into practices of inequality and exclusion, not only in slavery and then the legal apartheid called Jim Crow, but in their legacy, contemporary residential patterns, labor markets, criminal justice institutions, cultural practices, and state policies.

But just as high theory has narrated modernity in terms of capitalism or disenchantment, but not slavery and the color line, so for Baldwin American culture and politics are also engendered by *disavowal* of their traumatic origin and continuing ground in racialized domination. It is not possible to understand the shaping and character of American life, he argues, unless we credit the generative centrality of racial domination—and its disavowal. In Baldwin's version of what some theorists now call constitutive exclusion, American nationhood is constituted by disavowed domination; what he calls "innocence" of domination is a willful, and so culpable, form of bad faith, to use the existentialist idiom of his formative years, a willful not-seeing and disclaiming of responsibility, which fundamentally corrupts American life: every aspect of public and private life; every cultural practice, and every literary or theoretical production. Innocence names a condition not only moral and political but "spiritual," he claims, for it bespeaks a failure to acknowledge human finitude and the "tragedy" of life, a denial of the very nature of reality as well as the reality of others. In turn, he argues, those disenfranchised as "black" (and their allies) must name and confront the disavowals that both privilege and imprison those enfranchised as white. To move from innocence to the kind of acknowledgment he calls "acceptance" would reconstitute the American regime.

This project of provoking acknowledgment—which Baldwin witnesses in the Civil Rights Movement and enacts in his texts and worldly speech-acts—is a political practice meant to reconstitute a regime, by confronting the bad faith that sustains it and thus by recasting at visceral levels what and who are counted as real by the enfranchised. So the question becomes: by what language does he take exception to the racial state of exception constituting American liberal nationalism? Working not within a democratic frame, but to engage the domination and disavowal that both found and violate it, he echoes neither the idealization of reason and deliberation in liberal political thought nor the idealization of plurality and difference in its poststructural critics. He depicts himself as addressing not a problem of ignorance to remedy by knowledge, but a failure to acknowledge, as Stanley Cavell puts it, what people do know but disavow; he depicts himself as facing not so much a dogmatism of identity hostile to plurality, as an identity inseparable from domination.[1] Correspondingly, Baldwin does not speak like Habermas, as if to prove the validity of truth claims about the structure of society, nor does he quite speak like poststructuralists who expose the contingency of identity to foster irony and openness to difference. Rather he makes a claim about willful blindness, a claim that is not a contestable interpretation, but a truth those who call themselves white must accept, or they live in denial of the true meaning of their conduct and history. Given this claim, he must undertake a form of persuasion that expects resistance, values rhetoric, and relies on literary art.

For these reasons among others, I argue, he draws on the genre of biblical prophecy even as he inflects it in nontheist ways. This secularized prophecy enacts registers of voice—urgent, intense, uncompromising, probing, accusatory, demanding, provoking—that are devalued or even demonized both by liberal discourse and by prevailing genres of political theory. But as he uses prophecy to confront the issue of racial domination, we see how such speech, and the kinds of political claims it bears, are needful and not only dangerous in democratic politics.[2]

Disavowal, Acknowledgment, and Prophecy

One passage from *The Fire Next Time* especially exemplifies his critical practice and its characteristic idiom. In the first part of the book, "a letter to my nephew on the 100th anniversary of the emancipation," he says:

> The crime of which I accuse my countrymen, and for which neither I nor time nor history will ever forgive them, is that they have destroyed and are destroying hundreds of thousands of lives and do not know it and do not want to know it. One can be and indeed must strive to become, tough and philosophical concerning destruction and death . . . but it is not permissible that the authors of this destruction should also be innocent. It is the innocence which constitutes the crime.[3]

He then says: "This innocent country set you down in a ghetto in which, in fact, it intended that you should perish. You were born where you were born and faced the future you faced because you were black and for no other reason." Having positioned white readers to overhear him, he urges his nephew:

> Try to remember that what they do and cause you to endure does not testify to your inferiority but to their inhumanity and fear. In-

> deed, there is no basis for their impertinent assumption that they must accept you. The really terrible thing . . . is that you must accept them . . . with love. For these innocent people have no other hope. They are still trapped in a history they do not understand and until they understand it they cannot be released from it.[4]

Accordingly, "we, with love, will force our brothers to see themselves as they are, to cease fleeing from reality and begin to change it."[5] The alternative is not only the continuing subjugation of African Americans: switching to a we that joins blacks and whites as Americans, he adds: "If we, who can scarcely be considered a white nation, persist in thinking of ourselves as one, we condemn ourselves . . . to sterility and decay, whereas, if we could accept ourselves as we are, we might bring new life to Western achievements and transform them."[6]

A language of innocence as disavowal, and of acknowledgment as "accepting ourselves as we are," is Baldwin's way to address race and secularize prophecy as a language of politics. He thus imagines the critic not as God's messenger, but as an artist whose struggle with society he depicts in terms of love: "The war of an artist with his society is a lover's war, and he does, at his best, what lovers do, which is to reveal the beloved to himself and, with that revelation, to make freedom real."[7] Meaning love not "in the infantile American sense of being made happy, but in the tough and universal sense of quest and daring and growth," he links critics with artists and lovers to imagine not only himself but blacks as a collective subject, acting as a "disagreeable mirror" to "block the door to the spiritual and social ease" of whites.[8] "Love" thus names an engagement to move whites not from ignorance to knowledge, but from innocence to acknowledgment, and so from sterile repetition into the freedom of the unknown.

That engagement is a calling likely to fail: "A person does not lightly elect to oppose his society. One would much rather be at home among compatriots than mocked and detested by them. But the mockery of the people, even their hatred is moving because it is so blind: it is terrible to watch people cling to their captivity and insist on their destruction."[9] From his self-authorizing election to their blindness, captivity, and self-destruction, and so to the pathos of witnessing choices he has failed to change and suffering he cannot forestall, Baldwin forges a nontheist prophecy to confront white supremacy. To assess its political bearing, we must unpack his idea of innocence and then how he organizes critical and political practices around the idea of impelling whites to acknowledge what and whom they disavow.

The Concept of Innocence

Baldwin uses the moral category of innocence ironically: it denotes not excusable ignorance, but a blindness that is culpable because it is willful. Destruction and domination are commonplace in history; rendering others invisible is an injustice built into human life by hierarchy and power. But innocence is a refusal not only to recognize these others but to acknowledge that we enact this denial. Innocence is disowning social facts we in some sense know. It is disavowing the exercise of power, the practice of inequality, and their benefits.

In one dimension, this innocence signals a society invested both in egalitarian ideals and in slavery. "Confronted with the impossibility of remaining faithful to one's beliefs [because one is invested in slavery] and the impossibility of becoming free of them [because one remains committed to equality]," Euro-Americans are "driven to the most inhuman excess."[10] Excess is the idea of blackness, which they invent to justify inequality by racializing subalterns in demonic and debased terms. But masters are haunted and crazed:

> It was impossible for Americans to accept the black man as one of themselves, for to do so was to jeopardize their status as white men. But not to accept him was to deny his human reality, his human weight and complexity, and the strain of denying the overwhelmingly undeniable forced Americans into rationalizations so fantastic that they approached the pathological.[11]

In Baldwin's view, then, Euro-Americans invent fictions of race and melodramas of black pathology to justify domination and protect an innocence they voice in claims to whiteness, moral virtue, exceptional liberalism, and an exemplary nationalism.

But the symbolic meaning invested in blackness also signals another form of innocence:

> The racial tensions that menace Americans today have little to do with real antipathy—on the contrary indeed—and are involved only symbolically with color. These tensions are rooted in the very same depths from which love springs, or murder. The white's unadmitted—and apparently, to him, unspeakable—fears and longings are projected onto the Negro.[12]

Whiteness is formed by projecting blackness, which becomes a site not just of aversion, but of longing for what is split off.

Partly, the meaning of blackness is linked to death: "White Americans do not believe in death, and this is why the darkness of my skin so intimidates them." But "death" does symbolic work for Baldwin; it bears the meaning of a finitude he links to time, change, and mortality, thus to embodiment and incompletion, hence to desire and thereby to vulnerability, suffering, and violence. Accordingly, "My black flesh is the flesh that Saint Paul wanted to have mortified," for in the name of pure disembodied spirit, Christianity "splits itself into dark and light."[13] But secular liberalism also denies the meaning of carnal mortality by its idolatry of self-determination as sovereignty, a wish sustained by lodging license, irrationality, passion, dependence, and violence in racialized others, who signify what normative citizens must master to achieve "self-determination."[14]

"White" thus denotes not skin color, says Baldwin, but a "moral choice" to "opt for safety instead of life." [15] That choice is a symptom of *ressentiment* and a form of violence. Indeed, disassociating from their own destructiveness, those who call themselves white invoke morality to exorcize the specter of darkness in others, as if to master their own impulsive life, and life itself, by controlling the symbolically charged bodies of others. Blackness is then the Dionysian, and innocence is the bad faith that moralizes and racializes it. As racial categorization yields moral dichotomy, both make the "American" vision of life abstract and rigid:

> The American vision of the world—which allows so little reality, generally speaking, for any of the darker forces in human life, which tends to paint moral issues in glaring black and white—owes a great deal to the battle waged by Americans to maintain between themselves and black men a human separation which could not be bridged.[16]

Lastly, therefore, innocence connotes disavowal of the past:

> It is a sentimental error . . . to believe that the past is dead. . . . It is not a question of memory. Oedipus did not remember the thongs that bound his feet; nevertheless the marks they left testified to that doom toward which his feet were leading him.[17]

To address people invested in Christian ideas of rebirth, or in the liberal romance of self-making, Baldwin invokes the image of Oedipus—whose wish to make his own destiny seals his doom, whose insistence on escaping the past tightens its grip, and whose claim to know himself assures misrecognition of his identity. As a tragic truth-teller Baldwin might be a Tiresias, but in a biblical culture he calls himself "a kind of Jeremiah"[18] who must address citizens willfully blind to what is self-defeating in their self-making:

> White man, hear me! History . . . does not refer merely or even principally to the past. On the contrary, the great force of history comes from the fact that we carry it within us, are unconsciously controlled by it in many ways, so history is literally *present* in all that we do. It could scarcely be otherwise since it is to history that we owe our frames of reference, our identities, and our aspirations.[19]

To summarize, by casting whiteness as "innocence," Baldwin denotes: partly a denial of the Dionysian that he links to carnal mortality and what he calls the "tragic" nature of life; partly a denial of the reality of others and a disclaiming of this refusal; and partly a denial of history, the past constituting the inescapably situated particularity of every human life. In each regard, innocence is a dream of safety, sovereignty, or purity, of not being subject to sentience and dependence on others, to time, loss, and death. But finitude in these senses is socially mediated: people undergo "life" through subjection to—and privileging by—social categories, domination, and violence. Innocence also means denying this social landscape of power and our differential positioning in it. Whiteness thus signals a regime that disavows its investment in inequality and a culture animated by bad faith.

From Disavowal to Acknowledgment

As the weak invent true worlds or fixed racial categories to seek an impossible kind of protection from life, and as "those who cannot suffer never grow up," so "freedom and innocence" are antithetical.[20] The alternative to innocence, it is therefore crucial to emphasize, is not so much guilt as a capacity for responsibility Baldwin associates both with adulthood and with agency. To depict this alternative he uses the idiom of acceptance: white supremacy is an idolatry that produces sterility, "whereas, if we could accept ourselves as we are, we might bring new life to western achievements and transform them." Always naming "the price of the ticket," the cost not only of domination and its disavowal but also of their overcoming, he adds that "the price" of renewal is "the unconditional freedom of the Negro: it is not too much to say that he . . . must now be embraced and at no matter what psychic and social risk." Freedom means resisting innocence as bad faith, by "accepting" what (and who) has been disavowed.[21]

Partly, the freedom of those who call themselves white depends on "accepting" national origins in violence and slavery, not in consent, and "accepting" an abiding national investment in inequality, not equality. Partly, whites remain trapped by this history unless they accept how racial domination and black agency have shaped American culture in every regard: "What happened to the Negro . . . is not simply a matter of *my* memory and *my* history, but of *American* history and memory." For "the history the Negro endured . . . was endured on another level by all the white people who oppressed him. . . . I was here, and that did something to *me.* But you were here on top of me, and that did something to *you.*" Right now, what "this republic does to the Negro, it does to itself."[22] Indeed, the relation of white and black is not only oppressor to oppressed, he insists, but a blood bond of family and an erotically charged marriage:

> Love does not begin and end in the way we think it does. Love is a battle, love is a war; love is a growing up. No one in the world . . . knows Americans (i.e. whites) better or, odd as it may sound, loves them more than the American Negro. This is because he has had to watch you, outwit you, deal with you, bear you, and sometimes even bleed and die with you, ever since both of us, black and white, got here—and this is a wedding.[23]

Baldwin moves between metaphors of family in which one brother confronts another and metaphors of wedding in which a lover confronts a beloved, to register and engender investment in a bond readily disavowed but impossible to escape. What he calls "achieving our country" means accepting the gothic reality of this wedding and the people we have become by it: only if "we" "accept" that American history is shaped by domination and miscegenation can we initiate a democratic nation-building never yet attempted. Baldwin here "accepts" a national frame for politics, not because he loves an ideal America, but because freedom means wrestling with the fatality of the actual one. Whereas Richard Wright answers white disavowal with refusal, Baldwin forges a collective black subject by blocking ideas of divorce and of racial purity. Instead he encourages blacks to "accept," and in all ambivalence engage, a miscegenated attachment he depicts as grievously flawed. It may be irredeemably flawed, but until 1968 he believes a history of domination and miscegenation can be made into a condition of action.[24]

Baldwin himself models the acknowledgments he seeks from blacks and from whites as constituent members of a national subject. In "great pain and terror," he says, he grasped the depth of his own historical constitution, but "only then can one enter into battle with that historical creation, oneself," and attempt to re-create oneself according to a principle more humane and liberating:

> One begins the attempt to achieve a personal maturity and freedom which robs history of its tyrannical power and also changes history. . . . Obviously I speak as a historical creation which has had to bitterly contest its history, to wrestle with it, and finally accept it in order to bring myself out of it.[25]

He cannot escape his past or fix what went wrong in it, as if to change it. Only by accepting his historical constitution can he, paradoxically, make a future different from the one the past seems to dictate. In a Nietzschean sense, accepting the past diminishes the power it accrues from denial; those ruled less by resentment of it or by fantasies of escaping it can wrestle with it to act otherwise.

Baldwin does not want African Americans simply to "accept" hegemonic images of blackness; to accept that "categorization alone is real" and "surrender to the image" is to give life "no other possible reality" than self-hatred and hatred. Yet "bitter railing" at a category is "the only motion needed to spring the trap on us," for we reinstate it in our protest.[26] To elude the trap, paradoxically, means "accepting" that "the American image of the Negro lives in the Negro's heart," that "this dark and dangerous and unloved stranger is part of himself forever." For "only this recognition sets him in any wise free," and it is "this necessary ability to contain and even, in the most honorable sense of the word, to *exploit* the 'nigger' which lends Negro life its high elements of the ironic."[27] To "accept" this stranger within is to credit, at once, carnal humanity and internalization of its estranged white image; such doubleness yields the tragic insight and freedom that enable creativity.

Whites, too, must "wrestle" with the constitutive power of the past as the inherited categories they internalize and live by and as the segregated, unequal world they sustain. But one trapped within the safe sterility of whiteness must also seek "fruitful communion with the depths of his own being." To contact such "depths" is in effect "to become black himself, to become part of that suffering and dancing country that he now watches wistfully from the heights of his lonely power."[28] If whites can "accept and love themselves" by learning to accept the "dark stranger" within each person "—which will not be tomorrow and may very well be never—the Negro problem will no longer exist for it will no longer be needed."[29] They must risk the idol of racial identity, not by minstrel inversions, but by contacting the Dionysian:

> It is the responsibility of free men to trust and celebrate what is constant—birth, struggle, and death are constant, and so is love, though we may not always think so—and to apprehend the nature of change, to be able and willing to change. I speak of change not on the surface but in the depths—change in the sense of renewal. But renewal becomes impossible if one supposes things to be constant which are not, safety for example, or money or power. One clings then to chimeras, by which one can only be betrayed, and the entire hope—the entire possibility—of freedom disappears.[30]

Assessing Baldwin's Politics as a Practice of Prophecy

How shall we assess the political bearing of a critical practice cast in terms of disavowal and acknowledgment? Begin with the criticisms of white and black audiences at the point of Baldwin's greatest visibility and since. Many whites express rage at his view of their willful innocence, which makes any resistance to his view evidence of its truth. He imposes an interpretation of history as a truth whites must accept or, he insists, they live in self-denial. Resenting the judgment and aggression in such claims, they say that critics, to be effective, must use other registers of voice, to persuade by argument, not self-righteous testimony. Inversely, black critics object that Baldwin acquiesces to white power: by investing in dialogue and casting blacks in the role of redeeming whites, his idiom of love sacrifices black political autonomy in a vain effort to free people who cannot listen and to change a regime invested in racial rule.

We can translate these historic and recurring reactions into questions. First, what is the status of Baldwin's claims about innocence and disavowal: what kind of truth is this? Does it moralize white supremacy or politicize it? Does this idiom clarify how people know something, say about inequality and the humanity of excluded others, and yet do not acknowledge or count as salient, and so cannot act on, what they know? But what fosters such acknowledgment? Second, therefore, is his way of addressing the nation as a subject: does his analogy of the personal and the collective collapse the plural space of politics or conjure a subject of attribution to undertake what Hannah Arendt calls "collective responsibility"? Third, does his language of love romanticize nationhood and escape from politics, or rather, depict miscegenation and gothic ambivalence, to name the only terms on which a democratic politics in the United States could begin? Last, is he binding blacks not only to whites and a national frame, but also to the past and what Wendy Brown calls "wounded attachment"? Or on the model of Nietzschean redemption, does he use his art to "compose fragments, riddle, and dreadful accident" into *amor fati*? [31] I can't answer these questions in any detail here, but they suggest the many ways in which Baldwin enriches the conversation of political theory.

Most broadly, Baldwin's texts reveal a modernity whose legacy is divided because it is founded in slavery, not only enlightenment, and because secularism remains entangled in religious faith, as the subjection and resistance of African Americans attests. Through him we confront a modernity neither white nor secular, and we can thereby reimagine the meaning and making of a "countermodernity." More specifically, his account of white supremacy transforms how we view American liberalism.

His basic political claim is that democratically authorized racial domination has formed the regime of liberal nationalism: the liberal freedoms of the enfranchised depend on the material subordination and cultural exploitation of racially marked others. How does this change our view of liberalism? Carl Schmitt depicts liberalism as antipolitical because an inclusive and pluralist, consensual and procedural creed avoids the "decision," and refuses the "friend-enemy" distinction, by which he defines the properly political. What Schmitt laments as a loss is praised by defenders of liberalism, but Baldwin sees how race is what Schmitt calls "political theology," the organizing discourse defining the constitutive outside and internal other of American liberalism.[32] What Michael Rogin calls "counter-subversive" politics is thus Schmittian decision in American drag: a liberal regime forges sovereignty and normative citizenship by imposing a racial and sexual frontier.[33] A black man of "dubious sexuality," Baldwin stands with the enemy or subversive against which a nation forms itself as a political community. Naming the state of racial exception enabling liberal nationalism, he takes exception to American exceptionalism.[34] But what, then, could suspend the state of exception that sustains the liberal rule of the American ordinary?

The dominant story of equal rights, individual mobility, and ethnic pluralism is not so much invalidated by Baldwin's story of white supremacy, as recast as a form of innocence; as he makes ghettos signify not black inferiority but white domination, and as he makes riots signify not irrationality but insurrection, he shifts the gaze from black to white pathology, and he links black agency to justice not anarchy. Both stories seem validated by experience, but neither can be proven; each is a background narrative preceding what we even count as facts, let alone how we endow them with meaning. Baldwin's rhetorical and political task is thus to confront a prevailing narrative perspective and shift the deep judgments it sustains.

He provokes that shift in part by visiting the standpoint of whites to voice what is unspeakable by them, both their fearful fantasies of blackness and the meaning of unmarked whiteness. But he also testifies to what blacks do not directly say to whites. In effect he asks: how would your view of your conduct and history change, and how would our life together change, if you took my perspective seriously and counted as real my experience of domination and resistance to it? In this way he creates a textual space for dialogue that parallels the political space being taken and created in the fifties and early sixties by African American collective action. To craft these voices and mediate them, I believe, he draws on the biblical genre of prophecy, which depicts the public office of messengers who announce, witnesses who testify, watchmen who warn, and singers who lament.[35]

As messengers announce what is, so Blake argues that prophets are poets. For their seminal fictions—Wallace Stevens says supreme fictions—become truths that subsequent generations live by.[36] In this sense Baldwin voices a perspective that remakes the passionate frame of reference by which people orient self-reflection and agency. But messengers announce *unspeakable* truths, which people deny at great cost to themselves and others: Amos thus declares that God does not unconditionally support the Hebrews, but holds them accountable for injustice and declares war against them, while Nietzsche assumes the office of prophecy to announce the death of God. To announce the conditions we *must* acknowledge *if* we are to flourish—whether a just god or a universe beyond good and evil—is a prophet's office.

In this sense Baldwin speaks imperatively not because of dogmatism, but because of the kind of claim he makes; he seeks not obedient submission to dogma, but acknowledgment—of conditions of finitude we must accept, and of idolatrous fictions we must relinquish, if we are to escape imprisonment. Imperative assertions—about how we must see our situation and our history to bring ourselves out of it—take conditional form: you *must* stop doing x and start doing y *if* you would flourish. We feel we cannot argue back, but he is stating the price of the ticket, not commanding us to obey, and we are free to ignore him, albeit at our peril.

Baldwin also repeatedly insists that he speaks as a witness rather than as a spokesman. He says what he sees, like a legal witness, but like a prophet he also stands against it: making present voices long made absent or uncounted, he bears witness against the exclusion and disavowal by which a democratic regime constitutes and betrays itself, but he also bears witness to capacities for resistance and self-overcoming. His judgment is militant because he believes he addresses not a lack of knowledge to fix by information or a cognitive error to remedy by reasoned argument, as liberal reformers have argued since Gunnar Myrdal's *American Dilemma*, nor an inescapable partiality of vision due to our imbrication in discourse, as Foucault argues, but a motivated blindness about the reality of others that is culpable because it can be overcome. He testifies to no mere gap between people's professed ideals and their actual conduct, but to a denial of reality so profound that every value seems hollow, and people seem deranged, not just hypocritical.

As prophets therefore warn that self-destruction is the penalty paid by those who deny reality, so arguments about disavowal entail a prudential and futural dimension, and prophets call themselves watchmen who would forestall the danger they foresee. When he warns of "the fire next time," therefore, Baldwin does not decree or predict a fate; rather, he names the consequence of conduct as a contingent future we can avoid if we "amend our ways," as Jeremiah puts it. But like the biblical prophets, he also warns of the point when it may be too late to avert the relentlessly unfolding consequences of prior conduct.

What then is Baldwin's answer to disavowal and its penalties? Biblical prophets claim that what God requires is not esoteric, but accessible, not a transcendent Archimedean point to reach by abstraction, but a "turn" toward what is nearby, to become present to it. As the Hebrew for "turn" is translated as "repentance," so Baldwin uses narrative and personal testimony to turn us toward what we disavow. That turn reconstitutes political community by recasting at visceral levels whom we count as real, how we judge social practices, and the way we practice first principles.

He knows his perspective is contestable, but for him, we who contest it are denying the meaning of our history and conduct. Here he stands, and he cannot speak otherwise, for he would betray his vocation by moving if we are offended. Depicting amnesia, disavowal, and self-destruction, he expects our resistance, for he offers not opinions or stories whose comparable validity we must grant to achieve civility, but urgent judgments on which our lives depend. He does not attack dogmatism to pluralize valuable optics, then, but names a willful blindness about domination to reconstitute a regime. As Martin Buber argues that biblical prophets do not predict the future but demand a "decision" in the present, so Baldwin seeks a fateful decision about constitutive practices.[37]

What is dangerous and needful in prophetic speech, and in Baldwin's revision of it, is the claim that people are willfully blind to the truth of their conduct and history, and this demand for decisive choices between commitments, practices, and narratives depicted as antithetical. The danger shadows the Schmittian provenance of "decision," which seems to deny plurality as an axial principle of democratic politics, and yet for Baldwin, this register of speech is needful if the issue is domination and its disavowal. Jacques Rancière's *Dis-Agreement* suggests why.[38]

Rancière argues that any regime enfranchises some by excluding others; every "whole" is partial, presuming a "part that has no part." The subordinated exist demographically, so to speak, but become properly political subjects only as they translate their "injury" into claims about "wrong" that dispute who a regime counts, and how. By their speech and action those who Rancière calls "the part with no part" creates a "scene" of argument to engage the enfranchised and reconstitute the regime as a whole. What Baldwin calls love is thus the engagement Rancière calls dis-agreement, not a movement beyond it. For Baldwin knows that speech relating a part to a whole may fail to persuade the enfranchised, and his goal is not to produce an agreement that ends politics, but to suspend a state of exception that makes democratic politics stillborn.

I have used Cavell's idea of acknowledgment, therefore, to suggest that the political problem for Baldwin is not ignorance but disavowal and that his political remedy is not so much new information or public deliberation as a different relationship toward what we (individually and collectively) already know, say, and do. But contra Cavell, Baldwin must turn people not toward criteria of ordinary language they have refused, but toward practices of domination they have disavowed. In turn, taking seriously Baldwin's focus on disavowed domination would reorient how we theorize politics.

We would shift focus from epistemology (as if to guarantee the truth of claims or establish the shared truth that identities are partial and contingent) to rhetorical arts (which use vernacular idioms to "turn" people toward what they know but disavow). Rather than validate truth claims by deliberative procedures, pluralize avowedly contestable faiths and contingent identities, or foster an ethical ethos of openness to difference, our critical practice would seek conflict about constitutive (racial) practices we must end, not learn to forbear or work to pluralize. Politics does entail dialogue about plural identities and perspectives, as well as deliberation about action, but it also must be adversaries struggling to reconstitute regimes that privilege some by subordinating others. Baldwin thus seeks not only openness to excluded voices but judgments about which practices (and stories) to mandate or oppose. His voice intensifies our awareness of domination, and his intensity—of anger, grief, and judgment—signals dimensions of political speech that are not only scary and indeed dangerous but also needful and transforming.

I have invoked Schmitt to emphasize the register of decision in Baldwin's story of disavowal overcome by acknowledgment, but it is also important to see how Baldwin reworks the distinction between friend and enemy. As his famous encounter with Elijah Muhammad suggests, he neither reifies nor defuses the friend-enemy polarity. He does see a worldly adversary in whites invested in domination, but the "enemy" he faces is also internal to every person, a capacity for bad faith he impels each to name and overcome. He thus stands with some and against others, but also in an agonal stance toward each and every citizen. Still, he never chastens his judgment of white supremacy, which remains an evil fundamentally at odds with democratic life.

Since forbearance toward the other means complicity in racial domination rather than receptivity toward difference, the appearance (even the reality) of moralism is not the greatest danger that Baldwin sees. Indeed, it is no surprise that whites cast him as an invasive moral fanatic opposed to democratic process: a racial state of exception requires him to question the authority of law, majority rule, local self-rule, and the idioms of pluralism, for each is wholly contaminated by racialized exclusion and domination. Yet overcoming white supremacy remains *the* condition of democratic possibility, period; the alternative is a fraudulent pluralism among whites. For Baldwin, then, politics is not a process of deliberation or mediation of plural identities, but a structure of rule, and a *democratic* politics must struggle against it. Still, he insists that every accusation contains a plea for community, and he argues that overcoming white supremacy will truly benefit those who call themselves white, though they cannot yet see how. Instead of polarization or pluralization, therefore, he mediates parts and whole to reconstitute political community.[39]

If Rancière theorizes the constitutive exclusion that Baldwin interprets as a state of exception, it is but a step to say that amnesia is its symptom; to reconstitute community, political actors must mediate parts and wholes, as Rancière argues, but also, like prophets, remember what people forget. In a way Rancière does not emphasize, Baldwin (like other critics of white supremacy) turns to prophecy to emphasize the historical and thus narrative dimension in politics. We therefore should note the stories that he rejects. He refuses the story of a providentially chosen people, but also the nationalist jeremiad that redeems this people from corruption by making good their liberal creed. Unlike Abraham Lincoln he does not invoke an ideal America to make real by acts of dedication and sacrifice. Unlike Martin Luther King he does not redeem founding principles to authorize protest by African American sons and daughters, and unlike Hannah Arendt he does not return to 1776 to recover a "revolutionary treasure."[40] Depicting a nation founded in slavery, whose ideals have been practiced only in viciously exclusionary ways, he denies that progress is the telos of American history.

He instead narrates a tragic story in which a disavowed past generates barren repetition. He insists on this story not to produce despair, but as a condition of opening a possibility for new possibilities. To quote Jonathan Lear, he seeks not "an ordinary possibility, like all the others only new," but "an alteration in the world of possibilities."[41] Is there some other way forward, except by coming to terms with the past? Baldwin denies it. Possibility is not produced by deliberative rationality, nor is it inherently emergent in the ontological process of becoming; it is entirely dependent on coming to terms with the past. Again, his claim-making is both imperative and conditional, as he offers the kind of story that might, in turn, make other stories possible.

Baldwin quickly grasped the failure of the civil rights era as a second reconstruction, and he lived long enough to grasp, too, that the strange complexities of a post–civil rights era did not signal fundamental change. He had hoped to take strategic advantage of the opening for racial change created by Cold War public relations, though he also privileged nationhood as the scene of political redemption, but by the late 1960s he came to think otherwise. Some critics depict his decline into ideology and bitterness, rather than credit his view of the intractability of white supremacy.[42] But he never relinquished faith in the possibility of reconstituting the field of possibility: "I know that what I am asking is impossible. But in our time, as in every time, the impossible is the least one can demand—and one is, after all, emboldened by the spectacle of human history in general and American Negro history in particular, for it testifies to nothing less than the perpetual achievement of the impossible."[43]

In registering the "achievement of the impossible" Baldwin is attesting not only to the ontological fact of contingency, an apparently miraculous exception recurrently rupturing the rule, but also to the ongoing countersovereignty and communal rites of black agency, situated between nation and empire. Continuing to write despite political defeat, he leaves as a legacy a political ethos that holds in tension two necessary but incompatible ideas:

> The first idea is . . . acceptance totally without rancor, of life as it is and men as they are: in the light of this idea it goes without saying that injustice is a commonplace. But this does not mean that one can be complacent, for the second idea is . . . that one must never in one's life accept these injustices as commonplace, but must fight them with all one's strength.[44]

For as he declares at the end of *The Fire Next Time*, "everything now, we must assume, is in our hands; we have no right to assume otherwise."[45]

NOTES

1. See Cavell, *Claim of Reason*.
2. For my broader argument about prophecy, and for the full chapter on Baldwin from which this essay is drawn, see Shulman, *American Prophecy*.
3. Baldwin, *Fire Next Time*, 334.
4. Ibid., 334–35.
5. Ibid., 335.
6. Ibid., 374.
7. Baldwin, "Creative Process," 317–18.
8. Baldwin, *Fire Next Time*, 370; "disagreeable mirror" is from his "White Man's Guilt," 409.
9. Baldwin, *No Name in the Street*, 172–73.
10. Baldwin, "Stranger in the Village," 89.
11. Ibid., 88.
12. Baldwin, *Fire Next Time*, 375.
13. Baldwin, "White Racism and World Community," 440.
14. In *The Fire Next Time* he says that "we sacrifice the beauty of our lives" and

"imprison ourselves in totems, taboos, crosses, blood sacrifices, steeples, mosques, races, armies, flags, nations in order to deny the fact of death," whereas we should "rejoice" in and "earn" it "by confronting with passion the conundrum of life" (373–74).

15. Baldwin, "On Being White and Other Lies."

16. Baldwin, "Stranger in the Village," 89.

17. Baldwin, "Many Thousands Gone," 68.

18. Baldwin, "American Dream and the American Negro," 403.

19. Baldwin, "White Man's Guilt," 410.

20. Baldwin, *Fire Next Time*, 376–77.

21. Ibid., 374. My claim, which I cannot justify in this chapter, is that Baldwin criticizes innocence to move beyond guilt, not generate it; indeed, he is trying to free whites from the unconscious guilt they already feel. He is trying to evoke responsibility without reinstating the moral apparatus and guilty subject of Christianity. See also in this context Arendt, "Collective Responsibility."

22. Baldwin et al., "Liberalism and the Negro," 31.

23. "In Search of a Majority," 234. The relations of people of African descent and Anglo-Europeans is "more terrible, more subtle, and more meaningful than the relationship of bitter possessed to uncertain possessor" or of "master to slave." It is "literally and morally a blood relationship, perhaps the most profound reality of the American experience, and we cannot begin to unlock it until we accept how very much it contains of the force and anguish and terror of love" ("Many Thousands Gone," 76). The "interracial drama," by a literal and figurative miscegenation, has created "a new black man, and a new white man too" ("Stranger in the Village," 89).

24. Refusing the path of separation is one lesson Baldwin teaches in his famous story about meeting Elijah Muhammad in *The Fire Next Time*, though it often goes unnoted that Baldwin also agrees with Elijah's critique of white supremacy. But after 1968, Baldwin increasingly doubts the possibility of an interracial movement to reconstitute the republic; even as he continues to deny ideas of racial purity and to insist that black and white are in fact mixed, he rarely says "we" of "Americans," by which he now means whites, and he argues that blacks must redeem *themselves*, not whites.

25. Baldwin, "White Man's Guilt," 410.

26. Baldwin, "Everybody's Protest Novel," 32–33.

27. Baldwin, "Many Thousands Gone," 77.

28. Baldwin, *Fire Next Time*, 375.

29. Ibid., 340.

30. Ibid., 373.

31. Brown, "Wounded Attachments"; Arendt, "Collective Responsibility"; Nietzsche, "On Redemption."

32. Schmitt, *Political Theology* and *Concept of the Political.*

33. Rogin, *Ronald Reagan, the Movie.*

34. Baldwin, *No Name On the Street*, 18. Baldwin left America because of race, but he left Harlem because of homophobia: homosexuality still signifies as an internal frontier demarcating racially authentic community, that is, the internal dimension of the friend-enemy distinction.

35. I draw the idea of "visiting" from Hannah Arendt, and I draw the idea of saying the unspeakable from Toni Morrison.

36. Blake, "There Is No Natural Religion," 97–98, and "The Marriage of Heaven and Hell," 148–58; Stevens, *Necessary Angel.*

37. "The Israelite prophet . . . hardly ever . . . foretells a plainly certain future. God does not deliver into his hand a completed book of fate with all future events written on it. . . . It was something of this kind that 'false prophets' pretended. . . . Their main 'falsity' lay not in the fact that they prophesy salvation but that what they prophesy is not dependent on question and alternative. . . . The true prophet does not announce an inevitable decree. He speaks into the power of decision lying in the moment" (Buber, *Prophetic Faith*, 103–4).

38. Rancière, *Dis-Agreement.*

39. Rather than endlessly unmask the falsity of every claim to universality, Baldwin believes a greater good can be engendered by particular voices seeking freedom, if they see they themselves as reconstituting a whole. For an analogous argument, see Singh, *Black Is a Country.*

40. Arendt, *On Revolution.*

41. Lear, *Therapeutic Action*, 204.

42. See especially Gates, "Fire Last Time." See also Als, "Enemy Within"; Lester, "Some Tickets Are Better than Others."

43. Baldwin, *Fire Next Time*, 379.

44. Baldwin, "Notes of a Native Son," 145.

45. Baldwin, *Fire Next Time*, 379.

BIBLIOGRAPHY

Als, Hilton. "The Enemy Within: The Making and Unmaking of James Baldwin." *New Yorker*, February 16, 1998.

Arendt, Hannah. "Collective Responsibility." In Jerome Kohn, ed., *Responsibility and Judgment.* New York: Schocken Books, 2003.

Arendt, Hannah. *On Revolution.* New York: Viking, 1971.

Baldwin, James. "The American Dream and the American Negro." In *Price of the Ticket.*

Baldwin, James. "The Creative Process." In *Price of the Ticket.*

Baldwin, James. "Everybody's Protest Novel." In *Price of the Ticket.*

Baldwin, James. *The Fire Next Time.* In *Price of the Ticket.*

Baldwin, James. "In Search of a Majority." In *Price of the Ticket.*

Baldwin, James. "Many Thousands Gone." In *Price of the Ticket.*

Baldwin, James. *No Name in the Street.* New York: Dial Press, 1972.

Baldwin, James. "Notes of a Native Son." In *Price of the Ticket.*

Baldwin, James. "On Being White and Other Lies." *Essence*, April 1984.

Baldwin, James. *The Price of the Ticket: Collected Nonfiction, 1949–1985.* New York: St. Martin's Press, 1985.

Baldwin, James. "Stranger in the Village." In *Price of the Ticket.*

Baldwin, James. "White Man's Guilt." In *Price of the Ticket.*

Baldwin, James. "White Racism and World Community." In *Price of the Ticket.*

Baldwin, James, Nathan Glazer, Sidney Hook, Gunnar Myrdal, and Norman Podhorertz. "Liberalism and the Negro: A Roundtable Discussion." *Commentary*, March 1964.

Blake, William. "The Marriage of Heaven and Hell." In Geoffrey Keene, ed., *Blake: Collected Writings*. New York: Oxford University Press, 1972.

Blake, William. "There Is No Natural Religion." In Geoffrey Keene, ed., *Blake: Collected Writings*. New York: Oxford University Press, 1972.

Brown, Wendy. "Wounded Attachments." *Political Theory* 21, no. 2 (1993).

Buber, Martin. *Prophetic Faith*. New York: Harper and Row, 1949.

Cavell, Stanley. *The Claim of Reason*. New York: Oxford, 1979.

Gates, Henry Louis. "The Fire Last Time: What James Baldwin Can and Can't Teach America." *New Republic*, June 1992.

Lear, Jonathan. *Therapeutic Action: An Earnest Plea for Irony*. New York: The Other Press, 2003.

Lester, Julius. "Some Tickets Are Better than Others: The Mixed Achievement of James Baldwin." *Dissent* 33 (1986).

Nietzsche, Friedrich. "On Redemption." In *Thus Spoke Zarathustra*. New York: Vintage, 1980.

Rancière, Jacques. *Dis-Agreement*. Minneapolis: University of Minnesota Press, 1999.

Rogin, Michael. *Ronald Reagan, the Movie*. Berkeley: University of California Press, 1987.

Schmitt, Carl. *The Concept of the Political*. Chicago: University of Chicago Press, 1996.

Schmitt, Carl. *Political Theology*. Chicago: University of Chicago Press, 1985.

Shulman, George. *American Prophecy: Race and Redemption in American Politics*. Minneapolis: University of Minnesota Press, 2008.

Singh, Nikhil Pal. *Black Is a Country: Race and the Unfinished Struggle for Democracy*. Cambridge: Harvard University Press, 2004.

Stevens, Wallace. *The Necessary Angel: Essays on Reality and Imagination*. New York: Vintage, 1951.

SIX

Rendezvous with Life

Reading Early and Late Baldwin

ROBERT REID-PHARR

Stomp my feet
An' clap my han's
Angels comin'
To dese fair lan's.

Cut my lover
Off dat tree!
Angels comin'
To set me free.

Glory, glory,
To de Lamb
Blessed Jesus
Where's my man?

Black girl, whirl
Your torn, red dress
Black girl, hide
Your bitterness.

Black girl stretch
Your mouth so wide.
None will guess
The way he died

Turned your heart
To quivering mud
While your lover's
Soft, red blood

Stained the scowling
Outraged tree.
Angels come
To cut him free!

—JAMES BALDWIN, "BLACK GIRL SHOUTING"

James Baldwin was a bad poet, or so it is generally held within the settled and static critical and biographical traditions that bunch around Baldwin's infinitely interesting figure. He was a bad poet; a remarkable, if not always reliable, novelist; a talented orator; a forthright partisan of the Black American civil rights struggle; a breathtakingly interesting American exile; and a profoundly talented essayist. For many these are established facts, the clearly and incontrovertibly "known" truth about this most significant of twentieth-century Black American writers. That is to say, as a subject established *within* the practice of literary and cultural criticism, James Baldwin, the many attestations to his vibrancy notwithstanding, is, it seems, shockingly, surprisingly, frustratingly dead. What I hope to demonstrate and to work against in this essay then is a tendency toward ossification (mummification, one is wont to say) within the critical and biographical narratives that surround Baldwin and his work, narratives that structure not only which parts of Baldwin's corpus are deemed to be worth consideration (novels and essays are "in" while plays and poems are "out") but also which epochs within Baldwin's career it is imagined one might fruitfully approach.[1]

That I begin these comments with consideration of a poem that a precocious teenaged Baldwin published in the winter 1942 issue of the *Magpie*, the literary magazine of the Bronx high school that Baldwin attended, bespeaks, I hope, a desire to resuscitate devalued forms and underappreciated periods within Baldwin's oeuvre. At the same time, however, I must rush to say that, though I agree that there is considerable value in underappreciated parts of Baldwin's corpus, I am most concerned in these comments to focus as closely as I can on the discursive and ideological structures underwriting the ongoing process of Baldwin's valuation, institutionalization, and canonization. Thus my interest in this earliest poem by Baldwin (a work that with its predictable images, improbable dialect, and strained changes of diction and voice suggests that perhaps Baldwin was not so off the mark when he disparaged his own efforts as a poet) turns on my belief that it is precisely within undervalued precincts that one might most easily discern basic social, aesthetic, and ideological structure. Moreover, much the same can be said of the other work that we will examine in these pages, Baldwin's almost universally disparaged long essay *The Evidence of Things Not Seen*, a work predictably published at the end of a masterful, if presumably declining, career.

I am attracted to these texts precisely because they represent "failures" for Baldwin—though I stress again that my point is not to enter into what I take to be an overwrought concern with when, where, or how to assign value. Or perhaps to state the matter a bit more clearly, I find these works interesting precisely because they seem for many of us to be beyond the pale, (critically/aesthetically) inert. Indeed, I have gone so far as to attempt to provoke my readers by associating the process of Baldwin's canonization with the author's figurative death not to resuscitate Roland Barthes's now decades-old call for a necessary distinction between the critical and the biographical, but instead in order to remark my concern that the ossification of critical conceit regarding Baldwin and his work speaks less to innate quality than to only half-articulate attempts within our critical literatures and practices to place not so much Baldwin as *Baldwin studies* in service to specific class interests.[2] Perhaps I overstep myself then when I speak of the death of Baldwin. Instead it might be more precise to argue that the process of canonization in which many of us, myself included, participate, a process that is intimately connected to the strong tendency to discount significant portions of Baldwin's corpus, evinces a will to disestablish Baldwin as a vibrant, "live" participant within our critical practices by focusing too obsessively on the author as a sort of valuable, transferable, product. The point here is to remind you that while it may be unwise, and perhaps even vulgar, to subject works of literature to political or ideological analyses, the same cannot be said of processes of canonization.

It is, one hopes, not necessary to rehearse the long struggle by students of Black American literature and culture to make plain the ways that the question of not only who gets to speak but also how that speech is framed and judged is a matter that is obviously and—oftentimes explicitly—politicized. As Hazel Carby has written:

> The forms that signs take are conditioned by the social organization of the participants involved and also by the immediate conditions of

> their interactions. . . . We must be historically specific and aware of the differently oriented social interests within one and the same sign community.[3]

Here Carby stresses the necessity of ideologically aware and indeed partisan analyses of not so much processes of figuration as the values attached to these processes within the "sign communities" that both authors and their audiences share. That is to say, value, for better or worse, may be established *inter*textually but never exclusively *intra*textually. This is, I believe, a claim with which most of my readers will concur. What I take to be a more difficult matter, however, are the ways that the "*immediate conditions*" of our own critical interactions are quite profoundly implicated within what I have named class struggle within the "sign community" that encompasses both Baldwin's labors and our own.

In making these claims I would gesture toward the Saturday, July 14, 2007, appreciation of Baldwin and his career published in the *Guardian* by novelist Caryl Phillips, on the occasion of the fiftieth anniversary of the first of Baldwin's many returns from Europe to the United States. Therein Phillips, in a largely celebratory piece, makes a number of what have become standard claims about the arc of Baldwin's career and the nature of his artistic practice. He utilizes a highly schematic developmental narrative to structure his discussion of Baldwin's career, separating the author's body of work into three, biographically established periods, or "acts." The first act ends with a youthful, still-unknown, "private" Baldwin returning in July 1957 from Paris to New York. The second act finds Baldwin back in New York, actively taking part in the burgeoning Civil Rights Movement and fully inhabiting the role of mature, famous author, a role that, according to Phillips, left Baldwin little time or energy to devote to craft. The third act involved Baldwin's return to France in an attempt to recapture control over his prose.

The point is that Baldwin achieved what Phillips takes to be his major successes as a novelist, *Go Tell It on the Mountain* and *Giovanni's Room*, because of the relative obscurity and leisure he enjoyed during his first years in Paris. Moreover, even as Phillips rightly praises *The Fire Next Time*, he suggests that this work was already a concession to Baldwin's having relinquished hold over the apparatuses of the novelist in order to achieve his potential as an essayist and polemicist. Like many others before him, then, Phillips argues that what disrupted Baldwin's talent was precisely the fame that accrued to him once that talent was generally recognized.

> In the mid-60s he [James Baldwin] was arguably the most photographed author in the world; on May 17, 1963 he was on the cover of *Time* magazine the week after John F. Kennedy. He was in constant demand for lectures and readings all over the U.S. and around the world, and he was continually on television, radio, and in print. His performances were often dazzling and were generally delivered with authority that overwhelmed the audience. With this level of fame came a daunting travel schedule and it is astonishing that Baldwin found the time to get any work done.[4]

My concern here is not to quibble with Phillips over whether or not some innate quality in Baldwin's writing suffered because of his fame. Again, I would remind you that I have specifically opted not to enter into the treacherous waters where questions of literary value are debated. What concerns me instead are the commonsense beliefs that structure Phillips's assertions about the conduct of first-rate intellectualism. While bemoaning Baldwin's lack of time for work and private reflection, Phillips also seems to forward the assumption that artistic value is established by the ability of the creative intellectual somehow to obscure political and social investment. Phillips privileges a sort of peekaboo aesthetic practice in which the audiences for an artist's work gain satisfaction from the knowledge that there is, in fact, some private, unspoiled arena in which the public creations of the intellectual are incubated and hatched.

I would suggest, moreover, that this recognition allows one to understand better some of the stranger moments in Phillips's encomium to Baldwin. The first is his awkward musing about Baldwin's presumed lack of and longing for a single committed romantic relationship, a love that would have, in Phillips's words, allowed Baldwin to achieve security, "to find a kind of peace—a kind of invisibility." The second is Phillips's criticism that in Baldwin's more "performative" pieces, particularly the essay that we will take up briefly, *The Evidence of Things Not Seen*, the author indulges in "irrelevant autobiographical asides that continually lead the reader away from, rather than towards, the central subject matter." Without belaboring the point, I would argue that when one brackets the specific charges that Phillips makes in order to examine the implications of the rhetoric that he utilizes and celebrates, what one finds is a rather straightforward articulation of the value of a cloistered intellectualism. The artist's creations, all presumably produced in some well-established home protected from politics and publicity, ought to evince a certain social modesty and sobriety, a coyness about the difficulties of producing narrative.

The problem for me is not so much that I cannot appreciate the elegance of Phillips's claims. On the contrary there continues to be something valuable, something infinitely promising, about the dream of a "room of one's own." What concerns me, however, particularly within comments pitched so directly at the matter of Baldwin's canonization, is the fact that Phillips's largely biographical claims have the danger of leading one onto rather deadly critical terrain. Specifically, those of us interested in traditions of intellectualism established in relation to slavery, colonialism, imperialism, internationalism, and the African diaspora should, I believe, be extremely careful when deploying the assumption that homelessness, or living one's life in public, as it were, is always and ever so very enervating that the relative worth of a cultural artifact might be properly matched to how far from this reality that artifact's creator or creators have traveled.

It surprises me, in fact, that so few persons have challenged the idea that Baldwin's craft suffered because of his fame, even though the logic embedded within it would immediately break down if it were applied not only to musicians, actors, and other performance artists but also and importantly to the many critics of black diasporic life and culture whom we now regularly celebrate. A homebound W. E. B. Du Bois, a coy Frantz Fanon, a delicate C. L. R. James would, in most quarters, seem unthinkable. Part of what establishes these men's importance in our current critical endeavors is precisely the fact that their efforts make sense primarily or perhaps *only* in public. Or to state the matter from another direction, what Du Bois, Fanon, and James all demonstrate for us are the ways that public social and political exigencies have been profoundly articulated within our intimate and private lives.

I have chosen then to turn to what have been named as some of the worst moments in Baldwin's artistic and intellectual life because I want to stress the ways that part of what is effected through our negative judgments of both Baldwin's early poetry as well as his late essays and novels is the diminishment of Baldwin's importance in an engaged *critical* terrain. Thus, though I will not altogether leave off with assigning value in Baldwin's corpus, I do want to suggest that aesthetic value for Baldwin largely turned on the ability of the artist to make visible, *palpable*, the highly contested, highly politicized substance of structures of valuation, processes of canonization.

One might rightly argue, therefore, that context is the most obvious consideration when reading Baldwin's early poetry, work that demonstrates, I believe, a not properly obscured political and aesthetic orientation. That Baldwin wrote and edited a literary magazine in a largely white high school in segregated New York City should be enough to give even the least partisan of critics pause. Even more important, the *Magpie* was published at a moment when citizens of the United States were becoming increasingly self-congratulatory about the country's articulation of a so-called potent center, a space figured somewhere between communism and fascism that effected the *extra*literary contexts in which the apprentice Baldwin honed his craft, the very figuring structures of the author's—and his society's—work.

Volume 26, number 1, of the *Magpie*, entitled the "Star-Spangled Issue," was rather articulate in its representation of American exceptionalism. The first short story included therein, "Three Houses," written by one Solomon Stein, was a self-conscious allegory of the tensions underwriting World War II. The complexities of the war were pitched to the magazine's juvenile audience as the struggle between three families: the E Pluribus Unum(s), the Smiths, and the Uber Alles(es), who of course neatly confirmed stereotypes of honest, unified Americans; lethargic, impolitic Britons; and aggressive, acquisitive Germans. When it is read in relation to the magazine's treatments of German anti-Semitism, the presumed lack of fairness within socialism, and celebrations of a youthful, vibrant American "way of life," one begins to understand what the stakes for young Baldwin were in producing a poem established around the shouting, quivering, and bitterness of the black survivor. What may be most disappointing (at least for conservative readers) about Baldwin's early poem is not so much his obvious lack of authorial control, but instead the reality that he attempts to soil (a word I have chosen knowingly) transparent narratives of innocent, progressive nationalism through the use of the well-established metaphors of the wailing black girl and the lynched black man. That is to say, Baldwin's awkward piece rather self-consciously disrupts the smugly celebratory tendencies shared by both the *Magpie's* youthful readers and the larger community of which they were a part.

I take it to be supremely telling to find that Baldwin deployed similar strategies at the end of his writing career as well, specifically within his final monograph, *The Evidence of Things Not Seen*. Indeed, for reasons that I hope will become clearer later, I invite the thinly considered narrative of progression that I have just criticized. I do want us to think of *Evidence* as that spoiled, petulant, know-it-all younger brother whose childish personality nonetheless helps to complete Baldwin's noble line. It is, in fact, precisely this lack of what one might think of as proper socialization that I would suggest is the key to appreciating this clumsy, difficult late text, as well as the political and aesthetic tensions that it represents.

The much maligned work examines the murders in Atlanta during the early part of the 1980s of twenty-eight Black American individuals: two adult men, two girls, and twenty-four boys, in and around an area known as the Casbah, a heavy crop of low-income housing that directly abutted Atlanta's smug, faded downtown. The villain, the stranger inside, who was put on trial and convicted for the murders of the two men and thus assumed by city and state officials to have been responsible for all twenty-eight murders, was a somewhat nondescript, perhaps even dowdy black Atlantan named Wayne Williams. Those of us familiar with these events will remember that many members of the Atlanta black community doubted that Williams committed any of the crimes, much less all of them. And the weight of memory and history being what it is, one might very well imagine the variety of the alternative narratives of terror and death then circulating in Atlanta and throughout the nation. Baldwin writes, "Whoever was murdering the children . . . could, literally, have been anyone, of any color, from the teacher to the preacher to the cop to the bus driver to your neighbor to you: all would, or could, have had the same motive."[5]

It is to the matter of this presumably all too apparent motive that Baldwin commits himself in *Evidence*. And though I myself have criticisms of the work, particularly what seems to me a sort of knee-jerk nostalgia, a will to read contemporary black Atlanta as somehow only a pale reflection of the more inwardly focused, more clearly formalized Black American neighborhoods that Baldwin remembered from his youth, I nonetheless find myself stunned by the ambitiousness on display in the text, the manner in which Baldwin's aesthetic and theoretical sophistication is met, challenged, and extended by a certain flat-footed pragmatism. Or to rush to one of my final punch lines, it is the very clumsiness that many have noticed in *Evidence*, a clumsiness anticipated in "Black Girl Shouting" and presumably expressed in all those failed literary experiments bemoaned by Phillips, that I take as proof of the text's being uniquely capable of speaking to difficulties that specifically beset us as students and critics of "domestic" fictions produced in increasingly globalized, alienated, "strange" contexts.

What Baldwin is after in *Evidence* is the production of what one might call a poetics of terror, the enumeration of the many ritualistic forms individuals and communities develop to mark their inability to remember horror.

> What I remembered—or imagined myself to remember—of my life in America (before I left home!) was terror. And what I am trying to suggest by what *one imagines oneself to be able to remember* is that terror cannot be remembered. One blots it out. The organism—the human being—blots it out. One invents, or creates, a personality or a *persona*. Beneath this accumulation (rock of ages!) sleeps or hopes to sleep, that terror which the memory repudiates.[6]

Of course, any sophomore student of Freud's major works will rightly understand that Baldwin means to suggest that this moment of repudiation, that all-too-human blotting, might be properly understood as the very foundation of a specifically Black American culture. Moreover, as Baldwin makes absolutely clear, the forms, cultural and otherwise, we have created to address this reality (this void where a memory of violence ought to stand) are strongly, even viciously contested in the United States and elsewhere.

Even so, this "autobiographical digression," this insertion of the author's presumably private "life story" into the structure of the text, works against the production of what one might think of as elegant narrative. I must wonder, however, if this is not, in fact, the point. Of course, the complex structure of the narrative, the abrupt changes of voice and vantage point that we also saw in the efforts of young Baldwin, efforts that presumably were often repeated as the author gained a taste for fame, directly parallel the multivocality, the profound differences in opinion and perspective, that surrounded the Atlanta child murders. I would argue, therefore, that the true terror that Baldwin names in *Evidence* is that which goes largely unremarked, if not unnoticed, within societies structured by hierarchies of race, class, and gender. Within these contexts terror slips beneath memory, moldering in private, relieved only by the screams of childless mothers and the quivering of abandoned lovers.

It is not then a thing primarily produced during spectacular, public expressions of violence. Instead the terror that Baldwin announces is an aspect of the enforced silences that help to establish the structural, discursive, and ideological frameworks in which such barbarism takes place. Thus the broken body of the child and the scorched body of the lover are, in effect, signs of even more heinous realities. They are the proof, the evidence in Baldwin's language, that violence, exploitation, abuse, and antipathy are normal, *normative* realities within white supremacist societies.

As I have suggested already, Baldwin's problem with authority, his stumbling over words, can be found repeatedly in the work of many intellectuals who attempt to articulate the ways that subjugated individuals struggle within and against dominant narratives and values. This means that for the engaged critic, the name of the critical/aesthetic game is always to unsettle, through any means necessary, established narrative forms. Moreover, one of the major ways that Baldwin attempted to effect this disruption was precisely by courting, in early work and late, the strangely structured, immature, enfeebled modes of discourse available to both the novice and the so-called has-been. Part of what makes Baldwin's complex efforts in *Evidence* so interesting today then is that while he clearly wanted to demonstrate some of the ways that the suffering of Black American persons and communities, the patterning of a never quite properly remembered terror, is suppressed in our society, forcefully (dis)established beneath the level of polite public discourse, he was also extremely aware of the ways that these discursive patterns were universally, that is to say, transnationally and transracially, destructive.

I have suggested already that much of the rest of the world suffers what I will call the enforced privatization of terror just as readily as do Black Americans. Baldwin's addition to this somewhat obvious realization is to suggest that the white "oppressors" are just as disabled by these discursive processes as the "oppressed" blacks. "White Americans," Baldwin reminds us, "are probably the most abject victims of history the world has ever seen, or will ever know. (Yes: in spite of Iran, Ireland, England, Russia, and Jerusalem)."[7] The innocence of the so-called white subject is predicated on the ability to imagine that there is a racial identity, a whiteness, that remains somehow aloof from the political and the performative, an ability that Baldwin regularly struggled against during the course of his career, especially as he self-consciously broke out of standard narrative modes that tended to leave both authority and the difficulties of establishing—and disrupting—authority unspoken. Moreover, it is this refusal to reiterate normative narratives of value (the bourgeois distinction between an author's private life and his public creations) that I believe makes Baldwin an artist whose work might prove to be particularly useful for our own efforts at progressive literary and cultural analysis.

Much of what Baldwin does in *Evidence* and throughout his career is to demonstrate the lie of the notion of an essentially aloof, apolitical, and asocial cultural ideal announced by Matthew Arnold and kept alive by a bevy of his often quite unlikely students. What Baldwin seeks is a *formal*, sociological assessment of the structures that allow for this (black) process of mapping (and masking) spectacle at the site of an unknown, unspeakable, yet ever palpable terror. Enter messy, arrogant, brown-skinned Wayne Williams, an individual who, by presumably proving that Black Americans could, in fact, produce a serial killer on the fantastic scale so often demonstrated by whites, ushered increasingly less primitive and innocent Black Americans through yet another strange side entrance, leading into ever more advanced levels of modern depravity. (That is to say, Wayne proves that we can do "it" too.)

Here I would suggest that though Baldwin attempts to produce a sort of communal voice for the residents of the Casbah, though he correctly understands that one of the tragedies of this bloody episode was the way in which many competing narratives were overwritten by a whitewashed tale of localized horror, the truth of the matter is that the only figure who is fully developed in the text is Wayne Williams himself. Edward Smith, Timothy Hill, Alfred Evans, Milton Harvey, Yusef Bell, Angel Lanier, Jeffrey Matthis, Eric Middlebrooks, Christopher Richardson, LaTonya Wilson, Aaron Wyche, Anthony Carter, Earl Terrell, Clifford Jones—I dare say that none of these names have caught in the communal imagination, black, American, or otherwise, more securely than that of Wayne Williams.

What the unlikely figure of Wayne Williams does then is to give us access, even and especially as he evokes vulgarity and horror, to precisely the juvenile tendency to disrupt polite discursive modes. Thus the pages that Baldwin gives over to the fact that Wayne was generally thought to be disrespectful and abusive to his own parents suggest a certain fascination on Baldwin's part with the ways that vulgar disruption may, in fact, be a necessity if one is to break through the even more ugly and antihuman deadening of our awareness of how the ugliest, most thick-nailed processes of capitalist and racist domination structure our most precious moments of intimacy and privacy.

It is hopefully clear therefore why I will attempt to resist (at least in these pages) my own tendency to deal with the complexities of forming something like eloquent sentences with discordant elements by simply stressing ambiguity, undecidability, or a perhaps now old-fashioned retreat to half-baked ideas about postmodernity or, more current but at least not in this context, a particularly satisfying catch-all "queerness." Stuart Hall reminded us decades ago that the discursive structures of racism are often utilized by black individuals and communities themselves in order to produce resistant cultures.[8] Amy Kaplan has suggested that U.S. culture, particularly after the close of Reconstruction, was profoundly concerned with the figuration of empire, even and especially in texts and contexts that were self-consciously framed as domestic.[9] Penny von Eschen looks at the ways that the anti-Communist and often anti–"Third World" ideologies of the U.S. state, particularly the State Department and the Central Intelligence Agency, were forwarded by wildly popular, state-sponsored tours of black musicians.[10] Brent Edwards stripped away much of the obfuscation and frankly therapeutic mushiness that surrounded the concept of diaspora, arguing that the movement of African-derived cultures, and African-descended individuals, might not be as distinct as one would want to believe from the development of capitalism and white supremacy itself.[11]

I hope that my own efforts will lead you to realize that it is time for those of us seriously engaged in Baldwin studies, the revaluation and canonization of James Baldwin, to begin to pitch our efforts in the direction of these scholars, among many others, who have in various forms and contexts tried to focus ever more clearly on power within the power/culture nexus. I suggest that we do so, moreover, both by referring to devalued texts and periods in Baldwin's literary life *and* by focusing on the ideological structures in which these texts have been produced and articulated. The will to trap Baldwin and his legacy within a canonical process that turns on a sort of unrelenting sentimentalism is indistinct from the will to force the author back into the restrictive, deadening ideological structures that make both terror and the *resistance* to terror unspeakable. The challenge then for those of us dedicated to not simply celebrating Baldwin's memory but also to continuing and developing his literary/critical practice is not only to place the master on our reading lists but also to continue to take seriously his efforts to demonstrate the struggles around power and value that those lists represent. We must work to enliven Baldwin studies by pushing beyond the tired tendency to search for innate, *a*contextual value in his essays, poetry, and fiction. We must take up the difficult, profoundly unglamorous, if somehow angelic, labor of unsettling narratives of (black) aesthetic value. We must, that is, cut down that charred body, prune that scarred tree, and attempt (or at least begin to attempt) to set Baldwin—and ourselves, for that matter—free.

NOTES

1. My argument here builds on the work of D. Quentin Miller: see particularly "James Baldwin, Poet."
2. See Barthes, "Death of the Author."
3. Carby, *Reconstructing Womanhood*, 17.
4. Phillips, "Price of the Ticket."
5. Baldwin, *Evidence of Things Not Seen.*
6. Ibid., xi (emphasis in the original).
7. Ibid., 23.
8. Hall, "Race, Articulation."
9. Kaplan, *Anarchy of Empire.*
10. Von Eschen, *Satchmo Blows Up the World.*
11. Edwards, *Practice of Diaspora.*

BIBLIOGRAPHY

Baldwin, James. *The Evidence of Things Not Seen.* New York: Henry Holt, 1985.
Barthes, Roland. "The Death of the Author." In *Image, Music, Text*, trans. Stephen Heath. New York: Noonday Press, 1988.
Carby, Hazel. *Reconstructing Womanhood: The Emergence of the Afro-American Woman Novelist.* New York: Oxford University Press, 1987.
Edwards, Brent Hayes. *The Practice of Diaspora: Literature, Translation, and the Rise of Black Internationalism.* Cambridge: Harvard University Press, 2003.
Hall, Stuart. "Race, Articulation, and Societies Structured in Dominance." In Houston A. Baker, Manthia Diawara, and Ruth H. Lindeborg, eds., *Black British Cultural Studies.* Chicago: University of Chicago Press, 1996.
Kaplan, Amy. *The Anarchy of Empire in the Making of U.S. Culture.* Cambridge: Harvard University Press, 2002.
Miller, D. Quentin. "James Baldwin, Poet." In D. Quentin Miller, ed., *Re-Viewing James Baldwin: Things Not Seen.* Philadelphia: Temple University Press, 2000.
Phillips, Caryl. "The Price of the Ticket." *Guardian*, July 14, 2007.
Von Eschen, Penny. *Satchmo Blows Up the World: Jazz Ambassadors Play the Cold War.* Cambridge: Harvard University Press, 2004.

PART TWO

Stranger in the Village

SEVEN

"History's Ass Pocket"

The Sources of Baldwinian Diaspora

KEVIN BIRMINGHAM

The most important thing is somewhere else.
It always is—somewhere else.

—JAMES BALDWIN, 1969

In 1972, James Baldwin described a moment during his first trip to the American South in the late fifties, and the exhumed memory produced one of his most jarring and sophisticated metaphors of power:

> I have written elsewhere about those early days in the South, but from a distance more or less impersonal. I have never, for example, written about my unbelieving shock when I realized that I was being groped by one of the most powerful men in one of the states I visited. He had got himself sweating drunk in order to arrive at this despairing titillation. With his wet eyes staring up at my face, and his wet hands groping for my cock, we were both, abruptly, in history's ass pocket.[1]

This passage from *No Name in the Street* is more than an example of Baldwin's descriptive genius. In one striking phrase—"history's ass pocket"—he evokes what it means to be caught up in a regime that violates the same privacy it creates. Baldwin's image uncovers the qualities of history we often disregard: that the salient features of the past are found not in history's visible attire, but in the events concealed from public scrutiny; that past events are not stripped from the body of time so much as they are pocketed by power (sequestered as items of privacy, as shame, or close possession); and that it is only from a relentless innocence masquerading as decorum that we admire history's clothing and decline to check its pockets at all—especially the *back* ones.

As if inattentive to history's pockets, scholarship about the Baldwinian South often overlooks small moments like this in order to focus on Freudian readings of castration anxiety palpable enough in Baldwin's imagination of the Southern lynching ritual.[2] While critics are certainly right to demonstrate his preoccupation with the horrifying image of the lynched body,[3] readings of Baldwin have become overly preoccupied with whatever details reinforce the South's metaphorical value as a spectacular terrain of psychic trauma, and this preoccupation distracts us from noticing that, beyond the horrifying violence on display in the lynched body, we find violations of privacy through an elaborate system of small gestures and groping hands that is far subtler and far more pervasive than the lynch mob. As much as the South is a trauma erupting within the collective memory of black Americans, the imaginative structure of Baldwin's understanding of the relationship between power and race—history and identity—in the United States is primarily built upon the entire country's vexed privacy, which the South merely throws into relief.

As it happened, Baldwin gained international acclaim by describing the relationship between the failures of the private life and the abuses of the public sphere as explicitly as possible. Ten years before *No Name in the Street*, he wrote in *The Fire Next Time:*

> The political institutions of any nation are always menaced and are ultimately controlled by the spiritual state of that nation. We are controlled here by our confusion, far more than we know, and the American dream has therefore become something much more closely resembling a nightmare, on the private, domestic, and international levels. Privately, we cannot stand our lives and dare not examine them; domestically, we take no responsibility for (and no pride in) what goes on in our country; and, internationally, for many millions of people, we are an unmitigated disaster.[4]

If there is any subtlety to the metaphor of the ass pocket, it is not present here. Baldwin diagnosed the United States as a global disaster whose epicenter was the individual's nonexistent private life. He had long championed "the private life"[5] as the toughness of the soul that demands one take an honest reckoning of oneself, but what was new in *The Fire Next Time* was that Baldwin began to connect privacy—the "spiritual state" he associated with the artist's domain—to the structure of political institutions. In other words, the "Negro Problem" was a privacy problem.

For Baldwin, a country's private life was its relationship to the past. The damning criticism of *The Fire Next Time* was that a shared, usable past simply did not exist in the United States, and insofar as the past was excluded from the national consciousness there could be no genuine national identity. In 1960 (less than a year before he began working on *The Fire Next Time*) Baldwin described the peculiarly American incoherence as the empty verbal gestures performed between two friends when they both know that the closet next to them contains a corpse: "We can't talk about anything because we can't talk about that. No matter what I say I may inadvertently stumble on this corpse."[6] The undiminished body of material—a corpse, not a skeleton—in the national closet is the nation's violent history, and insisting upon the closeted presence of the past provided much of the force for Baldwin's voice. In fact, when we say that Baldwin writes in a prophetic mode, we are generally referring to his willingness to redeem the United States by recalling the shared past that Americans are so eager to ignore. Being a prophet meant redeeming a nation with an honest privacy held with the past rather than the false privacy of collective denial. Being a writer—an essayist or a novelist, a Jeremiah or a Henry James—meant creating a language out of the "incoherence" that the nation's disastrous private life created. Either way, any redemptive language would require more than simply putting the nation's corpse on display or turning history's pockets out. If the past is to produce an identity, history would have to be experienced as collective memory. This is why Baldwinian prophecy so often meant invoking the full presence of the past. He projected his prophetic voice through the authority of his memory: "I am one of the first Americans to arrive on these shores."[7]

Time and again, Baldwin's collective memory led him to the U.S. South, which served as his ancestral home and the site of his most elemental memories, despite his having been born and raised in Harlem. In an interview with Margaret Mead in 1970, we hear how the Southern past gave Baldwin his sense of artistic purpose:

> I have to talk about my beginnings, and I did begin here auctioned like a mule, bred as though I were a stallion. I was in my country,

> which I paid for and am paying for. Treated as not even a beast is treated. Died in ditches not even as a mule is murdered. And I have to remember that. I have to redeem that. I cannot let it go for nothing. The only reason I'm here is to bear witness.[8]

The urgency in his tone suggests that the ancestral memory of slavery is not just the reason why he is here. It is who he is. The memory that we summon when we claim to recall the trials of our ancestors posits a collective identity. In other words, Baldwin's prophetic voice insists that who we are is shaped by our membership in a cohesive group whose ancestral experiences we share. As he explained in another interview a few months earlier, bearing witness "doesn't mean I saw it. It means that I was there."[9] The Christian rhetoric of "bearing witness" carves out a subtle but crucial distinction for Baldwin. Seeing something, after all, already implies being there, but what he means when he says that he "bears witness" is that the past is a full presence—it is not an observed event, but an experienced environment. He is more than a bystander to slavery. He is thoroughly ensconced in it.[10]

This would seem to lead us to the moment in which Baldwin imagines himself inside of history's ass pocket, an image that evokes collective memory's notion that the past is an intimate alcove that we can inhabit rather than a cardboard box safely quarantined in the archive. And yet being ensconced in the presence of the past, and more specifically in ancestral memories of the South, had become sinister. Baldwin's ideas of home, memory and privacy—and of the very structure of identity that those ideas assembled—were deeply problematic by 1972. The very region that was supposed to provide the privacy of an ancestral home had become something else entirely. Power had corrupted the intimacy of collective memory by transforming it from an experience nestled within history into an experience suspiciously pocketed. The story of how Baldwin would find imprisonment in the ideals of privacy, homelands, and in ancestral memory takes us through Baldwin's elaborate (and seemingly endless) detours far from the South and from the United States itself. While we rightly think of *The Fire Next Time* as the most American of his essays (with its final rousing call to "achieve our country"), Baldwin discovered the complexity of the relationship between privacy and nationhood through a frame of reference that seems impertinent to both the private life and the national life: through his transnational life. Baldwin found the full depth of history's pockets not in the South, but in West Africa and Israel.

New World Negritude

Before the South was a problem it was an ideal, and like most idealizations it was conceived from a distance. Baldwin imagined his ancestral homeland in the United States through the idea of Africa he found in Paris. That is, Baldwin's interest in the collective memory of homelands was spurred by his encounter with the negritude movement that emerged before World War II as a cultural reaction to colonialism. Writers like Léopold Senghor, Aimé Césaire, and Alioune Diop conceived of an intrinsic pan-African sensibility uniting the African diaspora that was created by the slave trade. Negritude is antiessentialist insofar as the bond it references is the bond of shared historical circumstances, and yet the force behind the identitarian claims of negritude derives from collective memory. It insists that the historical facts and contingencies of slavery and colonialism deepened into a profound sense of kinship that Senghor called a "communion of souls" grounded in a common point of origins, an African diaspora.[11] As Bentley Le Baron describes it, "The physical homeland on the African continent is paralleled by a semi-mystical homeland of the soul—which is 'Negritude.'"[12] Over time, a Senghorian strain of negritude discourse would shift from the semimystical essentialism of souls to a more psychological essentialism positing a distinct "African personality."[13] For Abiole Irele, negritude is a cultural pan-Africanism that flows from a shared "psychological response" to the colonial situation, and negritude literature is produced by writers who are "dominated by the collective consciousness" of this response.[14]

Whether it is a collective consciousness or a communion of souls, the unity of negritude emerges at precisely the point when the history of colonialism becomes the memory of colonialism, when historical events become seamlessly integrated into an identity. The term "negritude" itself was necessary because "tradition" was incapable of bearing the full identitarian load of a community of souls. "Memory," on the other hand, bears this weight rather well. When Jean-Paul Sartre celebrated the poetry of the negritude movement in *Black Orpheus*, he identified negritude as the common memory that strings together all of the diaspora's far-flung differences: "From one end of the earth to the other, the blacks, separated by the language, the politics and the history of their colonizers, have in common a collective memory."[15] In the shift from history to memory, from pan-Africanism to negritude, the political had become personal.

The negritude movement was burgeoning in postwar Paris just in time for James Baldwin's arrival. Sartre's paean to negritude poetry appeared in 1948, the same year that Baldwin first left New York for Paris, and its publication helped to popularize the negritude writers for a wider circle of postwar intellectuals. The year 1956 proved to be a watershed moment. That summer, Paris hosted the First Congress of Negro Writers and Artists, where Senghor, Césaire, and Diop all spoke, and the major objective of the conference was cut from the cloth of the negritude movement: to define the culture that unites the African diaspora. Baldwin attended the conference and covered it in a detailed essay for *Encounter* called "Princes and Powers," which was guarded in its assessment of the conference's polemical stance. Baldwin agreed that the African diaspora shared an "unutterably painful relation to the white world," and yet he was skeptical that a full-fledged culture could be built entirely upon a historical antagonism: "Is this history enough to have made the earth's black populations anything that can legitimately be described as a culture?"[16] For Baldwin (as for the negritude writers) a culture was authenticity writ large, an expression of positive identity arising from within, and so he was skeptical that a dialectical reaction to colonialism alone could constitute an authenticity: "The anatomizing of the great injustice which is the irreducible fact of colonialism was yet not enough to give the victims of that injustice a new sense of themselves."[17] Baldwin's objection was that the conference featured much more discussion about casting off the colonial image of blackness than about what remained after that image was gone.

Despite his initial skepticism, the congress fueled Baldwin's nascent interest in collective memory by generating in him a deeper appreciation for collective memory's relationship to the land. In fact, he seems to have been cautious about the proceedings of the congress because he was busy imagining a negritude native to American soil. That is, he cast aspersions upon his ties to the African continent because he thought they weakened his ancestral claim to the United States, and, above all, Baldwin insisted that the black Americans attending the conference were different from all of the other delegates:[18] "We had been born in a society, which, in a way quite inconceivable for Africans, and no longer real for Europeans, was open, and, in a sense which has nothing to do with justice or injustice, was free. It was a society, in short, in which nothing was fixed."[19] Beyond their participation in an "open" and "free" society, with all of its qualifications, Baldwin boldly asserted that black Americans have had their roots viably (if not justly) transplanted in a unique slave experience.

Cultural roots were as important as ever, but the nourishing soil for the black American community was in the United States rather than in Africa. Baldwin continues, "The land of our forefathers' exile had been made, by that travail, our home . . . and nothing, in any case, could take away our title to the land which we, too, had purchased with our blood."[20] It was important for Baldwin that the travail and blood of slavery in the United States were arduous enough to obliterate whatever claims black Americans might have to Africa because he wanted the collective memory of the slave experience to stand as the singular provenance of black American identity. This is why Baldwin bristled when Senghor suggested that Richard Wright's *Black Boy* had an African heritage: "Senghor rather seemed to be taking away his identity. *Black Boy* is the study of the growing up of a Negro boy in the Deep South, and is one of the major American autobiographies."[21] The importance of diaspora—the pull of a homeland across space that mimics the pull of memory across time—was not lost on Baldwin, but the diaspora informing Wright's and Baldwin's identity was the black American diaspora disseminating rapidly from the South across the United States (and to Europe) throughout the twentieth century. The land to which Baldwin held an ancestral title—the "homeland of the soul" he recognized via collective memory—was the American South, the enduring, monumental site of his travail. In 1957, less than a year after the congress, Baldwin returned to the United States and traveled to the land of his ancestral origins for the first time.

The Americanization of negritude's diaspora nevertheless involved much more than new real estate. As much as Baldwin wanted to lay claim to an ancestral home, he also wanted to describe its originary influence over his identity as optional. Trading an African diaspora for an American diaspora was a move from a determined identity to a created one, which is why when Baldwin shifted ground from one continent to the other he made it clear that his roots had been transplanted into the soil of a "free" society in which "nothing was fixed." Baldwin imagined the United States, unlike Africa, as a land of rooted formlessness, a crucial example of the signature Baldwinian penchant for contradictions. C. W. E. Bigsby notes that Baldwin's essays indicate a "divided mind" in which he often lambastes Americans' denial of history's determining force, and yet when "it serves his purpose he too posits the existence of a primary self outside of and unaffected by history."[22] The "primary self" outside of history disarms the memories of slavery that would otherwise determine Baldwin. While he acknowledged his contradictions more than Bigsby seems to grant, it was a legitimate problem for Baldwin—not because it was contradictory (Baldwin was nothing if not willing to accept a conundrum) but because his involution of history as an ancestral memory necessarily made his relationship to the past less amenable to paradox. One might be both determined and self-created, but something about the intimacy of memory drains all insight from the act of both remember and forgetting. Did the boy from Harlem retain something from Africa or lose it entirely? How was Africa related to the boy from Harlem?

When Baldwin retreated to Loèche-les-Bains, a small village in the Swiss Alps, to finish writing *Go Tell It on the Mountain*, he imagined the isolated villagers as inherently kindred to centuries of European culture they may have never encountered. In "Stranger in the Village," he writes:

> The most illiterate among them is related, in a way that I am not, to Dante, Shakespeare, Michelangelo, Aeschylus, Da Vinci, Rembrandt and Racine; the cathedral at Chartres says something to them which it cannot say to me, as indeed would New York's Empire State Building, should anyone here ever see it. Out of their hymns and dances come Beethoven and Bach. Go back a few centuries and they are in their full glory—but I am in Africa, watching the conquerors arrive.[23]

Essentialized memories obeying the color line all the way back to the slave ships *should* connect Wright's *Black Boy* to Africa, and yet overlaying the ethnic memories estranging black Americans from the conquerors' *King Lear* is Baldwin's abiding belief in an American rebirth that obliterates the memory of the first slave ships altogether.[24] That is, while Baldwin-as-African is isolated from the culture of the arriving "conquerors," Baldwin-as-American is isolated from the entire scene of conquest unfolding among Africans and Europeans. Only a few months later, in "A Question of Identity," Baldwin maintains that American history

> has created an entirely unprecedented people, with a unique and individual past. It is, indeed, this past which has thrust upon us our present, so troubling role. It is the past lived on the American continent, as against that other past, irrecoverable now on the shores of Europe, which must sustain us in the present.[25]

There is no middle ground between the sharp historical rupture that makes "that other past" now "irrecoverable" for Americans and the collective memory that allows a black American to recall the arriving conquerors on the other side of the ocean and thus feel alienated from their traditions. There is either a diasporic recollection extending back to Africa or a national myth of origins that cannot recover memories of the Old World from the "American continent." This conflict between incongruent frames of collective memory was effectively a conflict between American exceptionalism and African diaspora. Baldwin's enduring bind was that as much as he wanted to invoke collective memories, he wanted to distance himself from their traumas.

The Dungeon and the Diaspora

While the ideas of Africa and the South intensified Baldwin's identitarian conflict, he would orient himself within that conflict by an entirely different landmark altogether: the state of Israel. It is in Israel that the conundrum of diasporic homelands appeared more like the sinister pockets of history and power than sites of memory and solidarity. Baldwin traveled to Israel in 1961 to do research for an essay about Israel and Africa commissioned by the *New Yorker*. Although he would never publish this piece, a series of letters to his agent during this trip[26] reveals just how much Africa and Israel are lurking in the margins of the essay Baldwin submitted in its place, the essay we now call *The Fire Next Time*.[27] In fact, Baldwin revised his manuscript twice—once after his trip to Israel in the fall of 1961 and again after his summer in Africa in 1962.[28] Israel provoked thoughts about collective memory and identity perhaps more than any single event since the congress in Paris, and he seemed to have used his letters to work through problems that were still unanswered in the South. At moments, he was amazed by Israel. "There are great faces here, in a way the whole world is here."[29] But the array of faces identifying themselves as Jewish only exacerbated his misgivings about what constitutes an identity in the first place. When he rhetorically asked in a letter, "What *is* a Jew?" he concluded that the Jewish people are united "by two things only (and perhaps 'united' is too strong a word)": "the memory of the six million" and "the resurrection of the Hebrew language," which prompted Baldwin to repeat the same question he asked about negritude five years earlier: "Is this enough to make a personality, to make an identity, to make a religion?"[30] If the connection between Israel and Africa was not clear, he made it clear later in the same letter: "To ask oneself, 'What is a Jew?' is also, for me, to ask myself, 'What is a black man?' And what, in the name of heaven, is an

American Negro?"[31] In September of 1961, Baldwin abandoned his travel plans for Africa at least in part because of the troubling questions Israel provoked. In a letter he sent from Switzerland, Baldwin tried to give his agent a sense of "how complex, once I got to Israel, the whole idea of Africa became."[32]

In Israel, Baldwin began to strip away the premises of shared culture (African, American, or otherwise) that merely made him skeptical and indignant during the congress. While the memory of the Holocaust could unite the Jewish diaspora, they were not united by the larger tradition of Judaism because "the Jews themselves do not believe in it anymore: it was simply one of the techniques for their survival—in the desert."[33] In any case, Baldwin was certain that the Jewish diaspora was not unified by the land they identified as their ancestral home. In fact, the fixed territory of Israel was somehow a *betrayal* of Jewish identity: "I am very struck by the realization that the Semites were nomads and this is still, somehow, the atmosphere of the entire country."[34] Putting aside the speciousness of this characterization,[35] Baldwin seems to have been thinking that Semitic identity was formed through a nomadic struggle for survival "in the desert" and a solidarity in the wake of the Holocaust rather than through the creation of a state. For Baldwin, the nation of Israel was not the recovery of a promised land ("the Jews themselves do not believe in it anymore"), but rather an indication that the land was no longer the site of Jewish travail and suffering. Presumably, this site was now in Europe, where the memory of the Holocaust's six million still united them. If it was the blood and travail of slavery that gave black Americans their title to the Southern soil—and obliterated their older ties to Africa—it was the blood and travail of the Holocaust that reshaped Jewish identity by obliterating the traditions that were once necessary "in the desert" had since become mere relics.

Yet Israel would have been a problematic source of Jewish identity even if the land retained its biblical tradition because the site of Jewish travail was now a site of power, a nation: "I personally cannot help being saddened by the creation, at this late date, of yet another nation—it seems to me that we need fewer nations, not more: the blood that has been spilled for various flags makes me ill. Perhaps I would not feel this way if I were not on my way to Africa."[36] It was nationhood that complicated Africa. The *New Yorker* presumably sent Baldwin to a newly created Israel in order to compare it with the new nations of West Africa. After Israel, Baldwin traveled to Senegal, Guinea, and Sierra Leone, all of which had gained their independence within the previous three years,[37] and the speed of this wave of new nations must have been especially powerful for Baldwin in light of the congress in Paris only a few years earlier. After all, Léopold Senghor, whom Baldwin saw only five years earlier claiming Richard Wright's *Black Boy* for negritude, had just been sworn in as the first president of Senegal. Baldwin, however, had mixed emotions. His journey to Israel and the mere prospect of a sojourn to Senegal had a surprising effect on him:

> The truth is that there is something unutterably painful about the end of oppression—not that it *has* ended yet, on a black-white basis, I mean, but it *is* ending—and one flinches from the responsibility, which we all now face, of judging black people solely as people.[38]

The pain of the end of oppression may be partly the pain of responsibility, but there must have been something deeper, something that accounts for the urgency and desperation of his tone in the letters leading up to his departure for Africa: "Write me, quickly, please, the morale is wildly fluctuating, I'm always afraid, and I'm pregnant with some strange monster."[39] Baldwin's monstrous suspicion was that the rapid transformations in Africa and Israel indicated that the travail that produces identity—negritude or Judaism—may also, in the end, produce new political regimes that will undermine genuine identity just as relentlessly as the old ones. *This* was the idea gestating in his mind before he left for Africa.

Baldwin's anxiety about the very nature of Israelis and Africans—what is a Jew? what is an American Negro?—now that their semimystical homelands of the soul were entirely real homelands of the government emerges in Baldwin's treatment of Elijah Muhammad and the Nation of Islam in *The Fire Next Time*. That is, Baldwin saw in the Nation of Islam another instance of nation-building based upon an identity that declares its ancestral title to land. Elijah "was saying that no people in history had ever been respected who had not owned their land. And the table said, 'Yes, that's right.' I could not deny the truth of this statement. For everyone else has, *is*, a nation, with a specific location and a flag—even, these days, the Jew."[40] These remarkable days, in which even the Jews have their land, were part of what Baldwin believed to be an "age of revolution" that lured young men and women to the Nation of Islam.[41] The prospect of a separate territory and economy seemed more plausible to the individual black American "because there were millions like him, coming soon, now, to power."[42] And this, Baldwin felt, was the corruption of identity. The private life begets the acquisitive life: "Years ago, we used to say, '*Yes*, I'm black, goddammit, and I'm beautiful!'—in defiance, into the void. But now—now—African Kings and heroes have come into the world, out of the past, the past that can now be put to the uses of power."[43] The monster gestating in Baldwin and birthed in *The Fire Next Time* is his suspicion that the end of oppression was really just the turning of oppression's crushingly endless cycle.

It should be no surprise, then, that conclusion of *The Fire Next Time* provides an image of the revolving power that had awakened his anxiety about collective identity. Baldwin suggests that the injustice perpetrated by the white world may have precipitated a

> historical vengeance, a cosmic vengeance, based on the law that we recognize when we say, "Whatever goes up must come down." And here we are, at the center of the arc, trapped in the gaudiest, most valuable, and most improbable water wheel the world has ever seen. Everything now, we must assume, is in our hands; we have no right to assume otherwise.[44]

Baldwin cannot lead us to our impending apocalyptic fire without using its ominous glow to light our escape routes. No sooner does he place us on the arc of the water wheel beginning its descent than he abruptly snatches us from it, telling us that "everything" is really "in our hands." Beneath his intonations of doom and remembrance lies a deep weariness of a past whose vicious cycle of vengeance is driven by identity.

Baldwin's fear was that collective identity closes off our escape routes. That is, solidarity promotes exclusive culture through the collective memory of oppression only to have its participants imprisoned by those memories when solidarity achieves power. Whether Israel was a nation because of the Holocaust or because of a religion that sustained a people in the desert, it was carceral: "You can't walk five minutes without finding yourself at a border," he explained to his agent, and "the Jews, who are surrounded by forty million hostile Muslims, are forced to control the very movements of Arabs within the state of Israel."[45] More important, Israel was but a local manifestation of the global problem that Baldwin would describe in *The Fire Next Time:*

> Perhaps the whole root of our trouble, the human trouble, is that we will sacrifice all the beauty of our lives, will imprison ourselves in totems, taboos, crosses, blood sacrifices, steeples, mosques, races,

> armies, flags, nations, in order to deny the fact of death, which is the only fact we have.[46]

Just in case we are skeptical, a more personal prison in *The Fire Next Time* shows us how imprisonment can result from what appears to be a freeing privacy. When Baldwin describes being a preacher at the age of fourteen, he says,

> I relished, above all, the sudden right to privacy. . . . There were hours and even whole days when I could not be interrupted—not even by my father. I had immobilized him. It took rather more time for me to realize that I had also immobilized myself, and had escaped from nothing whatever.[47]

The teenage preacher found a model for his lifelong dilemma of trying to remove himself from his immobilizing origins (his father, Christianity, the South, Africa) without sacrificing the memories they engendered and the voice they provided, a voice strong enough to shake the dungeons we create for ourselves. Ultimately, Baldwin found the best solution to this dilemma in the map of his questioning.

Paris, New York, Atlanta, Jerusalem, Istanbul, Loèche-les-Bains, Dakar. That formative period of restlessness for Baldwin (one of many in his lifetime) produced both *The Fire Next Time* and a sense of self that slips the knot of flags and races. In December of 1961, as he was anticipating his trip to Africa, he wrote to his agent from Istanbul: "I think that I must really reconcile myself to being a transatlantic commuter—and turn to my advantage, and not impossibly the advantage of others, the fact that I am a stranger everywhere."[48] I would like to suggest that Baldwin's endless commuting was not exactly the movement of a restless exile. Rather, it was a way to generate collective memory through something other than the centripetal pull of a diasporic homeland. Baldwin generated memory through what we may call a cosmopolitan nostalgia, a nostalgia without *nostos*, an impulse that draws one out to nowhere in particular with the faith that one's foundational memories are always in another country. In Paris he is American; in Switzerland he is African; in the South he is a New Yorker; in Harlem he longs for Europe. The nostalgia produced by his cosmopolitanism created an identity whose source is everywhere elsewhere, which is to say that Baldwin's diasporic homeland was not distant so much as distance itself.

A cosmopolitan form of nostalgia avoids the false intimacy of history's pockets and identity's prisons by imagining a global homeland whose permanent distance dissolves the determinism of origins while retaining their affective pull. In the end, this was Baldwin's response to the bind of remembering and forgetting. Being both inside and outside of history—making Africa both present and irrecoverable—was to find intimacy with homelands by remaining outside of them, by longing for them. While he located his homelands elsewhere, it was ultimately the United States' "unmitigated disaster" that compelled Baldwin's movement through so many landmarks but toward no particular point of origin. Baldwin's transnationalism was his reaction to the United States' most obsessive, systematic violation of his privacy: the thousands of pathological pages J. Edgar Hoover's agents would compile from years spent surveilling Baldwin's private life (his movements, his phone calls, his lovers) ostensibly at the service of that most global of ideological conflicts, the Cold War. The postwar political regime distorted space so fantastically that the most extreme scales—the international and the personal, the global order and the writer's bedroom—met in the same warped precinct that was patrolled, remarkably, by the FBI and black nationalists alike. When the FBI was no longer around to document Baldwin's sex life, Eldridge Cleaver and Amiri Baraka were more than happy to follow J. Edgar's lead. Although Baldwin was already "out," he was constantly being outed.[49]

The lessons Baldwin learned about the politics of privacy are still more crucial for us today. Rather than ending with the Cold War, the abutment of the personal and the international that Baldwin experienced fifty years ago appears to be a fixed feature of modern global politics. We live in an age when having your cock groped by a powerful man in the South is itself but a quaint, nostalgic version of the "enhanced interrogations" a nation uses to guarantee global freedom and protection from the hypothetical mushroom cloud always about to blow, all of which is possible because our blood and travail and our eagerness to protect "who we are" make us interlopers in a place where we document sexual torture on cell phone cameras, where wars no longer produce prisoners of war, and where the prisons themselves are only island detention camps. America's ass pocket.

NOTES

Standley and Pratt, *Conversations with James Baldwin*, 81.

1. Baldwin, *Collected Essays*, 390.
2. Freud is waiting in the wings of most discussions about James Baldwin,

though not without his tacit encouragement. In this passage, Baldwin goes on to say that because of the man's power "one had to be friendly: but the price for this was your cock" *(Collected Essays,* 391). When Freud takes the stage it is often for the spectacular performance of an Oedipal conflict involving Richard Wright, Henry James, Harriet Beecher Stowe, or some combination of the three. For Baldwin as both a Freudian and an existentialist, see Marcus Klein, *After Alienation;* Hernton, "Blood of the Lamb." For an Oedipal reading of Baldwin's influences, including a provocative interpretation of the struggle between Stowe and Wright as a literary rape that produced Baldwin, see Miller, "Maw of Western Culture."

3. It is an indelible image in Baldwin's imagination. There are several direct and indirect references to the lynched body in Baldwin's fiction and essays, which often lead to a form of textual psychoanalysis that explains Baldwin's writing all too neatly. Not only are Baldwin's sexuality and identity at stake in the castrated body, but his characteristic moments of anger may be as well. Horace Porter argues that the lynched black man provokes the "powerless and avenging rage" that afflicts many of his characters ("South in *Go Tell It on the Mountain,*" 69). Castration anxiety is flexible enough that we might even invoke it to explain the sentimental distance he keeps with the South. Notably, Paul Griffith avoids any discussion of castration anxiety in his reading of "Going to Meet the Man," Baldwin's short story that features one of his most explicit depictions of the mutilated body of a lynched, castrated man. Yet Griffith's formal analysis serves a different psychological reading: the story's flashbacks and fragmentation "depict racism as a disabling neurosis"—the disability primarily being impotence ("James Baldwin's Confrontation with Racist Terror," 508).

4. Baldwin, *Fire Next Time,* 89.

5. In 1959, Baldwin wrote, "The private life, his own and that of others, is the writer's subject—his key and ours to his achievement" (quoted in Gold, introduction to *Fiction of the Fifties,* 18).

6. Baldwin, *Collected Essays,* 228.

7. Baldwin, *Fire Next Time,* 98.

8. Baldwin and Mead, *Rap on Race,* 230.

9. Standley and Pratt, *Conversations with James Baldwin,* 92.

10. The moments of spiritual witness scattered throughout Baldwin's essays make them an important point of origin for what Kerwin Lee Klein calls the "memory industry" because they sweep aside the epistemological concerns about the knowability of the past that eventually surround memory studies and replace them with an unabashed metaphysics of presence. As Klein reminds us, the origins of the term "memory" are religious, and the Christian terms Baldwin uses to describe memory hearken back to these religious roots (Klein, "On the Emergence of Memory in Historical Discourse").

11. Senghor, *On African Socialism,* 49.

12. Le Baron, "*Négritude,*" 268.

13. Andrain, "Pan-African Movement," 11.

14. Irele, "Negritude," 499.

15. Sartre, *Black Orpheus,* 53.

16. Baldwin, *Collected Essays,* 152.

17. Ibid., 157.

18. Their unique status was dramatized during the conference by what Baldwin described as the American delegation's isolation: "There was also to be considered the delicate position of the American delegation, which had sat throughout the conference uncomfortably aware that they might at any moment be forced to rise and leave the hall" (ibid., 165).

19. Ibid., 147.

20. Ibid.

21. Ibid., 154.

22. Bigsby, "Divided Mind of James Baldwin," 126.

23. Baldwin, *Collected Essays*, 121.

24. Combining these two incongruent frames of identity—being black and being American—would replicate Du Boisian double consciousness precisely if Baldwin's memories were not defined by what they *cannot* remember. Where Du Bois sees a veil whose fabric permits the "second sight" of African Americans, Baldwin sees two sets of barriers, two memories that are collective because they selectively exclude.

25. Baldwin, *Collected Essays*, 100. In another example of Baldwin's eagerness to claim American exceptionalism, he mentions that the literary mantra "Only connect" belonged to Henry James, rather than to E. M. Forster, and embarrassingly suggests, "Perhaps only an American writer would have been driven to say it" (ibid., 385). Baldwin's dedication to the idea of black American exceptionalism was still prominent in *The Fire Next Time:* "The American Negro is a unique creation; he has no counterpart anywhere, and no predecessors" (84).

26. See Baldwin and Mills, "Letters from a Journey."

27. Baldwin's essay was published in the *New Yorker* (November 17, 1962) as "Letter from a Region of My Mind." This essay was renamed "Down at the Cross" and paired with a prefatory piece, "My Dungeon Shook," when it was published by the Dial Press as *The Fire Next Time* in 1963.

28. From Baldwin's letters to his agent, we know he was working on *The Fire Next Time* in Turkey on November 20, 1961 (one month after leaving Israel) and again a few months later in Switzerland in February 1962: "I am again reworking the interminable 'Down at the Cross.' . . . You'll see, I imagine, when you read it, why it has been so hard to do, and it probably also illuminates some of the unsettling apprehensions which have so complicated this journey" (Baldwin and Mills, "Letters from a Journey," 52). David Leeming's biography indicates that Baldwin revised "Down at the Cross" yet again in Switzerland *after* his trip to Africa in the summer of 1962 (*James Baldwin*, 211). "My Dungeon Shook," the first part of *The Fire Next Time*, was Baldwin's reaction to the Eurocentric history books schoolchildren were reading in Senegal (ibid., 212).

29. Baldwin and Mills, "Letters from a Journey," 49.

30. Ibid. (emphasis in original).

31. Ibid., 50.

32. Ibid., 52. Baldwin also notes, "Since this trip is clearly my prologue to Africa, it has become very important to me to assess what Israel makes me feel" (ibid., 49).

33. Ibid., 50. Baldwin seemed to dismiss Judaism for personal reasons as well: "One cannot help asking—*I* cannot help asking—if it is really desirable to resurrect the Jewish religion" (ibid.).

34. Ibid., 49.

35. Baldwin seems to be evoking the stereotype of "the wandering Jew," a characterization often associated with anti-Semitism. For Baldwin, however, the nomadic quality is a virtue, as I hope to show. See Mosse, *Toward the Final Solution*, for a discussion of the history of "the Wandering Jew," and Werner Sombart's *The Jews and Modern Capitalism* for an example of nomadism as a staple of anti-Semitic theory.

36. Baldwin and Mills, "Letters from a Journey," 50.

37. Guinea became independent in 1958, Senegal in 1960, and Sierra Leone in 1961. Senghor's Senegal may have been the centerpiece of Baldwin's travel plans, since Dakar was the only place Baldwin would actually visit on his original itinerary for 1961. Those plans included recently independent Ghana (independent in 1957) and Nigeria (independent in 1960), as well as Kenya, then in the process of becoming independent.

38. Baldwin and Mills, "Letters from a Journey," 49 (emphasis in original).

39. Ibid., 52.

40. Baldwin, *Fire Next Time*, 73.

41. Ibid., 91.

42. Ibid., 80.

43. Ibid., 77 (emphasis in original). Baldwin is just as cynical about the black American politics of identification in his letters to his agent: "Africa has been black a long time, but American Negroes did not identify themselves with Africa until Africa became identified with power" (Baldwin and Mills, "Letters from a Journey," 49).

44. Baldwin, *Fire Next Time*, 105.

45. Baldwin and Mills, "Letters from a Journey," 49–50.

46. Baldwin, *Fire Next Time*, 92. Baldwin would give a version of this prison idea in a letter as well: "There is a very grim secret hidden in the fact that so many of the people one hoped to rescue could not be rescued because the prison of color had become their hiding place" (Baldwin and Mills, "Letters from a Journey," 52).

47. Baldwin, *Fire Next Time*, 32.

48. Baldwin and Mills, "Letters from a Journey," 51.

49. See Cleaver, *Soul on Ice;* Baraka, *Home*.

BIBLIOGRAPHY

Andrain, Charles F. "The Pan-African Movement: The Search for Organization and Community." *Phylon* 23, no. 1 (1962).

Baldwin, James. *Collected Essays*. Ed. Toni Morrison. New York: Library of America, 1998.

Baldwin, James. *The Fire Next Time*. New York: Vintage International, 1993.

Baldwin, James, and Margaret Mead. *A Rap on Race*. Philadelphia: Lippincott, 1971.

Baldwin, James, and Robert P. Mills. "Letters from a Journey." *Harper's Magazine* 226 (May 1963).
Baraka, Amiri. *Home: Social Essays*. New York: Morrow, 1966.
Bigsby, C. W. E. "The Divided Mind of James Baldwin." In Harold Bloom, ed., *James Baldwin: Modern Critical Views*. New Haven: Chelsea, 1986.
Cleaver, Eldridge. *Soul on Ice*. New York: Delta Press, 1999.
Gold, Herbert, ed. *Fiction of the Fifties: A Decade of American Writing*. Garden City: Doubleday, 1959.
Griffith, Paul. "James Baldwin's Confrontation with Racist Terror in the American South: Sexual Mythology and Psychoneurosis in 'Going to Meet the Man.'" *Journal of Black Studies* 32, no. 5 (2002).
Hernton, Calvin. "Blood of the Lamb: The Ordeal of James Baldwin." *Amistad: Writings on Black History and Culture* 1 (1970): 183–225.
Irele, Abiola. "Negritude: Literature and Ideology." *Journal of Modern African Studies* 3 (1965).
Klein, Kerwin Lee. "On the Emergence of Memory in Historical Discourse." *Representations* 69 (2000).
Klein, Marcus. *After Alienation: American Novels in Mid-Century*. Cleveland: World Publishing, 1964.
Le Baron, Bentley. "*Négritude:* A Pan-African Ideal?" *Ethics* 76 (1966).
Leeming, David. *James Baldwin: A Biography*. New York: Knopf, 1994.
Miller, Elise. "The Maw of Western Culture: James Baldwin and the Anxieties of Influence." *African American Review* 38, no. 4 (2004).
Mosse, George. *Toward the Final Solution*. New York: Howard Fertig, 1978.
Porter, Horace. "The South in *Go Tell It on the Mountain:* Baldwin's Personal Confrontation." In Trudier Harris, ed., *New Essays on* Go Tell It on the Mountain. Cambridge: Cambridge University Press, 1996.
Sartre, Jean-Paul. *Black Orpheus*. Trans. S. W. Allen. Paris: Présence africaine, 1963.
Senghor, Léopold. *On African Socialism*. Trans. Mercer Cook. New York: Praeger, 1964.
Sombart, Werner. *The Jews and Modern Capitalism*. Trans. M. Epstein. New York: E. P. Dutton, 1913.
Standley, Fred L., and Louis H. Pratt, eds. *Conversations with James Baldwin*. Jackson: University of Mississippi Press, 1989.

EIGHT

Separate and Unequal in Paris

Notes of a Native Son and the Law

D. QUENTIN MILLER

It is December 27, 1949. James Baldwin, just released from a French prison, stands up on a chair. He is sweating as he holds the sheet in his hand, and he twists it, with bitterness and desperation, into a rope. He has left his home, his church, and his country in order to discover himself. He has published a short story, a dozen reviews, and a pair of essays. He is twenty-five years old.

His mind is filled with thoughts, as it always is: thoughts that gather steam and that tend to spill out of his mouth or out of his typewriter with an eloquent flow that never fails to startle his audiences or readers. Thoughts that barrel ahead like runaway freight trains, gathering intensity as they hurtle outward, threatening to explode. Fast as his thoughts are racing, his heart is racing faster. The blood in it is about to burst, like Arthur Montana's heart in the first sentence of Baldwin's final novel, to be published three decades from this moment. There is only one choice to make, only one that matters: to live or to die. This choice is more complicated than it might appear. To die this way does not mean to enter the Great Hereafter, the cornerstone of Baldwin's religious upbringing: suicide is murder, and murder is a sin. To die simply means to gain relief from the suffering of this world: the racism, the hypocrisy, the torment. And yet: one recurrent theme in Baldwin's work is that we must "say yes to life."[1] To die is to say no to life. His hands twist. He prays, if at all, for a sign.

The water pipe is as revolting as everything else in this fleabag hotel. As in the house of John Grimes, the protagonist of the novel he is working on, there is dirt everywhere; dust rising all around him; no end to it. Even the City of Lights offers no hiding place from the world's dirt, from the chaotic complexity of human consciousness. Aware that black American men have been dying with nooses around their necks for centuries now, Baldwin fashions his own hanging rope with bitterness, with tears in his eyes. The young, black, bisexual, expatriate writer destined to become famous, to appear on the cover of *Time* magazine, to be known as the spokesman for his race in its crucial hour, to be regarded as a prophet, a witness, a transcendent spirit, tosses the twisted sheet over the rusty pipe, secures it around his neck, and jumps.

When the water pipe breaks in the Grand Hôtel du Bac that day, Baldwin is saved, even "rebaptized by the flood," as David Leeming says.[2] The incident that caused Baldwin to spend over a week in jail before being laughed out of the French courts becomes the subject of an early essay called "Equal in Paris," and Baldwin's early suicide attempt is buried beneath an impressive body of work.[3] His career flourishes, and his literary reputation waxes and wanes from this point on. His death in 1987, though premature, becomes an occasion for celebration of the life rescued from what could have been the truly premature death in 1949 that would have rendered his life a tragedy. A tragedy like Richard's death in *Go Tell It on the Mountain.* A tragedy like Rufus's death in *Another Country.* A tragedy like Giovanni's death in *Giovanni's Room.* Artists are somehow able to survive in Baldwin's fiction, to get a second chance on life as Baldwin did when the water pipe broke, like Sonny in "Sonny's Blues," or like Fonny in *If Beale Street Could Talk.*

What do these characters have in common? What connects them with each other, with Baldwin, and with figures from Baldwin's three longest essays, Elijah Muhammad and Malcolm X in "Down at the Cross," Tony Maynard in *No Name in the Street,* and Wayne Williams in *The Evidence of Things Not Seen*?

One word: prison.

Baldwin's prison experience focuses a theme that flourishes throughout his career. These eight days in Paris, which were not the sum total of Baldwin's time in prison, clarified for him the reality of the law's power over lives like his. His time in jail aligns him with the "victims" H. Bruce Franklin describes in *The Victim as Criminal and Artist:* "Their art expresses the experience of being legally kidnapped, plundered, raped, beaten, chained, and caged—and the understanding that results."[4] It is this understanding that provides Baldwin with a keen insight into the legal system and the power structure that serves as its foundation. Imprisoned black authors in Baldwin's lifetime occasionally represented their period of incarceration as positive, even when the circumstances of their arrest were unjust or unjustified. Prison gave Malcolm X the opportunity to reform himself and to read and study in a way he would not have otherwise done;[5] for Martin Luther King, writing from prison was a way to raise the political consciousness of his readers and to demonstrate his political solidarity with other members of the oppressed black community.[6] George Jackson, in *Soledad Brother* (1970), also emphasizes the solidarity of the black community in prison, and Eldridge Cleaver in *Soul on Ice* (1968) uses the jail cell as a kind of platform to reinforce the connection between black militancy and the prison complex. Baldwin, however, never depicted incarceration in terms that could be considered even remotely positive, and even if he later regarded it as an opportunity to raise the public's political consciousness or to create solidarity among African Americans, he never would have declared it worthwhile to serve time in order to do so. If there are important reasons for being arrested, such as those Martin Luther King details in "Letter from Birmingham Jail" (1968) ("in order to arouse the conscience of the community"),[7] they are outside the Baldwin oeuvre. Prison for Baldwin was always the most depraved space in human existence, and his characters' consistent fear of it, and despondency if they are unlucky enough to experience it, is something his readers must engage with.

Baldwin is generally excluded from studies of prison literature. H. Bruce Franklin emphasizes that his work examines "'common criminals' whose understanding of their own situation developed directly as a consequence of their crime and punishment," as opposed to "those who were professional writers before they became convicts."[8] This trend has continued, but the field of prison literature has expanded to include professional writers such as Norman Mailer, John Cheever, and John Edgar Wideman, who have written about prison through close contact with prisoners as well as "uncommon criminals"—that is, incarcerated writers such as Leonard Peltier, Mumia Abu-Jamal, and Kathy Boudin, whose writing careers grew out of highly publicized legal cases. Since Baldwin's time in prison was brief and since it occurred just as he was becoming a professional writer, he fits into both of these categories and thus neither. He definitely does not fit into the political reform mode in which the narrator has been imprisoned "for an act many readers would commend,"[9] yet we can see in his early work the nascent development of a certain political attitude that will flourish in his later works: when incarceration is based on racial profiling, it should inspire outrage rather than despair so it can lead to political action. In his writings of the 1940s and 1950s, though, it is about despair.

Baldwin's initial engagement with the law was deeply personal and related to two facets of his early life in Harlem and his first period of exile in Paris: namely, the presence of the police on the streets of Harlem and the devastating effects of incarceration. Biographer David Leeming talks of two events in particular from Baldwin's childhood that led to his lifelong fear of the police: one was being roughed up at the age of ten, and the other was being "scared shitless" by policemen on horses at a May Day parade at the age of thirteen.[10] As a way to escape the dangers of the street—dangers represented by the cops as much as the criminals—Baldwin searches for personal spaces of refuge. His early works are dominated by the motif of the need to find a room of one's own—a space where one can discover the self away from the threats of society. Thus we see Peter in "Previous Condition" (1948), John in *Go Tell It on the Mountain* (1953), Baldwin himself in "Equal in Paris" (1955), and David and Giovanni in *Giovanni's Room* (1956) discussing in detail their own dingy private spaces. Peter is evicted from his room by a landlady who threatens to call the police; Baldwin is removed from his hotel room by Paris police and taken to jail; Richard (John's biological father) in *Go Tell It on the Mountain* is arrested for a crime he did not commit; and Giovanni is placed in jail and is on the verge of being executed at the novel's conclusion. Baldwin's early works illustrate that there is no safe haven, no room of one's own that can shelter one from the law. The complex intersection of themes related to racism, persecution of homosexuality, poverty, the abandonment of religion, and the need for exile in Baldwin's early works can be focused through a study of the law's power as it intrudes upon the individual's pursuit of self-improvement.

Baldwin scholars and biographers tend to point to three formative moments when they define the origin of Baldwin's story, three epiphanies that sketch out the portrait of this artist as a young man: (1) his violent conversion on the threshing floor of his church followed by his decision to leave the church, described in *Go Tell It on the Mountain*, *The Amen Corner*, and *The Fire Next Time;* (2) the incident in which he throws a water glass at a waitress in a New Jersey restaurant who refuses to serve him because he is black (discussed in "Notes of a Native Son" and reworked in many other works); and (3) his decision to leave New York for Paris, discussed in *No Name in the Street* and in numerous interviews. In his study *Exiled in Paris*

James Campbell notes Baldwin's claim for his own origin story, quoted from the essay "Equal in Paris," that his "life . . . began that year in Paris," but Campbell uses the quotation to illustrate Baldwin's promiscuity and profligacy; flanking the quotation are observations about how Baldwin brought a parade of "young French boyfriends" to his room as a way of breaking free from the morality of the church "with extreme fervor" and observations about how Baldwin's "motto" was "Go for broke."[11] To someone unfamiliar with Baldwin's work, it might sound from this description like Paris was a joyful, bacchanalian expatriate experience for the young author, that he had accessed the myth of Hemingway, of Richard Wright, of other American models who had gone to Paris to flourish as American literary artists and to live life with an expatriate's abandon. Although these features were certainly part of Baldwin's experience, it is crucial to return this quotation from "Equal in Paris" to its proper context: his observation that his life began that year comes as a direct result of a vision change he experiences in prison. Paris is merely the location: the setting is jail. This self-described beginning of life as detailed in "Equal in Paris" is born of despair, not revelry.

In style and tone, "Equal in Paris" stands apart from the other so-called Paris essays in *Notes of a Native Son* for two main reasons: first and most striking is Baldwin's use of the first-person singular pronoun. The other two Paris essays ("Encounter on the Seine: Black Meets Brown" and "A Question of Identity") are characterized by broad generalizations about American expatriates and Parisians, and Baldwin relies heavily on his early trademark pronoun "one" in those essays. The other feature separating "Equal in Paris" from its companions is its raw emotion, contrasted with the emotionally distant reportage that characterizes the other two essays. The personal nature and development of voice in this essay connect it to two of the strongest essays in *Notes of a Native Son*—the title essay and "Stranger in the Village"—and these features clear the path for his later, more ambitious attempts in *Nobody Knows My Name*, *The Fire Next Time*, *No Name in the Street*, and *The Evidence of Things Not Seen*. "Equal in Paris" has not received as much critical attention as others in the collection, but it marks an important shift in trajectory that results in the development of Baldwin's voice and provides a paradigm for a theme that unifies his career. To quote fully the final line of "Equal in Paris," "In some deep, black, stony, and liberating way, my life, in my own eyes, began during that first year in Paris."[12] It is deeply ironic that the liberation of Baldwin's voice occurs as a direct result of an eight-day stint in prison.

Baldwin attempts to describe the central incident, nearly an anecdote, of "Equal in Paris," in comic terms; he even refers to the essay as a "comic-opera,"[13] and James Campbell refers to it as Baldwin's "funniest piece," though he acknowledges that its humor does not obscure its fundamental serious purpose.[14] On December 19, 1949, Baldwin was arrested and held in a French prison after a friend, evicted from a hotel, left a stolen sheet in his room. The police officers assured him that the incident was of minor or no importance, but they held him regardless. The essay chronicles Baldwin's bewilderment: minutes turn into hours, and hours turn into days as he awaits a trial that seems like it will never arrive. Baldwin slows the pace of his essay nearly to a standstill in order to reveal his growing despondency, fear, and alienation from self. His attempts to write an essay reflecting the comic absurdity of the situation fail: we sense his bitterness and anger swelling under the surface of the essay, and these forces are so strong that they propelled his entire writing career thereafter.

What Baldwin does not tell us in "Equal in Paris" is that the experience in a Paris jail, far from being the catalyst for his writing life, nearly killed him. Having lived through this suicide attempt, Baldwin omits it from his essay but does give us some indication of his state of mind when he writes, "There was a real question in my mind as to which would end soonest, the Great Adventure or me."[15] The other element Baldwin omits from his essay is an overt connection between the force that kept him in a Paris jail cell for eight days and racism. The essay's comic notes indicate Baldwin's desperate attempts to write off the incident as a case of bad luck, of being in the wrong place at the wrong time, but the humiliation he experiences lays the foundation for the outrage that typifies the rest of his career, an outrage more frequently related to race than to poverty or to foreignness. In exile from America following his firsthand experience with racism, Baldwin is reluctant to admit that racism is not unique to America and that prison is one way racism can be legally reinforced even in the famously liberal City of Lights. Baldwin takes pains in the essay to avoid ascribing his arrest to race; he writes, "That evening in the commissariat I was not a despised black man. . . . For them I was an American."[16] Yet Baldwin published this essay in 1955, and in June of 1954 he and Themestocles Hoetis had also been arrested for no reason, this time in New York. On this occasion, according to Hoetis, Baldwin "*screamed.* All night long. . . . 'I'm a *nigger*; they picked me up because I'm black.'"[17]

Notes of a Native Son contains many instances of Baldwin's struggling with racial discrimination, so its apparent absence from "Equal in Paris" is curious, especially given the fact that he made the connection between racism and wrongful arrest so vociferously in New York the year before he published "Equal in Paris" and because other versions of wrongful arrest in Baldwin's early work are so clearly linked to racism: Richard in *Go Tell It on the Mountain* kills himself after he is the victim of racial profiling, for instance. Perhaps Baldwin was eager to place this incident in the broadest possible context; as he insists in his introduction to *Nobody Knows My Name:* "In America, the color of my skin had stood between myself and me; in Europe, that barrier was down."[18] And yet there is a nagging sense under the surface of "Equal in Paris" that racism is one of the main factors that contributed to Baldwin's feelings of powerlessness. The virtual absence of race from the essay might indicate that Baldwin felt it would do no good to draw attention to it as a relevant factor. He had not yet developed faith even in his outrage at the law's power to discriminate, and this surprising faltering of Baldwin's conviction can be interpreted by what Cornel West deems

> the nihilism that increasingly pervades black communities. *Nihilism is to be understood here not as a philosophic doctrine that there are no rational grounds for legitimate standards or authority; it is, far more, the lived experience of coping with a life of horrifying meaninglessness, hopelessness, and (most important) lovelessness.* The frightening result is a numbing detachment from others and a self-destructive disposition toward the world.[19]

Baldwin, having thoroughly rejected religion as hope and having not yet established his belief in the saving power of either art or love to the point that they could prevent despair, does indeed reflect the nihilism West identifies as pervasive. He was young, he was a foreigner, he had little money, and he hadn't mastered the language. These four factors *combined* with his race led Baldwin to be thrust into a rift he confronts throughout the Paris essays: namely, the black American's tenuous connection to his ancestral African past.

In the face of being judged as just another poor American drifter as opposed to an ambitious author, Baldwin is forced to confront his status as a Westerner of African descent. The question is one of identity, but also of a delicately evoked history. Led deeper and deeper into the hellish bowels of the French prison system, he feels a victim of the extraordinary way in which society enforces its power structure through its legal, judicial, and penal systems. Incarceration makes Baldwin understand this power and his own powerlessness in the face of it. In prison he observes:

> I was handcuffed again and led out of the Préfecture into the streets—it was dark now, it was still raining—and before the steps of the Préfecture stood the great police wagon, doors facing me, wide open. The handcuffs were taken off, I entered the wagon, which was peculiarly constructed. It was divided by a narrow aisle, and on each side of the aisle was a series of narrow doors. These doors opened on a narrow cubicle, beyond which was a door which opened onto another narrow cubicle: three or four cubicles, each private, with a locking door. I was placed in one of them; I remember there was a small vent just above my head which let in a little light. The door of my cubicle was locked from the outside. I had no idea where this wagon was taking me and, as it began to move, I began to cry.[20]

This passage is sure to elicit the vision of an African slave taken from his native land, being put in an absurdly narrow vehicle, taken from a home he would not see again, and led, against his will, he knows not where. Baldwin's response to the French prison testifies to what Foucault observes about prison construction in *Discipline and Punish* ("enclosed, segmented space, observed at every point, in which the individuals are inserted in a fixed place")[21] and anticipates a theme broader than (but related to) slavery: legal power. His arrest and prolonged imprisonment in Paris did not occur simply because he happened to be friends with a petty thief, but rather because of what might be called his "previous condition," the factors he cannot control, from society's perspective: his race, his poverty, and his nationhood. The essay is about the lack of control over one's destiny. To be "equal" is to be equally powerless wherever one goes.

In "Equal in Paris" Baldwin interprets his powerlessness most evidently in terms of poverty: he believes he is seen in terms of "the familiar poverty and disorder of that precarious group of people of whatever age, race, country, calling, or intention which Paris recognizes as *les etudiants* and sometimes, more ironically and precisely, as *les nonconformists*."[22] It is the presence of the policemen that causes Baldwin to see himself as mainstream Parisians must see him, not as an intellectual and an aspiring writer, but as an outcast: as he is marched out of the hotel room with his friend, he imagines the scene from the point of view of the hotel proprietor: "And so we passed through the lobby, four of us, two of us very clearly criminal."[23]

The very existence of police uniforms causes Baldwin and his friend to be labeled this way: the police presence immediately and irrevocably alters Baldwin's identity. Since he has been labeled "criminal," his fate is no longer in his control, and he contemplates his vulnerability in the context of incarceration: "I am not speaking now of legality which, like most of the poor, I had never for an instant trusted, but of the temperament of the people with whom I had to deal"[24]—that is, the jailers, judges, and police officers who held power over him. He observes, "It was quite clear to me that the Frenchmen in whose hands I found myself were no better or worse than their American counterparts. Certainly their uniforms frightened me quite as much, and their impersonality, and the threat, always very keenly felt by the poor, of violence, was as present in that commissariat as it had ever been for me in any police station."[25] This observation adds another layer of meaning to the essay's title, "Equal in Paris"—that is, the poor are treated equally poorly wherever they go—and it also reiterates the Baldwin theme that expatriation does not amount to escape: there is "no hiding place." At the same time, he has understood what it means to be disenfranchised—due to poverty, race, or foreignness—and the experience compromises his view of himself as a confident social and literary critic, advanced in the early essays of *Notes of a Native Son*, and as an honest man and a good writer, advanced in the preface and in the central essays.

The law, in the form of police officers acting according to the least rational interpretation of criminality, makes Baldwin keenly aware of the fear at the core of his being. Baldwin is frightened not only of the police officers but, in the alienating world of the prison cell, of his fellow prisoners: North Africans to whom he "could not make any gesture simply because they frightened [him]"[26] and other cellmates who warned him that he might mistakenly face the guillotine. He writes, "The best way of putting my reaction to this is to say that, though I knew they were teasing me, it was simply not possible for me to totally *dis*believe them. As far as I was concerned, once in the hands of the law in France, anything could happen."[27] The law, intended to be the most rational force holding together any society, becomes for Baldwin at this moment the most irrational force within society, one that would murder without remorse. His bewilderment and victimization not halfway into his eight-day detention are only to develop and to cause him to change the way he views not only the law in France but society in general and the ultimate powerlessness of individuals in response to it.

Baldwin is left with a fatalistic vision of humanity in marked contrast to the cheerful optimism of the "Autobiographical Notes" at the beginning of the collection, where he states, "I want to be an honest man and a good writer."[28] When he finally reaches the courtroom this phrase echoes hollowly: he observes

> that all the people who were sentenced that day had made, or clearly were going to make, crime their career. This seemed to be the opinion of the judge, who scarcely looked at the prisoners or listened to them; it seemed to be the opinion of the prisoners, who scarcely bothered to speak in their own behalf; it seemed to be the opinion of the lawyers, state lawyers for the most part, who were defending them. The great impulse of the courtroom seemed to be to put these people where they could not be seen—and not because they were offended at the crimes, unless, indeed, they were offended that the crimes were so petty, but because they did not wish to know that their society could be counted on to produce, probably in greater and greater numbers, a whole body of people for whom crime was the only possible career. Any society inevitably produces its criminals, but a society at once rigid and unstable can do nothing whatever to alleviate the poverty of its lowest members, cannot present to the hypothetical young man at the crucial moment that so-well-advertised right path."[29]

The fact that Baldwin has already chosen his own right path—honest man, good writer—seems irrelevant as he becomes aware of the immense and irrational power of the law to incarcerate the innocent, to assign a preordained criminal identity to the poor, the immigrants, the racial minorities. As Peter Caster writes, "Criminalization is . . . a jurisprudential process, not coincident with the commission of the crime but, rather, an effect of conviction. . . . Criminalization is thus a matter of interpellation, of being named."[30] Baldwin realizes that the law acts on behalf of society in naming him and thus preventing him from naming himself.

Baldwin's perspective on prison and the law in general as a society's most invidious way to enforce its power structure in terms of race and class was just beginning to develop in "Equal in Paris," though we can see evidence of it elsewhere in *Notes of a Native Son.* The first two essays in the collection—"Everybody's Protest Novel" and "Many Thousands Gone," about the artistic shortcomings of protest novels by Harriet Beecher Stowe and Richard Wright, respectively—are the essays in the collection that gained the most attention, and they continue to absorb

Baldwin's critics. Both *Uncle Tom's Cabin* and *Notes of a Native Son* are about the consequences of African Americans breaking the law. As Jon Christian-Suggs reminds us, "The very premise of the escaped slave's tale is that she or he has broken the law,"[31] and Stowe's novel is built on the genre of the slave narrative. Gregg D. Crane argues that "Stowe's images of good-hearted and law-abiding Northerners confronted by weary and shivering fugitives in *Uncle Tom's Cabin* were intended to and did bring home for many of her readers the momentous contest between conscience and law created by the Fugitive Slave Law."[32] In converting the slave narrative genre into the genre of the protest novel, according to Baldwin, Stowe fails to inspire true feeling in the reader, focusing instead on sentimentality and guilt. What is interesting about Baldwin's language in the essay is the prominence of prison metaphors in describing the human and American conditions. Protest novels, according to Baldwin, "emerge for what they are: a mirror of our confusion, dishonesty, panic trapped and immobilized in the sunlit prison of the American dream."[33] He also speaks of the "cage of reality"[34] that determines the fate of individuals deemed inferior by society. Protest novels are not the keys to unlock these prisons and cages, according to Baldwin; in fact, these novels are partially responsible for constructing the cages because they fail to bring us closer to the crucial concept of truth: "Truth, as used here, is meant to imply a devotion to the human being, his freedom and fulfillment; freedom which cannot be legislated, fulfillment which cannot be charted."[35] Baldwin is reaching for some lofty, abstract notions of freedom here and elsewhere in his early work: he refuses to equate freedom with something granted by law, something "legislated." Part of this perspective is optimism: he wants to think of freedom as something that is above the law. His prison experience, of course, weighs on this idea with heavy irony.

Baldwin's criticism of Wright's *Native Son* is even more focused in terms of the law, for Bigger Thomas, Wright's antihero, is an undisputed criminal whose trial occupies a fair portion of the novel. In "Many Thousands Gone" Baldwin begins to develop his theory that the fate of black Americans and the fate of white Americans are intertwined and that to separate them through such means as incarceration is to use legal power to deny the truth of American race relations. Wright's main flaw, in Baldwin's estimation, is that he approaches Bigger as a sociologist rather than as a humanist. Bigger is not allowed to develop his voice, particularly in the legal arena of the courtroom; Baldwin writes,

> It is useless to say to the courtroom in which this heathen sits on trial that he is [the white Americans'] responsibility, their creation, and his crimes are theirs; and that they ought, therefore, to allow him to live, to make articulate to himself behind the walls of prison the meaning of his existence. . . . Moreover, the courtroom, judge, jury, witnesses and spectators, recognize immediately that Bigger is their creation and they recognize this not only with hatred and fear and guilt and the resulting fury of self-righteousness but also with that morbid fullness of pride mixed with horror with which one regards the extent and power of one's wickedness.[36]

This observation links Baldwin's critique of *Native Son* to his own experience in the French prison: in both cases, he understands how the courtroom and the prisons function to manufacture a scapegoat who can serve to preserve society's power structure. In "Equal in Paris" he feels a victim of the notion that "any society inevitably produces its criminals,"[37] and he sees the same idea in *Notes of a Native Son.* In both cases there is no possibility for self-determination. Like Bigger, he is denied the opportunity to speak on his own behalf in the French courtroom, and he observes the way judges, juries, and witnesses condemn the accused anyway: if criminals are nothing more or less than criminals, in literature as well as in life, then there is no hope that their humanity can be fully developed. Baldwin believes that literature should be the realm where the accused, whether guilty or innocent, should have the opportunity to become human. His reaction to Wright's novel may have been not only a statement of his own aesthetic, but a solidarity with Bigger Thomas born of Baldwin's experience in a French prison: unable to speak, both Baldwin and Bigger were rendered powerless by the massive grinding wheels of the justice system.

One factor that develops out of Baldwin's first collection of nonfiction and that unites all of his early protagonists is roomlessness, a metaphor for isolation. This isolation is not merely a condition of a disenfranchised young man trying to find his place in the world in the absence of traditionally stable cultural institutions like family, religion, and higher education. It is a direct function of the realization of the law's monolithic power; as Foucault says of the first logical principle of the prison, "Isolation provides an intimate exchange between the convict and the power that is exercised over him."[38] In his early creative imagination, Baldwin interprets the criminal power of the law in terms of the way it exercises its influence unevenly based on poverty, race, and sexuality. Race is perhaps surprisingly underemphasized in "Equal in Paris," but in his later writings, the law will most often manifest its criminal power in terms of race. But sexuality and poverty are not unimportant in this formulation. The law has the ability to aid in the persecution of anyone who is relatively powerless in society's eyes. The only rooms available to the persecuted are jail cells, and these are rooms that belong to the state, not to the self.

NOTES

1. A phrase Baldwin used repeatedly; see, e.g., Baldwin and Avedon, *Nothing Personal*, part 3.
2. Leeming, *James Baldwin*, 72.
3. He also worked on a teleplay describing the incident with Sol Stein; also titled "Equal in Paris." It was never produced, but Stein recently published it in his book *Native Sons.*
4. Franklin, *Victim as Criminal and Artist*, xxii.
5. Malcolm X did not romanticize prison itself, though. He admits that he "wasn't framed. I went to prison for what I did," but he also says, "I firmly believe that it was the Christian society, as you call it, the Judaic-Christian society, that created all of the factors that send so many so-called Negroes to prison. And when these fellows go to prison there is nothing in the system designed to rehabilitate them. There's nothing in the system designed to reform them. All it does is—it's a breeding ground for a more professional type of criminal, especially among Negroes" (Clark, *King, Malcolm, Baldwin*, 38).
6. It is important to note that King's prison experiences involved racially segregated jails, even a decade after the *Brown vs. the Board of Education* decision; when Kenneth Clark asks him in a 1963 interview, "Have you ever been in an integrated jail? In the South?" King responds, "No, that's one experience I haven't had yet." The irony that jails were among the last segregated public institutions in the United States is self-evident. Clark puts the same question to Malcolm X in the same year about a Northern prison; Malcolm responds, "It was an integrated prison at the prison level, but the administrators were all white" (ibid., 22–23, 36).
7. King, "Letter from Birmingham Jail," 72.
8. Franklin, *Victim as Criminal and Artist*, 147, 148.
9. Ibid., 133.
10. Leeming, *James Baldwin*, 24, 16.
11. Campbell, *Talking at the Gates*, 25.
12. Baldwin, *Notes of a Native Son*, 158.
13. Ibid., 139.
14. Campbell, *Talking at the Gates*, 60.
15. Baldwin, *Notes of a Native Son*, 141.
16. Ibid., 146.
17. Campbell, *Talking at the Gates*, 90–91.
18. Baldwin, *Nobody Knows My Name*, 11.
19. West, *Race Matters*, 14 (emphasis original).

20. Baldwin, *Notes of a Native Son*, 150.
21. Foucault, *Discipline and Punish*, 197.
22. Baldwin, *Notes of a Native Son*, 142–43.
23. Ibid., 143.
24. Ibid., 144.
25. Ibid., 145.
26. Ibid., 153.
27. Ibid., 154.
28. Ibid., 8.
29. Ibid., 155.
30. Caster, *Prisons, Race, and Masculinity*, 13, 16.
31. Baldwin, *Notes of a Native Son*, 26.
32. Crane, *Race, Citizenship, and Law in American Literature*, 58.
33. Baldwin, *Notes of a Native Son*, 19.
34. Ibid., 20, 21.
35. Ibid., 15.
36. Ibid., 43.
37. Ibid., 155.
38. Foucault, *Discipline and Punish*, 237.

BIBLIOGRAPHY

Baldwin, James. *Nobody Knows My Name: More Notes of a Native Son*. New York: Dial Press, 1961.

Baldwin, James. *Notes of a Native Son*. Boston: Beacon Press, 1955.

Baldwin, James, and Richard Avedon. *Nothing Personal*. New York: Atheneum, 1964.

Campbell, James. *Talking at the Gates*. New York: Viking, 1991.

Caster, Peter. *Prisons, Race, and Masculinity in Twentieth-Century U.S. Literature and Film*. Columbus: Ohio State University Press, 2008.

Clark, Kenneth B. *King, Malcolm, Baldwin: Three Interviews*. Middletown, Conn.: Wesleyan University Press, 1985.

Crane, Gregg D. *Race, Citizenship, and Law in American Literature*. Cambridge: Cambridge University Press, 2002.

Foucault, Michel. *Discipline and Punish*. Trans. Alan Sheridan. New York: Vintage, 1995.

Franklin, H. Bruce. *The Victim as Criminal and Artist*. New York: Oxford University Press, 1978.

King, Martin Luther. "Letter From Birmingham Jail." In *Why We Can't Wait*. New York: Signet, 1963.

Leeming, David. *James Baldwin: A Biography*. New York: Alfred A. Knopf, 1994.

Stein, Sol, and James Baldwin. *Native Sons*. New York: One World/Ballantine Books, 2005.

West, Cornel. *Race Matters*. Boston: Beacon Press, 1993.

NINE

Exile and the Private Life

James Baldwin, George Lamming, and the First World Congress of Negro Writers and Artists

KEVIN GAINES

In the 1970 *No Name in the Street*, James Baldwin recalled his attendance at the First Negro Writers and Artists Congress, which took place at the Sorbonne, in Paris, from September 19 to 22, 1956. He recalled walking along the Boulevard St. Germain with Richard Wright and other speakers from Africa. "Facing us, on every newspaper kiosk on that wide, tree-shaded boulevard, were photographs of fifteen-year-old Dorothy Counts being reviled and spat upon by the mob as she was making her way to school in Charlotte, North Carolina." Suddenly the conference seemed insignificant in the face of Counts's ordeal. "It made me furious, it filled me with both hatred and pity, and it made me ashamed. Some one of us should have been there with her!" On that bright afternoon, Baldwin wrote, he knew he was leaving France. "Everyone else was paying their dues, and it was time I went home and paid mine."[1]

One readily sympathizes with Baldwin's outrage. Yet Baldwin's recollection of the conference at the end of the 1960s as he wrote *No Name in the Street* was flawed. For it was not during the Sorbonne conference, but a year later, in September of 1957, that Dorothy Counts, after four days of harassment by white mobs, abandoned her effort to integrate Harding High School in Charlotte. In conflating these two events in his narrative despite their separation in time, Baldwin, in effect, declared his solidarity with the black struggle then raging in the United States. He seemed to be apologizing for his self-exile, indeed, his very presence at the conference, which "I was covering for *Encounter*, or," by his own brash admission, "for the CIA." *Encounter* was the flagship organ of the Congress for Cultural Freedom, an organization dedicated to waging the West's ideological Cold War struggle against international communism. A decade later, it was discovered to have been covertly funded by the Central Intelligence Agency.[2] Baldwin was just as apologetic about being in France, where he "dawdled . . . for nearly yet another year, held by my private life and my attempt to finish a novel." Perhaps feeling a need to heal a rift with an imagined audience of young black activists, Baldwin owned up to his apparent complicity with U.S. propaganda. Even more significant in this regard is the reference to his "private life," an apparent allusion to his queer sexuality, as a diversion from the struggle at home, where, he claimed, he should have been engaged.[3]

Baldwin's candor on geopolitical and personal matters suggests a bid for authenticity and continued relevance as the black freedom movement stood at a dangerous crossroads. Traumatized by the death of his greatly admired contemporaries Martin Luther King and Malcolm X, Baldwin found that his message of redemptive love as a liberatory force lacked credibility to young militants, many of whom had rejected nonviolence for armed struggle. Despondent and helpless at the realization that the bloody struggles of the movement had brought so little change for the majority of African Americans, Baldwin felt obliged to reaffirm his loyalties to the struggle.

As recounted in *No Name in the Street*, Baldwin returned to the United States in 1957, and made his first trip to the South, a revelatory sojourn in which he reported on the movement for U.S. magazines. But by the late 1960s, Baldwin's faulty account of the Sorbonne conference, driven by the political exigencies of the moment, hints at perhaps a more painful form of exile, one to which he could give only partial, fleeting expression. This was the estrangement he, as a queer black man, was made to feel by his own people. The calculated mix of disclosure and dissemblance with which Baldwin references his sexuality in this recollection suggests an internal cold war waged against Baldwin by a younger generation of black militants. Taken together, Baldwin's "furious" fatherly expression of protective concern for Counts and his rueful intimation of questionable geopolitical and personal associations give the appearance of a man striving to remove the taint of suspicion and to prove his fidelity to the black struggle. Indeed, throughout *No Name in the Street*, Baldwin gives a poignant account of his alienation from his natal black community, by virtue of his lonely, jet-setting success and, inescapably, the complicated self he presented to the world. Little wonder that he would cast his exile in Paris in a negative light.

It is understandable, yet no less tragic, that the pressures of Cold War political repression, and Baldwin's turbulent relationship to black activists, obscured the memory of Baldwin's more immediate account of the conference, as recorded in his essay "Princes and Powers," published in *Encounter* in 1957. For despite its seemingly compromised provenance, the essay reveals the conference as a generative site of interaction with fellow writers of African descent, rather than the occasion for auto-critique it became in *No Name in the Street*. In "Princes and Powers," Baldwin gives an account of the speeches by prominent Western intellectuals of African descent, all grappling with questions of black unity and diversity, cultural identity, and their relevance for struggles against colonial and racial discrimination. Transitory Cold War concerns informed Baldwin's criticism of the anti-Western political grandstanding of some of the speakers. Yet "Princes" poses the more crucial matter of Baldwin's own development as a writer in relation to other black writers in the international arena. The Paris conference provides an important occasion for understanding Baldwin's evolution as a highly original commentator on racism, sexuality, and national identity.[4]

As is well known, it was often from the distance of self-exile that Baldwin elucidated the "private life" of the American racial imagination. This entailed an inquiry into the perverse tangle of intimacy and violence that characterized the history of blacks and whites in the nominally Christian United States. "Integration," Baldwin quoted a black man while reporting on the movement in Georgia, "has always worked well in the South, after the sun goes down," adding, "it's not miscegenation . . . unless a black man's involved."[5] But Baldwin was equally interested in exposing the psychological consequences of the racism he experienced in the Harlem ghetto of his youth and young adulthood. Baldwin's chilling exposure to the South's violent folkways of white supremacy informed his writing on the psychological violence of racism in the North, as well.

Baldwin's forte in the 1960s was to lend eloquent expression to African Americans' exclusion from the American dream. As the white South waged violent resistance to desegregation during the early 1960s, Baldwin increasingly took aim at the willful innocence and paternalism of Northern white liberals, blind to the fact that their privilege rested on the exclusion and disciplining of black people by business, labor, government, the banks, organized crime, the landlords, and above all the police.

Baldwin fled this regime of Northern racism to become a writer. Throughout his career, Baldwin's expatriate sojourns provided respite from the stresses of U.S. racism and the demands of fame in the United States. And due to the burdens of racism, poverty, and homophobia, his embrace of America as his native country, and African Americans as his natal community, remained qualified, ambivalent at best.[6] At the time of the conference, Baldwin had completed his second novel, *Giovanni's Room*, a bold departure for its foregrounding of homosexuality, its absence of African American characters, and its Paris setting. The conference was a pivotal moment between *Giovanni's Room* and his next novel, *Another Country*, for Baldwin's understanding of the linkages of racial and sexual oppression. "Princes and Powers" marks its author's shift in concern, away from a geopolitical U.S. struggle for influence abroad to an inner cold war waged within the hearts and minds of Americans, a clinical survey of the struggle for love and mutual understanding within the hostile territory of a racist society.

It would be mistaken to read "Princes and Powers" solely through the prism of Cold War politics, or the advocacy of negritude, or other assertions of communal solidarity. What Baldwin gained at the Sorbonne conference was an affirmation of his own individuality, his "private life."

To be sure, Baldwin could not escape Cold War tensions. His interest in specifying his relationship to America as an African American abroad was fodder for U.S. propaganda defending the image of America overseas. In "Princes," Baldwin notably contrasted what he called the relative openness of American society with the absolute exclusion practiced by colonial societies. And he criticized W. E. B. Du Bois's "ill-considered" protest at his exclusion from the conference by the State Department. Still, to dwell on such matters overlooks Baldwin's deeper investment, and that of others at the conference, in the seemingly less polemical, but no less vital, question of the struggle of black writers to find an independent voice in the shadow of a patronizing Western culture shaped by racism and colonialism. For Baldwin, the task taking shape in his imagination was exposing the racial and sexual phobias embedded in American nationalism, as well as the sexual hierarchies implicit in ideologies of racial solidarity and nationalism.

Like others at the conference, Baldwin was absorbed by the question of what the global community of people of African descent held in common despite their divergent histories and experiences. But he described the challenges facing the black writer with a keen awareness of his own difference and the distinctive nature of his own project. "Black men," as he put it, held in common

> their precarious . . . unutterably painful relation to the white world. What they held in common was the necessity to remake the world in their own image, to impose this image on the world, and no longer be controlled by the vision of the world, and themselves, held by other people.

Baldwin's gendered formulation of the black writer's struggle for manhood hinted at the inherently contested nature of manhood.

> What, in sum, black men held in common was their ache to come into the world as men. And this ache united people who might otherwise have been divided as to what a man should be.[7]

A major catalyst for Baldwin's quest for personal and intellectual integrity amid the clamor for unity was the Barbadian writer George Lamming's reflections on the lived experience of black writers (then viewed as a fraternal order referenced with the male pronoun) judged by the Eurocentric criteria of a racist Western culture. Baldwin wrote admiringly of Lamming's "refusal to be intimidated by the fact that he is a genuine writer" and of his skepticism toward facile assertions of identity. In Lamming's address "The Negro Writer and His World," he noted that while the conference's ostensible goal was to establish the Negro's contribution to world civilization, "the image of the [white] Other is always present in our conception of ourselves."[8] Owing his very existence to the history of slavery and colonialism, the Negro writer finds himself saddled with that condition that the Other has devised for them both: "He is not simply *there*. He is there in a certain way. The eye which catches him and cages him, has seen him as a man, but a man *in spite of*."[9] Like the nausea that overwhelms Fanon's West Indian migrant in Paris after he is accosted by the child—"Look, a Negro . . . I'm frightened"[10]—the Negro writer "is a little ashamed . . . the shame which touches every consciousness which feels it has been *seen*." Lamming's emphasis on shame as central to practices of racialization suggested to Baldwin an affinity with the stigma attached to homosexuality. In our contemporary language, we might say that implicit in Lamming's formulation of racial shame was a sense of the way in which anti-black racism, by definition, defines black people as "queer" through its accusation of their inherent deviation from dominant white, patriarchal, heterosexual norms.

The concept of racial shame was not news to Baldwin, who had witnessed, and written frequently of, the destruction of the daily humiliations visited upon his father. But Baldwin's gloss on Lamming's remarks suggests that they resonated with Baldwin's own sense of estrangement rooted in homophobia as well as racism. Baldwin gravitated to Lamming's idea of having found "something crippling in the obsession from which Negroes suffered as regards the existence and the attitudes of the Other—this Other being everyone who was not Negro." For Baldwin this meant the stigma of heteronormative authority—whether white, black, or religious—imposed on gay black men like himself. And to Baldwin's ears, Lamming implied that black people themselves were as susceptible as anyone else to wielding an oppressive power that would "be in no way distinguishable from the power they sought to overthrow."[11]

Baldwin praised Lamming for "insisting on the respect which is due the private life." "Private life" was Baldwin's Jamesian term for the interior life that served as the wellspring of his creativity. In a homophobic world that discouraged candor, "private life" was also a euphemism for his own sexuality. In yet another sense, the phrase "private life" signified "the immensity and variety of the experience called Negro," a field of possibility that should be recognized as wealth. Baldwin endorsed Lamming's "idea that part of the great wealth of Negro experience lay precisely in its double-edgedness." The conclusion Baldwin drew from Lamming was that Negro identity was much more than met the eye, constructed not only in relation to the white other but also in relation to other black people: "[Lamming] was suggesting that all Negroes were held in a state of supreme tension between the difficult, dangerous relationship in which they stood to the white world and the relationship, not a whit less painful and dangerous, in which they stood to each other." Baldwin evidently felt a keenly personal affinity with Lamming's view that acceptance of this duality by people of African descent was a source of strength and "their means of defining and controlling the world in which they lived."[12]

Baldwin's receptivity to Lamming's speech at the Sorbonne in the fall of 1956 invites us to view his novels *Giovanni's Room* (1956) and *Another Country* (1961) as experiments in exploring the similarities and connections between racism and homophobia, with the ultimate objective of dissecting the racial and sexual dimensions of midcentury American alienation. *Giovanni's Room* was the product of Baldwin's attempt to "define and control the world in which he lived" as a black writer, through his revolt against the expectation that he limit himself to "racial," or Negro subject matter. With its setting in France, and its story of a short-lived affair between a white middle-class American, David, and his dark working-class Italian lover, Giovanni, the novel provided Baldwin an opportunity for theorizing the social and public dimensions of his "private life." Baldwin's dedication of the novel, to his lover Lucien Happersberger, tellingly quotes Whitman: "I am the man, I suffered, I was there."[13]

The novel's study of American alienation, with its European metropolitan setting, is not overtly a matter of race, as it might have been for Lamming or Fanon. Rather, alienation is manifested in David's inability to love. In a manner reminiscent of Lamming's and Fanon's scenarios of racist interpellation, on several occasions, David, who narrates the story, voices an uneasy awareness of being watched by others and feeling exposed and shamed by their gaze. When he meets Giovanni, who works as a bartender, their conversation and evident mutual attraction are periodically interrupted by the demands of Giovanni's job, as he moves among the bar's patrons, taking and filling their drink orders.

> I watched him as he moved. And then I watched their faces, watching him. And then I was afraid. I knew that they were watching, had been watching both of us. They knew they had witnessed a beginning and now would not cease to watch until they saw the end.[14]

David's homophobic imagination, which trafficked in racialist tropes of filth and animality by comparing loud and garish drag queens to "monkeys eating their own excrement,"[15] nevertheless fought a losing battle against his desire for Giovanni. Now, David felt that "the tables had been turned; now I was in the zoo, and they were watching."[16]

Here and at other moments, David's relationship with Giovanni cannot escape the surveillance of David's desire, not only by others but by himself, as well. David has received a letter from his father, whose plea for information about David's social, that is, private, life was rooted in the fear that their estrangement would become permanent. His father's need for such information exacerbated David's uneasiness and shame at his compromising associations (shades of the Cold War) with members of the homosexual subculture he frequents, epitomized by his intimacy with Giovanni. Indeed, David's capacity for love and his relationship with his father have been eroded, if not altogether undermined, by David's internalized notion of respectable heterosexual American manhood. David's notion of what a man ought to be governs and controls, according to Baldwin, David's enactment of his desire. When David, in spite of himself, stares at an attractive young sailor with envy and desire, the sailor "gave [him] a look contemptuously lewd and knowing. . . . Had our contact lasted, I was certain that there would erupt into speech, out of all that light and beauty, some brutal variation of *Look, baby, I know you.*"[17] Humiliated, David feels exposed by his lust, recognizing in himself the conduct of an older, furtive homosexual whom he himself has exploited and whom he regards as loathsome.

When David, after a period of avoiding Giovanni, finally tells him that he is leaving him for his fiancée, Hella, an American woman whom he does not love, but who will publicly confirm his manhood through marriage and bearing his children, Giovanni berates David for his rejection of their love. Giovanni, whose dark complexion and vulnerable social status (he lacks a work permit) are made to imply not only his racialized (or colonial) otherness, but also the heightened social awareness of the oppressed, unleashes a tirade against David that seems evocative of the psychosexual basis of racism, the fearful association of sexual intimacy with the racial other as contamination. Giovanni does not believe David when he says he loves Hella:

> You never have loved anyone, I am sure you never will! You love your purity, you love your mirror. . . . You want to be clean . . . you do not want to stink. . . . You want to leave Giovanni because he makes you stink. You want to despise Giovanni because he is not afraid of the stink of love. You want to *kill* him in the name of all your lying little moralities. And you—you are immoral."[18]

It is not difficult to imagine Baldwin, through Giovanni, as addressing those in mid-twentieth-century America who would perpetrate or justify the lynching of a black man, as if to kill as well the very idea of consensual sexual intimacy, indeed love, across the color line. Indeed, despite the Old World setting in the ostensibly "free" Paris, the circumstances of Giovanni's demise are reminiscent of an all-too-familiar scenario of racial violence, that is, the lynching, judicial and extralegal, of black men in the U.S. South. Giovanni kills his homosexual employer, who has exploited Giovanni sexually, after the employer accuses Giovanni of theft and fires him. Giovanni is apprehended, tried and convicted, and executed by guillotine.

In abandoning Giovanni, David has, in effect, condemned his lover to death, transforming Giovanni's accusation into a prediction: "You want to *kill* [Giovanni] in the name of all your lying little moralities."

Giovanni's Room probes the narcissistic character of dominant white American masculinity that renders love and intimacy impossible by conflating sex with self-indulgence and power. The ostensible homosexual plot becomes an allegory for Baldwin's reflections on the discovery of what it means to be an American. White heteronormative masculinity was inseparable from racialized notions of queerness. Black and white Americans have been formed by their common history and are bound together by their search for identity. Both groups need to liberate themselves from identities distorted by national myths of sexualized racism.

Giovanni's Room and *Another Country* were crucial texts for Baldwin's evolving synthesis of the relationship of the private life—of human relationships warped by racism and its attendant sexual fears and anxieties—to the persistence of conflicts and institutionalized racism in American public life and policy. But located behind those novels was Baldwin's participation in the First Negro Writers and Artists Congress held in Paris in 1956, which provided an occasion for Baldwin to begin to question his assumptions about American freedom as he contrasted it with the closed nature of colonial societies and enlarge on the relevance of his own "private life" for a critique of the racial and sexual pathologies animating divisive myths of American nationhood. In the South, these myths incited that region's citizens to lethal violence in the name of white supremacy. In the Northern ghetto, these racial and sexual pathologies, permeating Harlem's institutions, rendered black men vulnerable to equally lethal forces of self-destruction.

In *Another Country*, Baldwin gives a sobering portrayal of an ostensibly integrated circle of friends in New York City. The novel is driven by its meditation on the psychological distance that separates the most intimate of friends, lovers, husbands, and wives. A crucial manifestation of that distance is the gulf between what African Americans know from their racialized experience and what white Americans refuse to know about African Americans and their plight. In the novel, desire is a double-edged wild card of sorts, carrying the promise of either self-acceptance and love or the betrayal of love through self-hatred and a perverse and dangerous will to power.

At the center of this circle of friends is a doomed young black man, Rufus Scott, born in Harlem, but whose modest success as a jazz musician has brought him in contact with a downtown white milieu and an apartment in

Greenwich Village. To his white friends, Rufus is attractive, an object of fascination. Rufus, though embittered by the tough Harlem streets and a humiliating beating by a white officer in a boot camp in the South, loves to be desired by his white liberal friends. But at the novel's inception Rufus is one of the city's numberless fallen, wandering the streets, homeless, broke, desperately hungry, unkempt, avoiding his friends, and hustling to survive. Banished to the streets in his visibly abject state, Rufus, in his misery, recalls an epiphany of his then-teenaged sister Ida's beauty, glimpsed when she wore a colorful shawl he had brought back from his travels as a serviceman: "He had never seen the beauty of black people before." But seeing the woman his sister was becoming, "watching her dark face in the sunlight, softened and shadowed by the glorious shawl, it could be seen that she had once been a monarch." The bitter reality of the streets and Rufus's self-hatred intrude; Rufus looks out the window, thinking of the whores on Seventh Avenue, of "the white policemen and the money they made on black flesh, the money the whole world made." He is glad Ida cannot see him now, for he himself has been reduced to that degraded condition of prostituted black flesh.[19]

Baldwin's clinical reckoning of all the things that have destroyed Rufus is narrated in flashback, through the memories of life-altering encounters that come to Rufus during the meanderings of what turns out to be his last night on earth. That night, Rufus struggles to come to terms with the violent end of his unlikely relationship with Leona, a white divorcée from the South, struggling to make a life in New York after losing custody of her children. Rufus had picked Leona up after a gig. Their flirtatious banter was interrupted by Rufus's memory of a bloody encounter with the "shoe of the white officer against his mouth,"[20] suggesting a vengeful undertone to the seduction in progress. Indeed, Baldwin describes their sexual encounter as an act of aggression, overdetermined as such in Rufus's mind as payback for the history of sexual domination of black women under slavery and segregation, a history that persists in the sexual trafficking of black women's bodies in Harlem. Enacting the oppressive white male prerogative of rape, Rufus subdues Leona on a balcony overlooking the river and the George Washington Bridge. Baldwin's rendering of Rufus's subjectivity makes clear that for Rufus the encounter is an act of power and objectification, not love, as he imagines Leona impregnated with his "venom." Though Leona cries as "he cursed the milk-white bitch and groaned and rode his weapon between her thighs," they reach out to each other once Rufus's fury is spent. Leona imagines a future with him: "I really do like you. Please don't hurt me." Rufus promises not to hurt her and, without knowing why, invites her to come stay with him.[21]

Leona sleeps over at Rufus's uptown apartment, where they are visited the next morning by Rufus's friend Vivaldo, an Irish Italian aspiring writer, who defers coming to terms with his bisexuality in part by compulsively visiting prostitutes in Harlem. The usual competitive cross-racial machismo that passes for conversation between Rufus and Vivaldo is amplified by the presence of the white woman. Without the shared ordeal of their being severely beaten by racists in a barroom brawl, there seems to be little basis for their friendship. With their off-color teasing, Rufus and Vivaldo have convinced themselves that they are free of racial hang-ups. But their adolescent hipster version of male bonding is a barrier to genuine friendship and may also hold a potential homoerotic attraction at bay.

The strength of the union of Rufus and Leona is tested by their going outdoors, venturing beyond the sanctuary of Rufus's apartment, while accompanied by Vivaldo, for a stroll through the park. When Vivaldo separates from them momentarily to talk to an acquaintance, Rufus is taken aback by the unsympathetic glances they encounter as partners in that most explosive of sexual taboos. Rufus begins to understand the high price of a future with Leona, from whites, landlords, his family, and all that the relationship would mean. Rufus is unable to ignore the curious, occasionally contemptuous stares of passersby: "Without Vivaldo, there was a difference in the eyes that watched them. Villagers, both bound and free, looked them over as though where they stood were an auction block or a stud farm."[22] If strangers regard them as akin to racial and sexual stereotypes of chattel, Rufus notices Leona is oblivious of everything but him. When he catches the hateful stare of an Italian adolescent, who signals his contempt for Leona as well, Rufus mutters, "Cock sucker." Feeling the heat of the afternoon sun and the hateful stares of whites, Rufus resents the hegemonic, normative, and privileged state of Vivaldo's whiteness.

> No one dared to look at Vivaldo, out with any girl whatever, the way they looked at Rufus now; nor would they look at the girl the way they looked at Leona. The lowest whore in Manhattan would be protected as long as she had Vivaldo on her arm. This was because Vivaldo was white.[23]

The thought triggers in Rufus's mind the memory of the melee in which Rufus and Vivaldo were beaten bloody and senseless after Rufus met Vivaldo and his white ladyfriend Jane in a "poor-man's bar" where they knew no one. The fight erupted when Jane loudly pulled rank on Rufus with a racist insult. Vivaldo was hospitalized for days; Rufus refused to accompany the others to the hospital, fearing that charges would be brought against him regardless of what Vivaldo might say. Rufus was holed up in his apartment, bedridden for a week.[24]

The outing with Leona and Vivaldo makes painfully clear to Rufus the risks of a future with Leona. When he muses about the struggles of musicians to make a decent living ("they sweeping musicians up off the streets every day"), Rufus rebuffs Leona's words and gesture of reassurance: "She put her hand on his head and stroked it. He reached up and took her hand away."[25] Noticing Rufus's surprise at her comment that Rufus's (white) friends "think you're somebody," Leona laughs. "You act like you don't know who you are."[26]

Though Rufus tries to make a go of it with Leona, in the end, he cannot shrug off the hostile stares of those, whether "bound or free," who feel he has crossed a forbidden line with Leona. But Leona's telling remark also indicates Rufus's unreconciled attitude toward his own highly compartmentalized sexuality. Leona pays a dear price for her relationship with Rufus. For we learn, in the course of Rufus's last night alive, that Leona is gone, returned to the South after having been hospitalized at Bellevue, driven insane by Rufus's jealous rages and physical, sexual, and emotional abuse. Rufus has lost his apartment and livelihood in the downward spiral that consumed them both. Now he wanders the streets, sleeping in subway trains, dodging the police. He has allowed a rough-looking, well-dressed middle-aged white man to buy him a sandwich and drinks, knowing that the man expected sexual favors of him in return. "I'm not the boy you want," Rufus told him, his refusal to fulfill his part of the exchange recalling the words he had spoken to his friend Eric, a gay white actor from the South.[27] Rufus said this to Eric after the latter confessed his love to Rufus. Rufus was touched, and "he felt his own power." On a whim, he approached Eric, and "affection, power and curiosity all knotted together in him—with a hidden, unforeseen violence that frightened him a little; the hands that were meant to hold Eric at arm's length seemed to draw Eric to him."[28]

Hours before his fatal leap from the George Washington Bridge, Rufus "remembered . . . that Eric had loved him; as he now remembered that Leona had loved him." But the evidence suggests that Rufus's sexual confusion is not simply a matter of his unreconciled attitude to his queerness, but fundamentally of his conflation of sex with power.

> He had despised Eric's manhood by treating him as a woman, by telling him how inferior he was to a woman, by treating him as nothing more than a hideous sexual deformity. But Leona had not been a deformity. And he had used against her the very epithets he had used against Eric, and in the very same way, with the same roaring in his head and the same intolerable pressure in his chest.[29]

Rufus, who now personifies the white racist's fearful projection of black male lust, and who angrily resorts to homophobic epithets (cock sucker) to voice his hatred of white racists, and seemingly, to renounce his own queer desires, has lost touch with his humanity.

Rufus resurfaces at Vivaldo's, where he struggles, and fails, to put the catastrophe of his relationship with Leona into words. With a recording of Bessie Smith's "Backwater Blues" playing in the room, a measure of self-awareness seems within Rufus's grasp. He is ashamed at the prospect of his family seeing him in his disheveled condition, and his thoughts return to Leona, who told him, time and again, "ain't nothing wrong in being colored," which baffled and enraged him.[30] They came to blows, and worse, and "he fled from the raped woman into the bars." Driven by some compulsion, "he began to pick fights with white men. He was thrown out of bars. The eyes of his friends told him he was falling. His own heart told him so." As he cries in Vivaldo's room he realizes that there will be no end to the guilt and shame he feels, that they are intrinsic to his flesh, his existence: "His body was controlled by laws he did not understand. Nor did he understand what force within his body had driven him into such a desolate place."[31] Rufus apologizes to Vivaldo for the horrific scene he caused the last time they saw each other. Vivaldo had come to Leona's rescue during a particularly vicious quarrel with Rufus, which ultimately turned out to be their final fight. Rufus had threatened to kill Vivaldo as the latter left the apartment with Leona. Later, Leona confided to Vivaldo that Rufus had been driven mad by the contemptuous stares of white men. Rufus was "all the time looking for it, he sees it where it ain't. He don't see nothing else no more."[32] Leona warned Vivaldo that Rufus was suicidal, and Vivaldo, heeding this advice, took him out for drinks, where they encountered their friends Cass and Richard Silenski. Like Vivaldo, Cass tries to help Rufus, imploring him to forgive himself for what he has done to Leona. As the Silenskis leave, Vivaldo's friend Jane appears. Rufus excuses himself, ducks out without saying goodbye, rides the subway uptown, and plunges from the bridge.

Rufus's pathological rage and self-hatred are the product of a racist society. Baldwin brought a great deal of his own youthful struggles over his sexuality and black identity to the construction of Rufus's character. But Rufus was primarily based on Baldwin's close friend Eugene Worth, who committed suicide by jumping off the George Washington Bridge in 1946.[33] Without denying the impact of Baldwin's own struggles with racism and prejudice against homosexuals, Baldwin's fictional account of this personal tragedy, I would contend, can be traced to the influence of George Lamming's reflections on racialization, shame, and the double-edged nature of black experience—encompassing interracial relations with whites and intragroup relations among blacks. By affirming the private life as a source for literary creativity and social critique, Lamming's speech at the Paris conference was a pivotal moment for Baldwin's formulation of his distinctive political project. Rather than reading Baldwin's early career in relation to the Cold War politics of American exceptionalism, or as locked in an Oedipal conflict with his mentor Richard Wright, one might more productively understand Baldwin's evolution as a writer in a transnational setting and with reference to Lamming, who also knew a thing or two about the enabling aspects of exile.[34]

NOTES

1. Baldwin, *No Name in the Street*, 49–50.
2. Saunders, *Cultural Cold War*.
3. Baldwin, *No Name in the Street*, 50.
4. Baldwin, "Princes and Powers," 13–55.
5. Baldwin, *Nobody Knows My Name*, 115.
6. Baldwin never referred to himself as a homosexual. As an African American writer whose career coincided with the U.S. Civil Rights Movement, and with the pervasive and virulent level of homophobia in U.S. society widely seen as a threat to the movement, let alone Baldwin's career and status as black spokesperson, he was understandably evasive about his sexuality. On the one hand, his nonnormative sexuality was a matter of public record. On the other hand, his public career predated the gay liberation movement and its premium on asserting an "authentic" gay identity. In this chapter, I have chosen to deal with the complex and ultimately deeply personal issue of Baldwin's identity by referring to him as a queer black man. On the public discourse on Baldwin's sexuality in the mid-1960s United States, see Spurlin, "Culture, Rhetoric, and Queer Identity," 103–21.
7. Baldwin, "Princes and Powers," 29.
8. Lamming, "Negro Writer and His World," 321.
9. Ibid.
10. Fanon, *Black Skin, White Masks*, 112.
11. Baldwin, "Princes and Powers," 42.
12. Ibid., 42–43.
13. Baldwin, *Giovanni's Room*.

14. Ibid., 53.
15. Ibid., 39.
16. Ibid., 53.
17. Ibid., 121–22.
18. Ibid., 186–87.
19. Baldwin, *Another Country*, 12.
20. Ibid., 17.
21. Ibid., 24–26.
22. Ibid., 30–31.
23. Ibid., 31.
24. Ibid., 31–35.
25. Ibid., 38.
26. Ibid., 39.
27. Ibid., 42.
28. Ibid., 44.
29. Ibid., 44.
30. Ibid., 49.
31. Ibid., 50.
32. Ibid., 54.
33. Leeming, *James Baldwin*, 201.
34. Lamming, *Pleasures of Exile*. Lamming corroborates that the talk he delivered at the Sorbonne, though in abbreviated form due to time limitations, was published in its entirety in Lamming, "Negro Writer and His World" (George Lamming to author, Jan. 10, 2009, in author's possession).

BIBLIOGRAPHY

Baldwin, James. *Another Country*. New York: Dell, 1965.
Baldwin, James. *Giovanni's Room*. New York: Dell, 1972.
Baldwin, James. *No Name in the Street*. New York: Dell Publishing, 1972.
Baldwin, James. *Nobody Knows My Name: More Notes of a Native Son*. New York: Dell, 1961.
Baldwin, James. "Princes and Powers." In *Nobody Knows My Name: More Notes of a Native Son*. New York: Dell Publishing, 1961.
Fanon, Frantz. *Black Skin, White Masks*. New York: Grove Press, 1968.
Lamming, George. "The Negro Writer and His World." *Présence africaine* 8–10 (June–November 1956).
Lamming, George. *The Pleasures of Exile*. Ann Arbor: University of Michigan Press, 1991.
Leeming, David. *James Baldwin: A Biography*. New York: Henry Holt, 1994.
McBride, Dwight, ed. *James Baldwin Now*. New York: New York University Press, 1999.
Saunders, Frances Stonor. *The Cultural Cold War: The CIA and the World of Arts and Letters*. New York: New Press, 2001.
Spurlin, William. "Culture, Rhetoric, and Queer Identity: James Baldwin and the Identity Politics of Race and Sexuality." In Dwight McBride, ed., *James Baldwin Now*. New York: New York University Press, 1999.

TEN

From Istanbul to St. Paul-de-Vence

Around James Baldwin's *The Welcome Table*

MAGDALENA J. ZABOROWSKA

In an interview with Ali Poyrazoğlu published in Turkey in 1969, James Baldwin stated, "It is very difficult to talk about American theatre. There is no such thing as an American theatrical tradition."[1] Well aware of what had been available to theatergoers and play readers in his home country, Baldwin expressed this view having just directed a play by the Canadian playwright John Herbert, entitled *Fortune and Men's Eyes* (1964), for the Gülriz Sururi and Engin Cezzar Theater in Istanbul.[2] *Düşenin Dostu*, as its translation read in Turkish, takes on the risky subjects of prison masculinity, homosexuality, homosocial bonds, and violence between men.[3] In the 1969 interview, which was published in the theater company's newsletter, *Tiyatro*, Baldwin discusses his difficult role as the director of *Düşenin Dostu*, looks back toward the United States, and voices "hopes for the future of the American theater." He mentions the "very noble projects" taking place off Broadway and explains that he is waiting for the mainstream theater of the United States to embrace and acknowledge all members of American society, including people of color.[4] Both the interview and Baldwin's long-term involvement in theater in Turkey and in the United States demonstrate his realization not only that any future transformation of the theater needed to take account of issues of race, gender and sexuality, but that, at the same time, it was necessary to think beyond the orthodoxy binaries.

Baldwin's third play and last completed work, *The Welcome Table* (1987), can be read as his response to the traditional American theater whose challenges he had in mind while talking with Poyrazoğlu in 1969. Originally conceived in Turkey around 1967, *The Welcome Table* was finally completed in draft form only two decades later, in the writer's house in St. Paul-de-Vence in southern France. Baldwin wrote its earliest parts soon after the opening of *Düşenin Dostu;* early work on *The Welcome Table* coincided as well with completion of *No Name in the Street* (1972), a two-essay volume about his female ancestry, the Civil Rights Movement, black masculinity, and his visits to the American South and Germany, which was also written in Turkey. Indeed, essays that comprised *No Name in the Street* anticipated some of the ideas, and even phrases, that were later echoed in *The Welcome Table.* Many word-for-word sentences that eventually found their way into his published works first appeared in his letters to friends and family, especially those to Engin Cezzar, a Turkish actor and director who was Baldwin's close friend during 1956–81 and who had first invited him to Turkey.[5]

Largely unexamined by scholars, critics, and readers, Baldwin's authorial exile in the East, which consisted of extended visits devoted to prolific writing between 1961 and 1971, was key to the completion of some of his most important—and arguably his most American—works: from his third novel *Another Country* (1962) and the two-essay volume *The Fire Next Time* (1963); through the play *Blues for Mister Charlie* (1964), the short story collection *Going to Meet the Man* (1965), the fourth novel *Tell Me How Long the Train's Been Gone* (1968); to his unrealized scenario on the life of Malcolm X, *One Day When I Was Lost* (1972), and the fourth collection of essays, *No Name in the Street* (1972), not to mention numerous occasional essays.[6] Arising from, and closing, this prodigious output, *The Welcome Table* can be seen as a work that represents Baldwin's Turkish decade, most clearly in its genesis in Istanbul but also in his preoccupation with new literary forms and themes that he first embraced while living in Turkey and that he was to develop further in his later works written in France.

As well as experimenting with the forms of the novel and the essay in the 1960s and 1970s, Baldwin saw his third play as exploring a new kind of theater. It was about "exiles and alienation' ";[7] like *No Name in the Street,* it came out of his need to witness history, but also to escape it, or "get away from . . . the horror of our time . . . to ventilate, to look at the horror from some other point of view."[8] Unlike his two earlier plays that were firmly rooted in black American culture, *The Amen Corner* (1954), which takes place in a Harlem storefront church community, and *Blues for Mister Charlie* (1964), which depicts a segregated town in the American South, *The*

Welcome Table is located outside the United States. Its action takes place in a Provençal house much like Chez Baldwin in St. Paul-de-Vence and features international characters and a tangle of interracial erotic and sexual attachments. The play's transnational context and content are amplified not only by Baldwin having been influenced by his Turkish experience and by his subsequent residence in southern France but also by his love for Russian literature and especially by his study of Anton Chekhov's plays. Baldwin greatly admired *The Cherry Orchard* (1904) and used it as an inspiration in his directorial debut in Turkey; he kept it in mind all the while he was writing *The Welcome Table.*

Baldwin's last play can be read as a lens through which to reassess his artistic experience and to reevaluate his earlier encounters within the American theater. It stands, too, as his artistic last testament. As in much of his previous work, by putting race, erotic attraction, sexual desire, and gendered performance at its center, he confronted directly questions of identity and the inner life. As in *No Name in the Street,* for example, he aimed it at the "children of our era," whom, he believed, needed to learn that "love is where you find it."[9] In *The Welcome Table,* as in his last novel, *Just Above My Head,* he also wrote against what Joseph Beam termed the "nationalistic heterosexism" embraced by many black writers of the time.[10] Baldwin sounded his bold creed on gender, race, sex, and representation most clearly in his 1985 collection of essays, *The Price of the Ticket* (1985), where, in "Here Be Dragons," he stated, "We are rarely what we appear to be. We are, for the most part, visibly male of female, our social roles defined by our sexual equipment."[11]

In the essay he drove home the transgender message he first embraced in *No Name in the Street,* one that had been inspired by his Turkish decade and that he made central to his last play: "We are all androgynous, not only because we are all born of a woman impregnated by the seed of a man but because each of us, helplessly and forever, contains the other—male in female, female in male, white in black and black in white." Echoing the jeremiad conclusion of *The Fire Next Time,* the androgynous-and-queer jeremiad of "Here Be Dragons" focuses on national unity that overcomes the boundaries of gender, race, sex, and sexuality: "We are a part of each other. Many of my countrymen appear to find this fact exceedingly inconvenient and even unfair, and so, very often, do I. But none of us can do anything about it."[12] This powerful closing is echoed in *The Welcome Table,* which links his exilic locations in Turkey and France and offers an important glimpse into Baldwin's thinking about the twin issues of Americanness and theater as the 1980s were coming to a close.

This chapter introduces *The Welcome Table*, which is still not available to American readers,[13] and examines it in the context of Baldwin's views on the articulation of questions of race, sexuality, and gender that were at the center of the works that emerged from his Turkish decade. It also takes a brief look at his two earlier plays and their reception. My wide array of primary material and the limited scope of this chapter prompt me to employ an eclectic methodology that brings together approaches from literary critical and cultural studies and especially feminist theory and black queer critiques of identity. This demonstrates not only how Baldwin's *The Welcome Table* puts traditional notions of Americanness in conversation with the transgender and queer sexualities that he advocated in that play, but also how it opens questions of U.S. national identity to a transatlantic perspective.

Gathering around the Welcome Table

Begun some time in 1967 in Turkey, *The Welcome Table* was completed around 1987, in collaboration with the African American theater director Walter Dallas, who had attended the Yale Drama School and now directs Freedom Repertory Theater in Philadelphia. Dallas dates the beginning of his working relationship with Baldwin to 1983, at a party at Coretta Scott King's house in Atlanta, after which Baldwin read to him from the first act of the play. Two years earlier Dallas had staged a powerful performance of Baldwin's first play, *The Amen Corner*, at the Center Stage in Baltimore. When Baldwin saw the performance, it so inspired him that he asked Dallas to become his collaborator. *The Welcome Table* was performed at the University of the Arts in Philadelphia during the 1990–91 season, following a videotaped reading of the play with Baldwin and student actors in 1986 and a studio reading in 1989.[14] On May 27, 1995, it was read at the Lincoln Center, in a performance directed by Dallas.[15]

The action of *The Welcome Table* takes place during one day, from early morning until "round around midnight," in a large Provençal house in the South of France.[16] The play's Turkish and transnational roots inflect its cast of main characters, all of them female and, as Leeming notes, all deliberate self-portraits of the author, who by the 1980s "had long since . . . assumed a more feminine character."[17] The protagonist, Edith Hemings, is an intriguing, turban-wearing[18] artist who can be read as a transgender

"So...nothing is resolved in the play. The play is simply a question posed – to all of us – 'how are we going to live; how are we going to live in this world with a vocabulary which is useless?' Forays, frontiers, and flags are useless. Nobody can go home anymore. I can't go back to Greece or back to Africa. I can't even go bact to the Bronx, you know. But that is what the play is about. It's not intended to resolve anything."

James Baldwin on The Welcome Table

The
Welcome Table

by James Baldwin

Director	*Dramaturg*
Walter Dallas	Orient Johnson

Cast (in order of appearance)

Peter Davis:	Troy Michael Rowland
Daniel King:	Ray Thomas
Bellboy:	Cory Einbinder
Mohamed:	Ké
Lavern Ross:	Laura Jones
Edith Hemings:	Anita Davenport
Rob:	Steve Salotto
Angelina:	Ana Ortiz
Regina Burke:	Stacey Martino
Mark:	Philip F. Lynch
Mlle. La Farge:	Jenny Seidl Foster
Terry:	Walter J. Slowe III

Time From early morning to around midnight, early summer, 1983.

Place A Paris hotel room; thereafter, the home of Edith Hemings, an ancient rambling stone house, in the South of France.

There will be two 10 minute intermissions.

No smoking please. This is a smoke-free building.
The taking of photographs during the performance is srictly forbidden.

Fig. 1. Playbill for performance of *The Welcome Table* at the Academy of the Arts in Philadelphia, directed by Walter Dallas. (Collection of Walter Dallas, reproduced by permission.)

figuration of Baldwin, a veritable hybrid of charismatic women he knew and admired in Turkey, in the United States, and in France: Gülriz Sururi, Eartha Kitt, Bertice Redding, Josephine Baker, and Nina Simone.[19] Given that Baldwin was working on the early sketches of this play around the same time he was finishing *No Name in the Street*, Edith, the famous aging Creole actress-singer-performer from a Louisiana bayou, may also have been foreshadowed in its opening and closing pages, which are devoted to Baldwin's female ancestors.[20]

Another character, Regina, is Edith's old friend, who has recently been widowed and who drinks heavily (possibly modeled on Baldwin's friend Mary Painter). Laverne, Edith's Creole cousin who runs her household (possibly inspired by Bernard Hassel, the choreographer friend and manager of Baldwin's house), employs Angelina, the maid, and Mohammed, the Algerian gardener (who was to be the hero of Baldwin's unrealized novel *No Papers for Mohammed*). There are also Rob, who is Edith's "protégé and lover," and Mark, a Jewish man who is also Rob's lover. Elderly Mlle Lafarge is a "pied noir," or a French woman exiled from Algeria (definitely inspired by Jeanne Faure, a local historian whose house Baldwin rented and then bought in St. Paul-de-Vence).[21] There are also Daniel, a former Black Panther and "clumsy arsonist" who is trying to become a playwright; Terry, a photographer; and Peter Davis, a black American journalist clearly modeled on Henry Louis Gates Jr.[22] The dramatis personae section ends with a note that specifies that Regina, Mark, and Rob are "in appearance" and "legally" white, as is, with "something of a difference," Mlle LaFarge. Terry's character is completely open to interpretation: male or female, black or white; Baldwin's idea of his/her gendered or racialized identity is never revealed or defined through dialogue or stage directions.

The play toys with drawing-room drama conventions and revolves around Peter Davis's interview with Edith on the day when the household is celebrating Mlle Lafarge's ninety-third birthday. As we progress toward the party and the late-night interview following it, we glimpse the complex erotic entanglements between the characters. While Peter and Edith keep talking, the dialogue travels from one group of interlocutors to another. Such a structure allows for a mixing of main and marginal characters, which invites the reader or audience to glimpse the complex social forces that underwrite the characters' dialogue. Because the play is not available to the general reader, let me describe its contents briefly at the same time as I link its purpose to the main argument of my chapter.

By far the longest and thickest in terms of dialogue, Act 1 begins with

Peter Davis, a journalist from a Detroit paper, the *Sentinel*, a hard-working man with no time "to piss and moan," who arrives in a French hotel and prepares for an interview with Edith Hemings later on that day. He takes a phone call from Serena, who seems to be his ex-wife and the mother of his son, who is "in trouble." While hinting that both the father and the son favor recreational drugs, from alcohol to harder stuff, Peter insists that the young man get himself out of this trouble on his own. We then see the "home" of Edith Hemings, where Daniel King, the "genuine born-again" Black Panther, as he talks about himself, is writing and studying and where Edith's cousin Laverne picks up the call that Peter has placed to inquire about his interview. We witness Laverne "holding" Edith's hand, or managing her household and affairs: she receives calls about the birthday party for Mlle LaFarge that Edith is hosting; haggles with vendors; and directs the Muslim gardener, Mohammed, to prepare the garden for the party. She also complains about the help and having to pay them.

Daniel briefly joins Edith at the piano, where they sing a few tunes together and discuss the progress of his work as a budding writer. Echoing Baldwin's vision of the "artist as lover," she advises him to get his hands on "a codpiece" and "a Bible," no matter that he is shy of both the Word and the Word "made flesh." Daniel has been at Edith's house for three weeks and is grateful for the haven she has provided him; much like young Baldwin when he first came to France, Daniel can now "breathe" and try to learn how to write and thus channel his anger and politics into art. Emboldened by his position as a protégé of the famous artist, he tells Edith that she drinks too much. She refrains from promising any improvement and speaks to him with parental authority, referring to him and her lover, Rob, as the "children." Regina, Edith's friend, who has just lost her diplomat husband and is trying to "drink herself to death," arrives at the house. While waiting for the other guests, Edith and Rob discuss Mark, who is also Rob's lover, and their exchange sketches the central love triangle of the play.

In his defense of what may be read as male androgyny and bisexuality, Rob argues that as long as the situation is clear to all involved—Mark knows about Rob and Edith as lovers, and Edith knows about Mark and Rob as lovers—all should be fine. Edith reminds him she is old enough to be his mother, to which Rob replies that love defies convention and is not anything one could take back to the "store for a refund." Echoing "Here Be Dragons," Rob pronounces that nobody "makes" himself or herself and that a man who "digs" both men and women can be "trusted" more than others. One's lovers are "key" to one's identity; they open one up as a person, and being wide open about one's desires makes honest erotic and emotional attachments possible. As the Baldwinian creed goes, love is "where you find it." Edith responds with what may be read as the first female pronouncement hinting at homoeroticism in Baldwin's works, when she mentions "some of the [unexpected] places" where she has found, and lost, love.

When Regina and Edith reunite and chat in the next scene, Mark appears fresh from a shower and exchanges a passionate kiss with Rob. The men comment on Regina, who is wearing white and is visibly drunk, calling her a "lush." In the meantime, the women talk about having lived apart for fifteen years—Regina as a wife, having been "Mrs. Paul Burke" and endowed with lovely stationary, and Edith as an artist, having become the "twisted and possessed" star who feels fully alive only when impersonating someone else. Mlle LaFarge, who is bitter as a result of having been driven away from Algeria after the revolution, joins the members of the household. Throughout the evening, she talks about the long-lost, idealized Algeria of her childhood, where everyone knew his or her place in the colonial order of things.

During the formal party that follows, Mlle LaFarge describes her aristocratic roots and the loss of her family's riches and status. She also proclaims France to be free of racism, which provokes comments to the contrary from Rob, Daniel, and Mark. But they are Americans, she accuses them. Echoing Giovanni's discussions with David in *Giovanni's Room*, she claims that "Americans" know nothing about "suffering." When Mark's Jewishness is revealed, and he and Rob wonder if Jews are better off in "America" or "France," the old lady reconfirms the superiority of her country and boasts of having helped Jews hide in her house through the Nazi occupation. From this discussion of race and ethnicity in the context of World War II and French imperialism, the conversation veers back to sexuality and gender. While Rob toasts free love—"Vive la difference!"—drunken Regina proclaims that physiological features do not make gender. A woman is not a woman only because she can bear a baby, and a man is not a man only because he can "pump" one into her.

Daniel takes center stage at this point and explains the historical underpinnings of the American psychosexual landscape using as a metaphor the "mint julep," a drink that comes from Louisiana. In his story, a "delicate, transplanted" French lady is sitting on a verandah, waiting for her husband's return. She is bored and "*untouched*" and so takes a little "refreshment" of mint with her bourbon to stave off the "heat." She has a male "darky" slave fan her—and perhaps help her pass the time in other ways as well. The result is the great "civilizing arrangement," with the white husband being "fucked *out*" and the mixed "darkies" being born, presumably, both to the French lady and to the master's slave women. Laverne is scandalized by this miscegenation parable of national origins and chastises Daniel for bringing up the subject. Her mother and grandmother were never the "play-things" of white men; in her Louisiana parish, she insists, women were respected, "*everywhere.*" Daniel apologizes, explaining that he was merely trying to "clue-in" the "old lady," Mlle LaFarge, about her beloved country's former colony in North America.

Echoing Baldwin's essay "Princes and Powers," the ensuing discussion links the transatlantic history of slavery to European colonial empires and to the then-current political events in the Americas. Regina confesses that her late husband was a supporter of the Pinochet regime when he was in Chile (his diplomatic status meant that he operated with the tacit blessing of the U.S. government). As if picking up where Daniel's story ended, she raves drunkenly about young men being beaten, hanged, castrated, and tortured in Chile and admits to feeling that she had been her husband's "accomplice." A passive wife who sat on her porch drinking mint juleps, she well knew "what he was doing," but like the French lady in Daniel's story never did anything about it.

In Act 2, Peter Davis arrives for his interview with Edith, and we see Terry photographing the star with much flash activity. The guests scatter around the room as the maid, Angelina, is clearing the space after dinner. For a moment, Peter and Regina talk and flirt, and he resists her efforts to get him a drink. As Peter's interview with Edith begins at her piano, the lights dim and focus on them. They talk more like friends than like a star and a journalist: she tells him about the surgery and fateful prognosis she has hidden from Laverne, and he speculates about her religious beliefs. All the while, in snippets of dialogue and stage directions, we keep track of the conversations of the other guests: Mlle LaFarge raving about the bygone Algeria of her childhood; Rob and Mark teasing each other about love (Rob argues that they can share a good life as a male couple with all of his female lovers in the wings); Regina drinking and talking with Laverne about their respective marriages (of which Laverne had three); Terry and Daniel getting to know each other; and Daniel being introduced in passing to Peter, who takes an interest in interviewing him.

When Peter tells Edith about his stint in the U.S. Army in Germany following World War II, he admits that he was haunted by the smell of the "burning flesh." Edith explains to Peter—who comes from Natchez, Mississippi—that he should not be surprised at his sensation, that as a black man from the American South he has carried this smell with him across the Atlantic. Peter also tells Edith about having met and interviewed a young German Army soldier, who had served in Poland during the war, and about his surprise at actually liking and befriending the former Nazi. Linking American and European histories of racism and genocide in a way that echoes the message of *No Name in the Street*, this moment in *The Welcome Table* sums up Baldwin's view of the West's shared responsibility for the "civilizing experiments" of the twentieth century.

When they discuss Edith's birthplace in a Louisiana bayou and her ancestry "entangled as the weeds," she tells him that as a small child she sneaked out to a local brothel to listen to the piano player. At that house of ill repute, which was also her first concert hall, she discovered unexpected connections between sexuality and race. The Madame, Lady Jones, who was a "*nice*, nice" woman, was very dark, while Edith, a Creole, was lighter skinned, which was supposed to "make" Edith "better." Edith confesses that she did not understand colorism, or what was "wrong" with that epidermally charged situation. She thought the "wrongness" had to do with either Lady Jones's "color" or her "job," and she ended up with her mind "fucked" or, as we might read it, convinced that Lady Jones's skin color and job, as much as her gender, sexuality, and class, were inseparable. Edith also mentions her envy of Laverne's beauty and her prestigious marriages and recalls her own thwarted college love, a "ginger-bread"-hued track star, Romeo, who could have been the love of her life had he not "moved away." Romeo's possible fate is symbolic of American black men of Edith's generation: he could have died on the needle or in prison, or he could have become a black entrepreneur, if not someone like Peter. An exchange between Laverne, Regina, and Mlle LaFarge adds another layer to that between Peter and Edith, as Laverne reveals her own envy of Edith, the "star . . . but the shy one." Laverne compares Edith to Bette Davis and calls her "bull-headed," a "maverick," and a "black sheep" of their family, who lived as if in an "echo of France" as Louisiana Creoles. Laverne resents that she had to leave her life in Ireland to follow Edith to France; she had to "save" her cousin from a "devastating" love affair, as Edith did not know how to "protect herself."

As Rob assures Mark of his love in Spanglish, Daniel and Terry talk about "Uncle Sam," whom they love but with whom they do not "get along," as he had once placed Daniel in prison. While they contemplate which of the European cities Daniel may visit next in his trek from one friend's place to another, the French-speaking Mohammed, whom Daniel calls "mon frère," or his Algerian brother, enters, and they invite him to have a drink with them in clear violation of Laverne's house rules. They comment on how those living in France perceive Americans and their country. Mohammed finds things American "strange" and is surprised when Daniel tells him that all the people in Edith's house, no matter their differences of status, appearance, and gender, are all equally American. He also complains of the racist treatment his people get in France, wishes he could invite Daniel to Algeria, and hopes that he can one day accept Daniel's invitation to the United States. At that point, Edith tells Peter that her secret surgery was a result of a long-ago abortion that followed her teenage pregnancy with Romeo, who was forced to leave town because her family disapproved of him, viewing him as being too dark skinned and hence unable to pass the proverbial "paper-bag test" that was de rigeur in her social caste. Dutiful Laverne told on them, and so Edith's youthful love story ended tragically, only to be followed by other abortions. Peter responds with the story about his only son, "little Pete," who is his "soul's salvation," but who lost respect for his father's work as an ad writer for beauty products for blacks. Like Daniel, little Pete has been in jail and is now "kicking his habit" in a "clinic." Barren bride and failed father, Edith and Peter can exchange sorrows but cannot comfort each other.

The brief third act begins with the lit-up birthday cake. The three candles Mlle LaFarge blows out for good luck have been set up by Edith: one for Algeria, another for France, and the last one for Mlle LaFarge as the daughter of both countries. The old lady is photographed with Edith by Terry, and soon Peter and Terry are invited to spend the night at the house, while Mohammed is about to drive the ancient heroine of the evening home. Peter and Edith briefly resume their interview at the piano, but as it deteriorates, they decide to continue next morning. As Laverne and Regina return to their gossiping about Edith's excesses, we learn that Edith's "French" lover, Xavier, from whom Laverne had to save her, was a black man from Haiti, who had arrived via Marseilles and "by way of North Africa"; he supposedly ran away from "her love for him." While some guests are moving into the garden, Daniel and Peter begin talking at the bar, and Daniel reveals that he has an older sister who lives in Copenhagen and is married to a Dane. He also confesses to having been a Black Panther, a "clumsy arsonist," and someone who was ready to commit murder for his convictions. He received an indeterminate prison sentence but was released after five years due, as he thinks, to his sister having married a white

European. Soon Daniel is crying and confesses to missing "his people" and being able to talk about this with "nobody." He is especially stricken by the separation from his parents.

Like the characters from Baldwin's novels *If Beale Street Could Talk* and *Just Above My Head*, they are simple people: a cook and a porter from Birmingham, who followed their son to Oakland when he went to jail. They sold all they owned to help him get to Europe, where he sought refuge with a trustworthy "black singer." As Peter ministers to Daniel, he joins him in drinking and takes on the paternal role that he did not succeed in with his own son. As Mlle LaFarge leaves and the party slowly disbands, Peter promises to give Daniel the addresses of his friends who could help him. He then rejoins Edith at the piano. Tender and easy with each other now, they listen to Edith sing as Laverne, who has been seeing the old lady to the car, hesitates on the threshold between the garden and the house. At this liminal moment, the curtain falls.

From Istanbul to St. Paul-de-Vence

As Walter Dallas assured me, when writing *The Welcome Table*, he and Baldwin aimed at a more "Chekhovian" rather than a "Baldwinian" approach.[23] Given its location, its cast of characters, and especially its kaleidoscopic focus and thematic reach—which contentious political issue of the day does it not contain?—it shares virtually nothing with *The Amen Corner* and *Blues for Mister Charlie*, which Dallas classifies as "folk drama." In its form, flow, and mood *The Welcome Table* owes much to Baldwin's love for *The Cherry Orchard*, as well as to his engagement with Tyrone Guthrie's adaptations and explications of Chekhov's play, which he was reading while directing *Düşenin Dostu* in Istanbul. *The Welcome Table* represents a "slice-of-life" theater, dependent on the "Chekhovian innuendos," on "the subtext, the unspoken"; it shows "history happening."[24] At the same time, it locates its action and its characters' lives in a rich and complex context of national and international histories and cultures.

The Welcome Table marked a new turn in Baldwin's writing, in both literary and personal terms. He was "terrified" of this play, as Dallas remembers, because he was trying "new things" in it both as a playwright and as an intellectual.[25] In an unpublished letter to Dallas written on August 18, 1983, Baldwin apologized for a long silence and reported that he was living under "unmentionable" stress and was struggling in a "sea of troubles" so vast that he feared drowning; still, he was eager to collaborate on their project.[26] In a note dated March 20, 1984, he asked Dallas to take over the revisions, as he had "nothing to say about it."[27] Almost four years later, just months before his death, he wrote about putting the finishing touches on *The Welcome Table* and cutting it by "about twenty pages." He felt he was done with it at that point and wanted Dallas to "take it over."[28] The letter also dwells on Baldwin's efforts to concentrate on the "coherence" and "precision" of the characters he calls "my people." Baldwin explained that Daniel, for example, was originally modeled on "a couple of Black Panthers," specifically Huey Newton and Bobby Seale, who had been among the inspirations and audience he had in mind while writing *No Name in the Street.* But by that time he had revised his view of the masculine dilemmas in the play. What he called "our troubles," he argued, certainly "didn't begin" and "haven't ended" with the political example of the Panthers. The "ball is in your court," he concluded. Dallas, who had his own Black Panther period complete with the requisite wardrobe, as he told me, understood well that the dilemma of the play's black male characters existed both inside and "outside politics" and welcomed the opportunity to refine the characters of Daniel and Peter in his own way.

The most intriguing part of Baldwin's letter to Dallas, however, is the moment when Baldwin refrains from discussing the play's main, female characters because "losing [his friend, the actress] Gerry Page was such a blow." Page was the same age as Baldwin when she died. When he wrote Dallas, Baldwin was ill with cancer and might have sensed that he was not going to recover. Focusing on the vicissitudes of his "convalescing" and on how "everything is new," but also "old" and "frightening," when one's body refuses to be "taken for granted," the last part of the letter makes it clear in powerful and moving ways that, apart from a new genre of theater, Baldwin was embarking in *The Welcome Table* on "a kind of self-examination he was not quite ready to attempt," as Leeming confirms.[29] This last work, then, performed on two levels: marking his farewell to authorship and celebrating his sociability and circle of friends, whose meeting he reimagined in his last dwelling place.

Henry Louis Gates Jr. describes the welcome table at Baldwin's house in St. Paul-de-Vence in a series of essays based on his 1973 interview with Baldwin and Josephine Baker, which Gates conducted as a young reporter for *Time* magazine. The specific piece of furniture that Gates refers to is the "long welcome table under the arbor, [where] the wine flowed, food was served and taken away, and James Baldwin and Josephine Baker traded sorties, gossiped . . . and remembered their lives."[30] Nicholas Delbanco, a

Fig. 2. The “welcome table” in the living room chez Baldwin, St. Paul-de-Vence, France, 2000. (Photo by author.)

frequent guest in 1971 and 1973, remembers the Baldwin entourage at his "Provençal court": "a chauffeur large enough to double as a bodyguard, a cook, a companion named Philippe . . . a dancer or painter in attendance—old lovers or associates from some project . . . [who] came from Italy, America, Algeria, Tunisia, Finland. Brothers and nephews passed through."[31] As Leeming notes, the "house itself is a metaphor for his mind, for his many selves."[32] Baldwin's stage directions for the play link the outdoor and indoor spaces and state that the rooms in Edith's abode exist "by suggestion," with the main one appearing as a "combination" of a dining room and office by virtue of a "prominent," large wooden table that holds the tools of the trade of the author: a typewriter, paper, and books. In *The Welcome Table*, as much as in the realities Baldwin had discovered in Turkey, the space of writing was also the space where social gatherings took place, where the words typed on the page echo the conversations of friends, lovers, and hangers-on.

While *The Welcome Table* clearly imaginatively reworked the "biracial, bisexual, confessional milieu" of the "scene" at Chez Baldwin in St. Paul-de-Vence,[33] it also grew out of and reflected the gender-bending social scene that Baldwin had been part of in Turkey throughout the 1960s. In its explorations of the ways in which gender roles and bipolar notions of sexuality imprint and imprison men and women, it took further the focus of *Düşenin Dostu* on the conflict between love and power, as well as the focus of *Another Country* and *No Name in the Street* on interracial and transgender romance and representations of black and white masculinities. Engin Cezzar, who followed the writing process of *The Welcome Table* over the years, claims emphatically that the play's genesis goes back to the lively gatherings that his friend Jimmy and his Turkish friends held throughout the 1960s. These gatherings included readings, discussion, and casual socializing and were especially intense during the production of the play *Düşenin Dostu* and during the last sojourn that Baldwin and Cezzar took as friends and collaborators in 1981 in Bodrum, a southern resort on the Aegean Sea. As Cezzar emphasized in our interview, "Jimmy *always* had a welcome table in Turkey!"[34]

Open to the newest innovations in the art world, in many ways, Turkish theater of the 1960s was more radical than American theater, at least in Baldwin's eyes. While he had only seen several plays and had a rather vague notion about Turkey's long and rich theatrical history, he was certain that American theater was lacking in comparison. His fourth novel, *Tell Me How Long the Train's Been Gone* (1968), whose main character, Leo Proudhammer, is a middle-aged bisexual black actor recovering from a heart attack, and that focuses on how American theater refracts and re-creates social divisions of class and race, sexuality and gender, spells out some of his disappointments. One of Baldwin's parable-novels, according to Leeming, *Tell Me How Long the Train's Been Gone* was "painful" to write[35] and carries a strong autobiographical message that puts the writer into the actor's shoes: "Leo Proudhammer is James Baldwin, complete with large eyes, 'pigeon toes,' and 'jiggling behind.'"[36] *Train*, as Baldwin liked to call it in his letters, arose from his longtime fascination with the world of the stage, a long sequence of ideas about the stage, indeed, that in the end led to *The Welcome Table*.

Baldwin's first play, *The Amen Corner* (1954), was a theatrical rendering of the themes related to the black church and family life in Harlem that preoccupied him in his first novel. Sister Margaret, the Pentecostal minister of a small congregation and the play's main character, shuns sensuality and joy from her life as they remind her of her estranged jazz musician husband. She demands that her congregation embrace similar "mortification of the flesh." Her world comes crashing down when her husband returns home to die, and their only son, whom Margaret has been grooming for the church, announces that he wants to leave home and pursue unholy music like his father. In the end, Margaret is demoted by scheming competitors in the congregation. But she triumphs spiritually in her final sermon, in which she embraces humanistic love and compassion that transcend religious creed and petty power struggles. Leeming emphasizes the fact that the inspiration for that character was Mother Horn, "the minister who presided over Baldwin's own 'salvation.'"[37]

In 1958–59, just a few years after Baldwin had finished *The Amen Corner* (1954), he assisted Elia Kazan, the Greek Constantinople/Istanbul-born immigrant director, while Kazan was directing Archibald MacLeish's *J.B.* (1958) and Tennessee Williams's *Sweet Bird of Youth* (1959) on Broadway. Baldwin attended rehearsals and took notes for his mentor. While he loved Williams's play, he "disliked *J.B.* with a passion" because he felt that MacLeish was patronizing.[38] In his autobiography, Kazan refers to this as the clash of the "different cultures, Harvard and Harlem."[39] *Tell Me How Long the Train's Been Gone*, written in Istanbul a whole decade after, reflects some of that experience, as well as Baldwin's memories of his collaboration with the Actors Studio on the production of *Giovanni's Room* in 1956 and their fraught Broadway staging of *Blues for Mister Charlie* eight years later. Baldwin disliked the Method approach worshipped at the Actors Studio;

vocal about the racial politics on the main stages of the United States, he was an enthusiast of new projects and embraced Lorraine Hansberry's *Raisin in the Sun,* as well as serving as a role model and mentor in his last years to such playwrights and writers as Suzan Lori-Parks, Randall Kenan, Melvin Dixon, and Hilton Als.[40]

In *Blues for Mister Charlie* (1964), Baldwin responded to Elia Kazan's suggestion that he write a play inspired by the murder of Emmett Till in Mississippi in 1955. *Blues* was one of those works that Baldwin felt he had to write as part of his involvement in the Civil Rights Movement, and it centers on the killing of a young black activist, Richard, by a small-town white racist, Lyle. It features the responses of the citizens of Whitetown and Blacktown—as the color-coded parts of the town are called—to the murder and to the ensuing trial that ends with Lyle's acquittal by an all-white, all-male jury. The play was performed by the Actors Studio and opened on Broadway on April 23, 1964, "to an audience of highly appreciative blacks and sometimes angry and often shocked whites."[41] Its production was contentious and fraught with emotional difficulties for Baldwin, who felt that the Actors Studio's Lee Strasberg and Cheryl Crawford did not understand his motives and were afraid to shock the white audience: "the scenes that occurred . . . are now fixed in Broadway legend."[42] Because Baldwin insisted on a low admission price in order that uptown audiences could see the play, income was low, and after one month the theater wanted to close the production. In an ironic twist, *Blues for Mister Charlie* was saved by a substantial donation from the Rockefeller sisters, Ann Pierson and Mary Strawbridge. In addition a petition signed by famous actors and artists—Marlon Brando, Sidney Poitier, Lena Horne, Richard Avedon, Harry Belafonte, Sammy Davis Jr., and June Shagaloff—urged the theater management to extend the production. As a result the play's run continued through to late August.[43] When a truncated production was taken to London, Baldwin publicly protested the Actors Studio's handling of his material and would later take up his disagreement with the studio in fictional form in *Tell Me How Long the Train's Been Gone.* When he began planning *The Welcome Table* soon afterward, he intended it to offer a new kind of drama in which all his ideas could meet. While the degree to which this succeeds can be debated, it deserves our close attention.

Baldwin never saw this last play performed: only rehearsed. As his last, and arguably least American work, *The Welcome Table* can perhaps be seen as a rehearsal of sorts. Yet in an early letter to Cezzar dated in late 1958, which has been recently published in Turkish translation in the volume entitled *Dost Mektupları* [Letters from a Friend], Baldwin offered what we may take to be an enigmatic reflection on the themes it encapsulates:[44] "I know I don't really need to say it, but I was very sad after our last conversation. Remember what you told me about the water wheel; and think back, friend, think back. We may seem to be moving slowly but the point is, we're moving. And that doesn't say it very well, either, but you know what I mean."[45] Like the ebb and flow of conversation, the changing shades of meaning, and the often-unspeakable feelings that pass between interlocutors, letter writers and readers, Baldwin's last play both resists and invites interpretation. Once published, and I wish that this could happen soon, it is certain to inspire rich readings both on stage and on paper and will certainly deserve a gala opening night.

NOTES

1. Some of the ideas explored in this chapter have appeared in their earlier incarnations in chapter 3 and the conclusion of my book *James Baldwin's Turkish Decade.*

2. The play's title, inspired by a line from Shakespeare's Sonnet 29, was freely translated into Turkish as *Düşenin Dostu,* or "friend of the fallen."

3. Poyrazoğlu, a copartner in the theater company at the time, played one of the main characters in the play and, along with the British Council employee and theater critic Oktay Balamir, served as its Turkish translator. For a detailed account of this production, as well as details on Baldwin's stays in Turkey, see Zaborowska, *James Baldwin's Turkish Decade.*

4. Poyrazoğlu, "Interview with James Baldwin."

5. See Campbell, "Room in the East."

6. He may have also worked there on the early drafts of *The Devil Finds Work* (1976).

7. Leeming, *James Baldwin,* 373.

8. Ibid., 373–74.

9. I am referring to the 1987 manuscript of the play, annotated by Baldwin, that Walter Dallas kindly shared with me in 2006. As with the rest of the Baldwin papers, direct quotations are not permitted by the estate.

10. Beam, "James Baldwin," 185. Beam confirms Baldwin's stature as a father figure for black queers: "Because he could envision us as lovers, our possibilities were endless. We could be warriors, artists, and astronauts; we could be severe, sensitive, and philosophical. . . . Not a bad legacy for someone whom the Republic wished deaf and dumb by age fourteen" (186).

11. Baldwin, *Price of the Ticket,* 690.

12. Baldwin, *Price of the Ticket,* 689–90. The essay, "Freaks and the American Ideal of Manhood," was first published in *Playboy* in January 1985 and later appeared retitled as "Here Be Dragons" in *The Price of the Ticket.*

13. I have read the play in two manuscript versions, one available at the

Schomburg Center for Research on Black Culture and another provided to me by Walter Dallas.

14. For Ruby Dee, David Baldwin, and other friends (Leeming, *James Baldwin*, 378).

15. Interview with the author, November 14, 2005. Dallas told me that the play was staged in London but was unable to give me more detailed information. The reading at the Lincoln Center starred Novella Nelson as Edith, Oni Faida Lampley as LaVerne, Faran Tahir as Mohammed, Mari Nelson as Regina, Robert Knepper as Rob, and Mark Feuerstein as Mark. The Lincoln Center project was never staged due to lack of permission from the Baldwin estate.

16. The Baldwin estate does not allow direct quotations from the play. I regret that I will have to limit my references to this text to situation descriptions and paraphrases of dialogue.

17. Leeming, *James Baldwin*, 376.

18. Baldwin, *The Welcome Table*, manuscript, 9. I am referring here to the copy of the play that is available at the Schomburg Center for Research on African American Culture.

19. Leeming mentions other "sisters," Maya Angelou, Verta Mae Grosvenor, Louise Meriwether, Paule Marshall, and Eleanor Traylor, as possible inspirations (*James Baldwin*, 377).

20. Baldwin began writing the play in 1967, while living in the Pasha's Library house in Rumeli Hisar in Istanbul, and completed it in a "rough form" the year he died (ibid., 275, 320). It began as a work clearly focused on sex and gender, tentatively titled *The 121st Day of Sodom*, "a takeoff on Sade's *120 Days of Sodom*," and was to be "'a drawing room nightmare of six adventurers' in the south of France" (ibid., 275).

21. Faure "had written a history of Saint-Paul de Vence, and had a particular aversion to blacks, whom she associated with those who, from her point of view, had exiled her from Algeria, the land of her birth. . . . Later Mlle Faure would come to admire and respect her tenant, and he her" (ibid., 312).

22. Gates, "Welcome Table," 318.

23. Walter Dallas, interview with the author, June 20, 2006, Freedom Theater, Philadelphia.

24. Leeming, *James Baldwin*, 373, 374.

25. Dallas, interview, June 20, 2006.

26. James Baldwin to Walter Dallas, August 18, 1983, Walter Dallas private collection, in his hands.

27. James Baldwin to Walter Dallas, March 20, 1984, Dallas Collection.

28. James Baldwin to Walter Dallas, July 21 (or 27), 1987, Dallas Collection.

29. Leeming, *James Baldwin*, 356.

30. Gates, "Welcome Table," 306.

31. Delbanco, *Anywhere out of the World*, 29.

32. Leeming, *James Baldwin*, 376.

33. Ibid., 374.

34. Engin Cezzar, interview with the author, May 30, 2001, Istanbul, Turkey.

The play's title also echoes a line from a popular gospel song, "I'm Gonna Sit at the Welcome Table."

35. Leeming, *James Baldwin*, 280.

36. Ibid., 278, 279. The book was not a hit with reviewers in the United States. Eliot Fremont-Smith wrote that it was "a disaster in virtually every particular" ("Another Track," 27), while Mario Puzo followed other negative critiques in the *New York Times Book Review* by calling it "one-dimensional" ("His Cardboard Lovers," 155).

37. Leeming, *James Baldwin*, 107. The play was first performed by the Howard University Players under the direction of Owen Dodson on May 11–14, 1955, and attended by such notables as E. Franklin Frazier, Strerling Brown, and Alain Locke (ibid., 107). The complete published version of *The Amen Corner* appeared in 1968 from Dial Press. For more detailed information, see ibid., 106–13, 247–50.

38. Ibid., 155.

39. Kazan, *Life*, 583. Kazan confesses that the "merits of that play eluded me," no matter that it won the Pulitzer Prize (582). Interestingly, Kazan considered himself a kind of immigrant "nigger" due to his southern European origins and emphasizes in his book that for that reason he and Baldwin got along well.

40. It was rather "uncharacteristic" of Baldwin "not [to] resist the urge for revenge in his treatment of Saul and Rags [stand-ins for Lee Strasberg and Cheryl Crawford], who are depicted [in *Train*] as arrogant, pedantic hypocrites—representatives of the white liberal establishment" (Leeming, *James Baldwin*, 279).

41. Ibid. 238.

42. Ibid., 233.

43. See also the detailed account in Weatherby, *James Baldwin*, 236–55.

44. Baldwin with Cezzar, *Dost Mektupları*.

45. Quoted in Campbell, "Room in the East," 5.

BIBLIOGRAPHY

Baldwin, James. *The Price of the Ticket: Collected Nonfiction, 1948–1985*. New York: St. Martin's, 1985.

Baldwin, James, with Engin Cezzar. *Dost Mektupları* [Letters from a Friend]. Trans. Seçkin Selvi. İstanbul: Yapı Kredi Yayınları, 2007.

Beam, Joseph. "James Baldwin: Not a Bad Legacy, Brother." In Essex Hemphill, ed., *Brother to Brother: New Writings by Black Gay Men*. Boston: Alyson Publications, 1991.

Campbell, James. "Room in the East: James Baldwin's Letters to Istanbul." *Times Literary Supplement*, June 15, 2007.

Delbanco, Nicholas. *Anywhere out of the World: Essays on Travel, Writing, Death*. New York: Columbia University Press, 2005.

Fremont-Smith, Eliot. "Another Track." *New York Times*, May 31, 1968.

Gates, Henry Louis, Jr. "The Welcome Table: James Baldwin in Exile." In Susan Rubin Suleiman, ed., *Exile and Creativity: Signposts, Travelers, Outsiders, Backward Glances*. Durham: Duke University Press, 1996.

Kazan, Elia. *A Life*. New York: Da Capo Press, 1997.
Leeming, David. *James Baldwin: A Biography*. New York: Henry Holt, 1994.
Poyrazoğlu, Ali. "Interview with James Baldwin." Trans. Asli Gür. *Tiyatro* 12 (October 1969).
Puzo, Mario. "His Cardboard Lovers." In Fred L. Standley and Nancy V. Burt, eds., *Critical Essays on James Baldwin*. Boston: G. K. Hall, 1988.
Weatherby, William J. *James Baldwin: Artist on Fire; A Portrait*. New York: D. I. Fine, 1989.
Zaborowska, Magda. *James Baldwin's Turkish Decade: Erotics of Exile*. Durham: Duke University Press, 2009.

ELEVEN

What Is Africa to Baldwin?

Cultural Illegitimacy and the Step-fatherland

DOUGLAS FIELD

> Baldwin's nose, like the North-seeking needle on a compass, is forever pointed toward his adopted fatherland, Europe.
>
> —ELDRIDGE CLEAVER, SOUL ON ICE

In an intriguing interview with Harold Isaacs, presented at the Third Annual Conference of African Culture in 1960, James Baldwin recalls how his first thoughts of Africa were inextricably linked to his father. "I don't know when Africa came in first," Baldwin told Isaacs, adding, "It *must* have been from my father":

> Somehow my first association with Africa comes through him. I compared the people in my father's church to African savages. This was because of my relation to my father. . . . I was ten or twelve. The church and my father were synonymous. Music and dancing, again sweat, out of the jungle. It was contemptible because it appeared to be savage. But this was also my image of my father. I guess I was hipped on being American and things they did seemed so common, so vulgar.[1]

Baldwin's early associations with Africa are not in the context of a longed-for motherland, but through his father and his church. By connecting

Africa with his father, Baldwin not only illustrates his uneasy relationship with David Baldwin but also hints at his complicated relationship with Africa, illustrated by his striking use of the words "contemptible," "savage," and "vulgar."

Baldwin's troubled relationship with his father, David, had already been well documented by the time Isaacs' paper was published in 1960. In "Notes of a Native Son," the title essay of his first collection, Baldwin recalled how he "had got on badly" with the man he called his father, noting how his father disapproved of his desire to become a writer. David Baldwin "looked to me," the young writer recalled, "like pictures I had seen of African tribal chieftains: he really should have been naked, with warpaint on and barbaric mementos standing among spears."[2] Baldwin's discussions of Africa elsewhere in *Notes of a Native Son* (1955), like those of his father, are characterized by uncertainty and unease. In "Encounter on the Seine: Black Meets Brown," Baldwin quashes notions of fraternity between "the Negro and the African," instead emphasizing "the gulf" between the two.[3]

Baldwin's links between his father and Africa gain further significance in "Autobiographical Notes," the opening essay of *Notes of a Native Son.* For Baldwin "the most crucial time in my own development came when I was forced to recognize that I was a kind of bastard of the West," a statement that surely refers back to his own illegitimacy.[4] Born James Jones, Baldwin never knew the identity of his biological father, and this question of lineage haunts his fiction and nonfiction—not least in the title of his first collection of essays, *Notes of a Native Son.* In the interview with Isaacs, Baldwin refers once again to his father, noting that "my father thought of himself as a king . . . and he would have said something like we were descended from kings in Africa," a comment that would have sidelined the young James Baldwin.[5] Again, in his first novel, *Go Tell It on the Mountain* (1953) (titled "In My Father's House," in an early version), the protagonist's father, Gabriel, envisages "a royal line," with John on the outside as the bastard stepson.[6] In "Notes of a Native Son" Baldwin had recounted his painful and embittered relationship with his father, whose patrimony was "bitterness," which "now was mine."[7]

This chapter focuses on Baldwin's complicated, shifting views on Africa, tracing his early writings on the continent until the 1980s.[8] According to James Campbell, "Baldwin never came to a coherent or thought-out position on the Afro-American's predicament *vis-à-vis* his ancient African cousins," adding that "it is impossible to discern a meaningful pattern."[9] Campbell is right to suggest that Baldwin's views of Africa vacillated over the years and that it can be difficult to make sense of the writer's conclusions. In sharp contrast to African American writers who dream of a connection with the motherland, Baldwin's at times acerbic comments suggest removal and distance, echoing his strained relationship with his (step)father.

During speeches Baldwin at times invoked his African past for rhetorical effect, claiming he hailed from Sierra Leone; and yet he also admonished black American students at Bowling Green University for claiming to be African.[10] On occasion his comments on Africa dance between astringency and belligerence. Recollecting his years in Paris in the conversation with Harold Isaacs, Baldwin recalled how he was both "frightened" and "disgusted" by his encounters with Africans in Paris.[11] Not surprisingly, some African critics, including the Nigerian writers Femi Ojo-Ade and Ezenwa-Ohaeto, have accused Baldwin respectively of evincing "his superior attitude towards Africans" and of demonstrating an "inability to grasp the predicament of the African."[12]

Before exploring Baldwin's views on Africa it is important to point out that he was by no means the only African American writer to express ambivalence or uncertainty about the continent, what Femi Ojo-Ade has called the "love-hate relationship" between "Blacks from Africa and those in the United States."[13] In "Heritage," one of the most well-known African American meditations on Africa, the Harlem Renaissance poet Countee Cullen (Baldwin's former teacher) begins with the line "What is Africa to me . . . ?," where the pagan beat of the poet's imagined Africa troubles the writer, setting the tone for a number of African American writers.[14] In Ralph Ellison's interview with Harold Isaacs, for example, he expresses his interest in African art but makes it clear that "I have great difficulty associating myself with Africa."[15] While Richard Wright's relationship with Africa is complex, he made no secret of his suspicion of Marcus Garvey in *Lawd Today!* (1963). For the Nigerian writer Chimalum Nwankwo, Wright's account of his travels in the Gold Coast, *Black Power* (1954), is little more than "an obscene travelogue," a book that is replete with stereotypes about savagery and barbarism.[16]

Baldwin's writings on Africa fit into the wider sense of unease felt by a number of African American writers toward the continent. Africa continues to trouble and preoccupy him long after his famous essay "Princes and Powers" and beyond his first visit to Africa in 1962. Notwithstanding the shifts that do occur, from moment to moment, overall a reading of his work reveals a coherent if surprising picture. Beginning with a discussion of Baldwin and the church, I trace Baldwin's views on Africa through a reading of his criticism of colonial powers through to his fictional and nonfictional descriptions of Africa, including one of his last published essays—a commentary on African art.

The Church, the Father, and Africa

> When I joined the church at fourteen . . . I imagined myself as an African boy, dancing as I might have danced thousands of years ago.[17]

In "Notes of a Native Son" Baldwin describes a pivotal moment where his stepfather challenged him with the question, "You'd rather write than preach, wouldn't you?"[18] Baldwin's reply was that he wished to write, and yet his early writing is filled with his life as a preacher and his years in the church, where his father looms. Baldwin's decision to write—rather than to preach the Word—is reminiscent of Derrida's claim that "writing is parricidal," where writing undermines the spoken authority of the father/king who cannot write—particularly when we recall the title of Baldwin's early story about his father, "The Death of a Prophet."

And yet Baldwin's decision to write, and not to preach, had not been his first act of defiance. By moving from a Baptist church (his father's tradition) to a Pentecostal church at the age of fourteen, Baldwin entered a less mainstream Protestant tradition whose links to Africa, important commentators suggest, were close. According to Zora Neale Hurston, Pentecostalism was not, as many claimed, "a new religion," but "the older forms of religious expression asserting themselves against the new," a point echoed by Robert M. Anderson, who claims that Pentecostalism was an "attempt . . . to preserve or restate what was believed to be the old-time religion, and as such it was an authentic expression of that older, folkish culture."[19] Historically, as I have traced elsewhere, the formal birth of Pentecostalism is marked by the Azusa Street revivals of 1906, an event that precipitated the formation of the Holiness Church.[20] Pentecostalism, in its attempts to rescue a more authentic religion, can be traced to much older African religions. Hurston famously claimed that the Pentecostal church represented an attempt to reintroduce an earlier African religion that was lost during slavery.[21] Like Hurston, James Tinney argues that Pentecostalism shares at least four distinct Africanisms in worship: "the congs, the dance, the percussion, and the tongue-speaking."[22] In fact, according to Tinney, not only do "few [theologians] express doubt about the Blackness of Pentecostalism," but "nowhere is there a religion [Pentecostalism] which is as truly Afro-American as this," a claim that echoes Baldwin's pronouncement that "when Black people talk about true religion, they're 'speaking in tongues' practically. It would not be understood in Rome."[23]

I am not concerned here with tracing the contested links of Pentecostalism to African forms of worship, but I want to explore the ways in which Baldwin's early writing hints at a relationship between ecstatic worship in the Holiness Movement and West African religious practices. For a handful of critics, Baldwin's first novel has direct parallels or overt connections to African cultural practices.[24] For Ernest Champion, Baldwin's first novel "can be seen as the fulfillment of what began in [Chinua Achebe's] *Things Fall Apart*," whereas for Babacar M'Baye, *Go Tell It on the Mountain* "reflects distinctive African retentions that affirm his reverence for his African heritage."[25] This idea of Baldwin's "reverence for his African heritage" simplifies his cautious and occasionally caustic views on the continent, but both Champion and M'Baye are right to emphasize the links between possession, the "shout," and the ring dance in Holiness and West African religious practices.[26]

Critics have long been divided about the degree to which African cultural heritage survived the Middle Passage and slavery, and it's difficult to argue against (or find convincing evidence of) the notion that *Go Tell It on the Mountain*, as M'Baye argues, "reflects cultural patterns that have parallels in Africa."[27] Similarly, it is unlikely that Carolyn Holmes's claim that "Baldwin's search for his identity could very well have been the same search for unity that his ancient ancestors in the Nile Valley had struggled to attain thousands of years ago" would have enthralled him.[28] Even so, Holmes's bid to uncover the connections between Baldwin and Zora Neale Hurston through an Afrocentric reading of *Their Eyes Were Watching God* and *The Fire Next Time* is of interest. For Holmes, "Baldwin's cosmology had a deeper structure [than critics supposed] and possibly an Ancient Kemetic source." For both writers their "early connections with the church were natural (or perhaps unnatural) outgrowths of their lost African ancestral heritage."[29]

This emphasis on the connections between Baldwin and Hurston is, I think, productive, not least because the latter was one of the earliest writers to comment on the Sanctified Church. Unlike Holmes, I am not concerned with proving, once and for all, the African heritage of the two writers. But I want to read Baldwin's short story "The Outing" alongside a brief interpretation of Hurston's *Jonah's Gourd Vine* (1934) in order to illustrate how both writers probe the links between the Christian church and African worship.

Baldwin's "The Outing," first published in *New Story* (1951), closely mirrors his first novel. Johnnie and his brother Roy accompany their father, Gabriel, to a trip down the Hudson River on a trip organized by the Mount of Olives Pentecostal Assembly. Anticipating the strained relationships in *Go Tell It the Mountain*, the illegitimate Johnnie struggles to contain his dislike of Gabriel, seeking solace in his (homoerotic) friendship with David as the holy Elisha proffers religious guidance to the teenage boys.

During the service on board the boat, David and Johnnie enter the blissful throes of the saints while Elisha is in agony on the threshing floor. Baldwin describes it:

> As though their youth, barely begun, were already put away; and the animal, so vividly restless and undiscovered, so tense with power, ready to spring had been already stalked and trapped and offered, a perpetual blood sacrifice for the Lord. Yet their bodies continued to change and grow, preparing them, mysteriously, and with ferocious speed, for manhood. No matter how careful their movements, these movements suggested, with a distinctness dreadful for the redeemed to see, the pagan lusting beneath the blood-washed robes.[30]

In contrast to the Saints who long to soar "far past the sordid persistence of the flesh," Baldwin emphasizes the irrepressible body beneath the veneer of the holy robes. By describing the boys' lust as "pagan," and by drawing attention both to the "bestial sobs" and to "the music [that] grew more savage," Baldwin implicitly links the boys to a pre-Christian era, tacitly suggesting that the African roots of Pentecostalism have burst through.[31]

Baldwin's muted reference to Pentecostalism's pre-Christian origins is strongly reminiscent of the work of Zora Neale Hurston, whose repeated insistence that the "Negro is not a Christian really" echoes Baldwin's claim that the "essential religion of Black people comes out of something which is not Europe."[32] In her novel *Jonah's Gourd Vine*, Hurston depicts a service among African American workers that transmutes into a pre-Christian celebration. As the workers discard the instruments of the white folks (guitar and fiddle), they clap, invoking the "voice of Kata-Kumba, the great drum," so that "the shore of Africa receded."[33] Similarly, Hurston's preacher protagonist, John Pearson, fails to recognize the division between spirit and flesh; when he preaches, Hurston draws explicitly on his African heritage, as he "rolled his African drum up to the altar, and called his Congo gods by Christian names," reciting his "pagan poesy."[34]

Hurston's explicit references to Pentecostalism's African heritage illuminate Baldwin's attempts to collapse the divisions between body and flesh. In *Go Tell It*, John's conversion is described explicitly as a "possession," an experience, as Joseph A. Brown has noted, that "is traceable through all African-based cultures in the Americas."[35] But at the very moment when John is in agony on the threshing floor, as "the Holy Ghost was speaking," he feels "a tightening in his loin-strings" and, crucially, "a sudden yearning tenderness for Elisha," a feeling Baldwin describes as "desire, sharp and awful."[36]

On the one hand, as various critics have pointed out, Pentecostalism—in particular the Fire-Baptized churches—is noted for its puritanical views governing sexual relations, a theme that Baldwin explores in *Go Tell It on the Mountain* and that he condenses through his use of the phrase of "walking disorderly." And yet, as Robert Anderson has argued, while the Holiness Church is noted for its "preoccupation with sexual mores," it has also been accused of propagating the convention that "'sins of the flesh' glorified God because they gave him an opportunity to manifest his grace—a belief that allegedly led to 'free love.'"[37] This contradiction, I argue, is central to Baldwin's exploration of the relationship between sexual and religious communion, where the church becomes not just a site of sexual prohibition, but a place that mediates sexual encounters.[38]

My aim here is not to oversexualize the African American concept of "soul," a point that the critic Amitai Avi-Ram has warned against, but to stress that the Puritan strictures on Pentecostalism are not as straightforward as they appear.[39] Critics such as Avi-Ram and Michael Dyson have made the point that African American religious beliefs do not always reflect the Western dualism of body and soul.[40] Rather than a polarization of the body and the spirit, Avi-Ram notes, "one tends to find a smooth continuity between body and soul,"[41] a point echoed by Michael Ventura, who notes that black culture has "transcended the split between mind and body inherited from Descartes and certain forms of Christian theology."[42] In the case of Pentecostalism, a religion that most closely retains its African heritage, there is, as some critics argue, not only less of a division between the spirit and the flesh but, more specifically, an acceptance between Africanisms and homosexuality.[43] Despite Baldwin's tentative articulation of a pre-

Christian sensibility in "The Outing," his subsequent essays questioned any straightforward relationship between the African American and the African.

1956: The First Negro Writers and Artists Congress

In an extraordinary recollection of his participation at the First Negro Writers and Artists Congress, Baldwin revealed how the Africans whom he met at the conference "frightened him." Singling out Alioune Diop, Baldwin recollected that the Senegalese writer "frightened me because of his extraordinary way of being civilized and primitive at the same time." Baldwin in fact claimed that the participants at the conference "disgusted him," keenly aware that "this meant sooner or later a great clash between myself and someone like that."[44]

The "clash" that Baldwin refers to, between the African American and the African, punctuates his writing and interviews, most famously in two of his essays: "Encounter on the Seine: Black Meets Brown" and "Princes and Powers," his report on the 1956 conference. In what follows I want to trace Baldwin's complex views on Africa by focusing on these two essays and by attempting to make sense of what Ezenwa-Ohaeto calls the "haziness in the perceptions of Africa" in his works.[45]

In "Encounter on the Seine," first published in *The Reporter* in 1950 as "The Negro in Paris," Baldwin begins by stating that, "at least from the American point of view," the African in Paris "is exceedingly primitive."[46] For Baldwin, the African student is characterized by his position as a colonial subject. In contrast to the African American in Paris, "the African has not yet endured the utter alienation of himself from his people and past." Baldwin's brief comparison of the African American and the African in Paris does not move beyond generalized comments. "All the students in the Latin Quarter," Baldwin writes, "live in ageless, sinister looking hotels," adding that "they are all forced continually to choose between cigarettes and cheese at lunch."[47]

Baldwin's discussion of the nameless Africans (who are not distinguished by gender, class, or country) surprisingly makes no mention of the long-established history of African students in the French capital, where he himself had lived since 1948. He probably would not have been aware of the short-lived *Légitime défense*, organized by Antillean students in 1932, and it is very unlikely that he would have ever come across the sporadically published *L'étudiant noir*, set up by Aimé Césaire, Léopold Senghor, and Léon-Gontrand

Damas in 1934. More surprisingly, however, Baldwin makes no reference to Alioune Diop's famous quarterly, *Présence africaine*, founded a year before Baldwin arrived in Paris, with contributions by African American writers including Richard Wright and Gwendolyn Brooks.

Baldwin's comments in "Encounter on the Seine" seem to question the cultural and political interchange signaled by *Présence africaine*'s inclusion of African American writers. For Baldwin,

> They face each other, the Negro and the African, over a gulf of three hundred years—an alienation too vast to be conquered in an evening's good will, too heavy and too double-edged ever to be trapped in speech.[48]

Baldwin's surprising choice of the colonially inflected verb "conquered" pits the African and the African American at odds, far removed from a notion of transcultural interaction. For Baldwin, the African and the African American, who do not share a common language, are unable to communicate, anticipating his later comment that "we almost needed a dictionary to talk."[49]

The African in "Encounter in the Seine" is little more than a cipher, a springboard for Baldwin to articulate his early and insightful views on the African American's peculiar relationship to the United States. He is less concerned here with communication between the African and African American than he is with the African American's struggle to explain his "birthright which he is struggling to recognize and make articulate."[50]

Unlike the American participants at the First Negro Writers and Artists Congress (who included Richard Wright, Mercer Cook, and John A. Davis), Baldwin was present in the role of reporter for *Encounter* (or, he added wryly, for the CIA).[51] According to David Macey, who fills in many of the details that Baldwin's account skips over, this occasion was "so important that it was widely described as the cultural equivalent to the Conference of Afro-Asian Nations held the previous year in the Indonesian city of Bandung to inaugurate the non-aligned movement." As Macey notes, sixty-three delegates from twenty-four countries were invited, with the majority coming "from the Francophone Africa and the Caribbean."[52]

Baldwin's article veers between observant comments about the wider geopolitical significance of the conference ("hanging in the air . . . were the great specters of America and Russia, of the battle going on between them for the domination of the world") and wry observations from an amused and bemused Westerner.[53] The Nigerian poet M. Lasebikan, Baldwin writes, was "dressed in a most arresting costume"; Baldwin notes that "he was wearing a very subdued but very ornately figured silk robe, which looked Chinese, and he wore a red velvet toque, a sign, someone told me, that he was a Muhammadan."[54] Baldwin's cavalier description and his hazy attempts to describe Lasebikan's national dress (which is conflated as oriental, foreign) not only echo his own earlier discomfort at being observed by the Swiss villagers, as he recalled in "Stranger in the Village," but firmly place the author as Western observer.

Despite his initial distance from the speakers at the conference, he is attracted to Senghor's theories on the lack of division in African culture between life and art. And yet, echoing his earlier comment in "Encounter in the Seine" concerning the gulf between the African and the African American, Baldwin believes that "Senghor's thought had come into my mind translated." Although Senghor's theory of "creative interdependence" (a term that I will come back to) chimed with the "active, actual, joyful intercourse . . . sometimes created among jazz musicians," Baldwin concludes that "social art had no reality whatever in western life."[55]

Baldwin questions Senghor's claim that the heritage of the African American is straightforwardly African. Senghor's conclusion that Richard Wright's *Black Boy* illustrates Wright's African roots, Baldwin argues, overlooks the specificity of his Mississippi upbringing. To view *Black Boy* as a great *African* autobiography, Baldwin writes, is not to restore Wright's African heritage: "rather it seemed to be taking away his identity."[56]

In "Princes and Powers" Baldwin repeatedly observes how identities are forged in specific historical conditions, illustrated by his well-known question, "For what, beyond the fact that all black men at one time or another left Africa, or have remained there, do they really have in common?"[57] Like most of the American delegates at the 1956 conference—including Richard Wright, John Mercer, and John A. Davis—Baldwin, as Bennetta Jules-Rosette notes,

> objected to imposing the concept of colonialism on black Americans and argued that their situation of racial oppression was historically different because it involved an active, legal, educational, and political struggle within an established national framework.[58]

At one point, Baldwin concedes that people of black descent *did* have something in common—"their precarious, their unutterably painful relation to the white world"—although this was a comment that he would later redress. In an interview eight years after the 1956 conference, he not only noted that he "profoundly distrust[ed]" negritude but again argued that "oppressions do not necessarily unify so many millions of people all over the world":

> Well, how in the world is this going to connect to so many different experiences? To be born in Jamaica, Barbados, or Portugal, or New York, or to be black, wouldn't seem to me to be enough . . . and the situation of the man in Jamaica is not the situation of the man in Harlem at all.[59]

In "Princes and Powers" Baldwin is careful to distinguish between the colonial experiences of Africans who wished to overthrow European white rule and the complex relationship between black Americans and white authority in the United States. "It had never been our interest to overthrow" the dominant white power, Baldwin writes. Rather, "it had been necessary to make the machinery work for our benefit and the possibility of its doing so had been . . . built in."[60]

Baldwin's emphasis on the relationship *with*—rather than separation *from*—the dominant white world characterizes much of his writing of the 1950s and 1960s. For Baldwin, America is the blood relation—with Africa, like the man he called his father, a stepparent. "It is not simply the relationship of oppressed to oppressor," writes Baldwin in "Many Thousands Gone," or "of master to slave . . . it is also, literally and morally, a *blood* relationship."[61] Drawing on the image of bondage, Baldwin insists in "In Search of a Majority" that black and white are now yoked together: "Whether I like it or not, or whether you like it or not, we are bound together for ever. We are a part of each other," a conviction that also underwrote his understanding of the relations between colonizer and colonized.[62] The Africans at the conference, Baldwin argued, "were all, now, whether they liked it or not, related to Europe, stained by European visions and standards, and their relation to themselves, and to each other, and to their past had changed."[63] Or, as he later wrote in *No Name in the Street*, "a representative from Dakar is not necessarily a man from Senegal. He is much more likely to be a spiritual citizen of France, in which event he cannot possibly convey the actual needs of his part of Africa, or of Africa."[64]

At the time of the 1956 conference, Baldwin had not yet visited the African continent, and it would be another six years before he would do so.

In the interview with Isaacs, he stated, "I want to go to Africa one of these days," adding, "I think there's a great deal I can discover about myself there."[65] Baldwin's ideas of self-discovery abroad echo those of David in *Giovanni's Room*, who hopes to "find himself," and like David, as I discuss in the following section, who realizes that the self that he hoped to find was "the same self from which I had spent so much time in flight," Baldwin found that visits to Africa did not fulfill the promise of self-revelation.[66]

Africa and Beyond

Baldwin's comments on Africa prior to visiting the continent suggest a certain degree of apprehension. Asked in 1961 why he had not been to Africa, Baldwin replied that once he had visited the continent, he would "not be able to dream anymore."[67] In an interview with Ida Lewis he claimed that he "didn't dare go to Africa" when he was first supposed to.[68] His reluctance to visit Africa may have been connected to his mistrust of black Americans who had started to identify with African culture, a theme he would return to on many occasions. David Leeming notes that Baldwin was "frankly skeptical of the interest among American blacks at the time in their African 'homeland.'"[69]

According to William Shawn, the former editor of the *New Yorker*, Baldwin suggested writing several articles for the magazine about a proposed trip to Africa in late 1959 or early 1960. "We gave him an advance," Shawn recalls, "and then we didn't hear from him again. For years."[70] Baldwin visited several African countries for the first time in July 1962. Accompanied by his sister Gloria, he spent time in Sierra Leone, Guinea, Monrovia, and the Ivory Coast. Although there are no detailed accounts of his first trip, most biographers seem to agree with Fern Eckman's conclusion that "Baldwin had no sense of homecoming in Africa." (Any notion of homecoming would no doubt have been tarnished by problems with visas that Baldwin encountered on his entry into Dakar.)[71]

David Leeming recalls that Baldwin took copious notes on his trip but was uncomfortable in his role as reporter. In interviews and biographical accounts of his first trip to African countries, Baldwin struggled to articulate his thoughts. Leeming recalls that Baldwin was struck by "the sheer beauty of the landscape, the farms, the people," although these were things that "really attracted him but which he was unable to pursue in any depth."[72] After an enjoyable start to the trip in Sierra Leone (where his sister would meet her future husband, Frank Karefa-Smart), Baldwin realized that he did not want to write the articles on Africa for the *New Yorker,* and he instead handed William Shawn a long essay on America, "A Letter from a Region in My Mind." In interviews Baldwin talked of writing a book on Africa—but not for a long time—and instead wrote what would become *The Fire Next Time*, his most incendiary engagement with the state of the American nation.[73]

Baldwin's second trip to Africa—a brief visit to Kenya to celebrate the country's independence—gives some indication of his growing awareness of, and commitment to, the anticolonial movements in Africa. Again, though, Baldwin's stance is hard to gauge. Much later the critic Ezenwa-Ohaeto wrote of how, on the one hand, in *The Devil Finds Work*, Baldwin was "aware of the economic and political dimensions to the suffering of the Africans," arguing that he "had become sensitive to the African reality," adding that in *No Name in the Street*, "Baldwin was gradually coming to terms with the African reality." And yet, Ezenwa-Ohaeto also notes, Baldwin had always expressed disenchantment with Africa, claiming that he "does consider them [Africans] inferior to him."[74]

Ezenwa-Ohaeto does not mention Baldwin's participation in Kenya's independence celebrations nor his participation in a forum sponsored by the Liberation Committee for Africa, published in 1961 as *Nationalism, Colonialism and the United States: One Minute to Twelve.* Baldwin's essay, though hardly his most fluent, attempts to map out the connections between nationalism and colonialism, turning back, once again to the United States: "The only hope this country has is to turn overnight into a revolutionary country, and I say revolutionary in the most serious sense of the word."[75]

Published a year before *Another Country*, Baldwin's appeal to radicalism seems out of place. After all, this is a writer who would become ignored and dismissed by a generation of younger writers—including such luminaries as Amiri Baraka and Eldridge Cleaver. In *Soul on Ice*, Cleaver takes Baldwin to task for his "antipathy toward the black race" in "Princes and Powers."[76] According to Cleaver, Baldwin "the reluctant black" expressed "revulsion" at the Africans at the 1956 conference through "the perfumed smoke screen of his prose." For Cleaver, Baldwin's homosexuality means that he can, in fact, never be "truly black," connecting the latter's sexuality with a "racial death-wish." And, in a comment that must have infuriated Baldwin, Cleaver concludes that the writer echoes "the black bourgeoisie who have completely rejected their African heritage."[77]

Despite criticism by Cleaver and other younger writers, Baldwin refused to embrace what he saw as the fashion of African culture. In an interview with Eve Auchinloss and Nancy Lynch in 1969 he dismissed neo-Africans as "romantic American Negroes who think they can identify with the African struggle, without having the least idea what it's about."[78] Although Baldwin would, as Ernest Champion recalls, on occasion invoke his African heritage, he would more frequently admonish students at Bowling Green for referring to themselves as "we Africans."[79]

In Baldwin's last novel, *Just Above My Head*, published at the end of the 1970s but set in the turbulent decade before, Baldwin briefly discusses his character Julia's visit to the West African city of Abidjan, where she lived for two years. As Andrew Shin and Barbara Judson astutely point out, "Julia's trip to Africa offers a kind of secular redemption for the religious hypocrisy that she unwittingly contributed to as a child."[80] In Africa she meets a "*really* black" man who is old enough to be her father, the only male who "understood something" about her.[81] And yet, as Shin and Judson note, Baldwin suggests that "pan-Africanism is not really a viable solution for the problems of American blacks."[82] "A black girl in Africa," Julia concludes, "who wasn't *born* in Africa . . . is a very strange creature for herself, and for everyone who meets her."[83]

Conclusion

I want to conclude by suggesting that Baldwin's opinions on Africa shifted in the late 1970s and that, by his death in 1987, there was a notable if not fully articulated change in his views. For a number of critics—not least for Ernest Champion—Baldwin's participation at the 1980 meeting of the African Literature Association marked a turnaround in his otherwise shifting responses to Africa. In his encounter with the Nigerian writer Chinua Achebe, Baldwin, it seems, found kinship and companionship, despite the cultural and geographical differences. Commenting on Achebe's *Things Fall Apart*, Baldwin stated, "I recognized everybody in it. And that book was about my father."[84]

Although the Baldwin-Achebe encounter was a profound event, it seems to me that Baldwin's ideas of Africa had already started to shift by the late 1970s. In an interview with *Africa: International Business, Economic and Political Magazine* in 1978, he began to articulate the need and desire for a dialogic encounter between black Americans and Africans, engaging with what he termed their "cultural interdependence."[85] Here Baldwin explicitly reworks his earlier notion that the "only thing that really unites all black men everywhere is, as far as I can tell, the fact that white men are on their necks."[86] In the *Africa* interview Baldwin pointedly discusses a relationship that is "much deeper than the common experience of colonialism or neo-colonialism," what he later termed "cultural interplay."[87] Noting how his nephew had found his visit to Africa "tremendously liberating," Baldwin speaks of his hope for more cultural interaction between the United States and Africa for the younger generation. And as he stated in a later interview with Jordan Elgrably and George Plimpton, "If I were twenty-four now, I don't know where I would go. . . . I don't know if I would go to France, I might go to Africa."[88]

In the Elgrably and Plimpton interview, Baldwin seems to revise his earlier insistence on the African American's disconnection from European culture that he had articulated in "Stranger in the Village," a shift that had begun in *No Name in the Street.* In the earlier essay, Baldwin had written of how "the most illiterate among them [the villagers] is related, in a way that I am not, to Dante, Shakespeare . . . Chartres."[89] In *No Name,* far from looking wistfully at European culture, Baldwin wrote that the "South African coal miner, or the African digging for roots . . . have no reason to bow down before Shakespeare, or Descartes . . . or the Cathedral at Chartres."[90] In the Elgrably-Plimpton interview, this position is again stated more clearly: "Europe is no longer a frame of reference, a standard bearer, the classic model for literature and for civilization. . . . When I was a kid, the world was white . . . and now it's struggling to *remain* white—a very different thing."[91]

Baldwin's comments here and elsewhere in the last decade or so of his life suggest the ways in which his aesthetic and political outlook had shifted to include a broader, transcultural perspective. As Baldwin stated in the late 1970s, "America is vast by itself, and yet the sense is that one no longer wishes to be isolated on the American continent"; he added that "we have to know what is going on in Africa and Africa has to know what is going on in Black America."[92]

Baldwin's reference to what he later called "cultural interdependence" is illustrated in an essay that he wrote in the year of his death, published in *Perspectives: Angles on African Art.* He was one of a number of writers and artists asked to select objects from the exhibition of African art that ran from 1987 to 1988 and to be interviewed by Michael John Weber. A large photograph of a regal-looking Baldwin wearing a corduroy jacket and an African-inspired bangle begins his section, where the text is placed alongside photographs of African sculpture. The interview responses (the questions are not shown) are frequently cryptic as Baldwin comments on his selected objects. "I feel reconciled to myself and my past," Baldwin states. "I come more directly from this than from Rembrandt." In sharp contrast to his criticism of negritude or "authentic blackness," Baldwin claims that "it says something to me because I am black."[93]

During the interview there are two notable, recurring themes. The first is Baldwin's recognition of kinship with the African art. Commenting on a woman with a Luba staff, Baldwin states, "I recognize the women; I met them in Harlem."[94] And yet even as he approaches some sense of cultural interdependence, he struggles, like Julia in *Just Above My Head*, to articulate his connection to the art of Africa. You "cannot *hear* another language, unless you've heard it already," claims Julia in the novel.[95] "It's hard to describe these things in a Western language," Baldwin himself states at one point, later adding, "I can't go there. I'm not equipped at all to discuss that." Pressed by the interviewer to comment further on a piece, Baldwin states simply, "I recognize it. I don't know how I recognize it. I don't know how to put it you." During the interview Baldwin seems worn out, exhausted by his attempts to translate his experience: "I'm not sure I can articulate it," he notes at one point, adding, "I'm also very weary, weary, weary of trying to deal with this."[96] These late reflections do not resolve the questions about Africa that he asked himself throughout his lifetime . It is clear, however, that Baldwin was increasingly open to the idea of a transcultural—or, to use his term, interdependent—relationship between the African and the African American. "It's not a Western face," Baldwin said in discussion of a Yoruban mask. "One could say an African face, but it's something deeper than that. I can't find the word for it. *Africa*, for lack of a better term."[97]

NOTES

1. Isaacs, "Five Writers and Their Ancestors," 327.
2. Baldwin, "Notes of a Native Son," in *Price of the Ticket*, 128.
3. Baldwin, "Encounter on the Seine: Black Meets Brown," in *Price of the Ticket*, 39.
4. Baldwin, "Autobiographical Notes," in *Collected Essays*, 7.
5. Isaacs, "Five Writers and Their Ancestors," 328.
6. Baldwin, *Go Tell It on the Mountain*, 125.
7. Baldwin, "Notes of a Native Son," 129.
8. Ezenwa-Ohaeto writes how "real Africa [in Baldwin's writing] is clearly the sub-Sahara zone" ("Notions and Nuances," 110), and I'm mindful of not replicating this view. It is beyond the scope of this chapter, however, to discuss Baldwin's

writings on Algeria: see in particular "This Morning, This Evening, So Soon" (in *Going to Meet the Man*) and *No Name in the Street* (in *Price of the Ticket*).

9. Campbell, *Talking at the Gates*, 109.

10. Eckman, *Furious Passage of James Baldwin*, 24; Champion, *Mr. Baldwin, I Presume*, 47–48.

11. Isaacs, "Five Writers and Their Ancestors," 324.

12. Ezenwa-Ohaeto, "Notions and Nuances," 108.

13. Ojo-Ade, "Introduction," in *Of Dreams Deferred*, 1.

14. Cullen, "Heritage," in *Color*, 36.

15. Isaacs, "Five Writers and Their Ancestors," 319.

16. Nwankwo, "Richard Wright: A Dubious Legacy," 58.

17. Baldwin, quoted in Isaacs, "Five Writers and Their Ancestors," 328.

18. Baldwin, "Notes of a Native Son," 142.

19. Hurston, *Sanctified Church*, 103; Anderson, *Vision of the Disinherited*, 7.

20. See my essay "Pentecostalism and All that Jazz."

21. Hurston, *Sanctified Church*, 105–6.

22. Tinney, "Blackness of Pentecostalism," 31. He also notes that "James Baldwin calls the drum the indispensable element in Pentecostal religion, the same as in African religion" (32).

23. Ibid., 28; Standley and Pratt, *Conversations with James Baldwin*, 182.

24. See, e.g., Sivan, "Out of and Back to Africa."

25. Champion, *Mr. Baldwin, I Presume*, xviii; M'Baye, "African Retentions," 43.

26. M'Baye, "African Retentions," 47–48.

27. Ibid., 44.

28. Holmes, "Reassessing African American Literature," 49.

29. Ibid., 49, 41.

30. Baldwin, "The Outing," in *Going to Meet the Man*, 44.

31. Ibid., 41, 45.

32. Hurston, *Sanctified Church*, 103; Standley and Pratt, *Conversations with James Baldwin*, 182. See also Baldwin, "Introduction," in *Price of the Ticket*, where he compares black and white churches: "We do not . . . share the same hope or speak the same language" (xix).

33. Hurston, *Jonah's Gourd Vine*, 59, 62.

34. Ibid., 145–46, 221.

35. Brown, "'I, John Saw the Holy Number,'" 55.

36. Baldwin, *Go Tell It on the Mountain*, 224, 225.

37. Anderson, *Vision of the Disinherited*, 159.

38. This is also explored in detail in my forthcoming article "Pentecostalism and All that Jazz."

39. Avi-Ram, "Unreadable Black Body," 37.

40. See Dyson, "When You Divide the Body and Soul," in *Race Rules*, 93. Dyson focuses on the physicality of black worship, calling for a "theology of eroticism."

41. Avi-Ram, "Unreadable Black Body," 36.

42. Quoted in Dyson, *Race Rules*, 92.

43. See Bergman, *Gaiety Transfigured*, 172–83. However, see also Asante, who

in *Afrocentricity* sees homosexuality as "un-African," writing that it is "a deviation from Afrocentric thought" (64–65).

44. Isaacs, "Five Writers and Their Ancestors," 324.
45. Ezenwa-Ohaeto, "Notions and Nuances," 110.
46. Baldwin, "Encounter on the Seine," 38.
47. Ibid., 39, 38.
48. Ibid., 39.
49. Isaacs, "Five Writers and Their Ancestors," 324.
50. Baldwin, "Encounter on the Seine," 39.
51. James Baldwin, *No Name in the Street*, in *Price of the Ticket*, 475.
52. Macey, *Frantz Fanon*, 279.
53. Baldwin, "Princes and Powers," in *Price of the Ticket*, 43.
54. Ibid., 46.
55. Ibid., 47, 48.
56. Ibid., 51.
57. Ibid., 49.
58. Benetta, *Black Paris*, 53.
59. Bondy, "James Baldwin," 16.
60. Baldwin, "Princes and Powers," 45.
61. Baldwin, "Many Thousands Gone," in *Price of the Ticket*, 76–77.
62. Baldwin, "In Search of a Majority," in *Price of the Ticket*, 234.
63. Baldwin, "Princes and Powers," 54.
64. Baldwin, *No Name in the Street*, 474.
65. Isaacs, "Five Writers and Their Ancestors," 328.
66. Baldwin, *Giovanni's Room*, 25.
67. Campbell, *Talking at the Gates*, 153.
68. Standley and Pratt, *Conversations with James Baldwin*, 85.
69. Leeming, *James Baldwin*, 207.
70. Campbell, *Talking at the Gates*, 152.
71. Eckman, *Furious Passage of James Baldwin*, 169; Leeming, *James Baldwin*, 207.
72. Leeming, *James Baldwin*, 210.
73. Standley and Pratt, *Conversations with James Baldwin*, 34–35.
74. Ezenwa-Ohaeto, "Notions and Nuances," 111.
75. *Nationalism, Colonialism and the United States*, 25.
76. Cleaver, *Soul on Ice*, 99.
77. Ibid., 99, 100, 103.
78. Standley and Pratt, *Conversations with James Baldwin*, 71.
79. Champion, *Mr. Baldwin, I Presume*, 47–48.
80. Judson and Shin, "Beneath the Black Aesthetic," 257.
81. Baldwin, *Just Above My Head*, 561, 564.
82. Judson and Shin, "Beneath the Black Aesthetic," 257.
83. Baldwin, *Just Above My Head*, 564.
84. Champion, *Mr. Baldwin, I Presume*, 86.
85. Standley and Pratt, *Conversations with James Baldwin*, 169.
86. Ibid., 17.

87. Ibid., 169.
88. Ibid., 246.
89. Baldwin, "Stranger in the Village," in *Price of the Ticket,* 83.
90. Baldwin, *No Name in the Street,* 473.
91. Standley and Pratt, *Conversations with James Baldwin,* 246.
92. Ibid., 169.
93. Baldwin et al., *Perspectives,* 115.
94. Ibid., 119.
95. Baldwin, *Just Above My Head,* 565.
96. Baldwin et al., *Perspectives,* 116, 122, 119.
97. Ibid., 127.

BIBLIOGRAPHY

Anderson, Robert M. *Vision of the Disinherited: The Making of American Pentecostalism.* New York: Oxford University Press, 1979. Reprint, Peabody, Mass.: Hendrickson Publishers, 1992.

Asante, Molefi Kete. *Afrocentricity: The Theory of Social Change.* Buffalo: Amulefi, 1980.

Avi-Ram, Amitai F. "The Unreadable Black Body: 'Conventional' Poetic Form in the Harlem Renaissance." *Genders* 7 (1990).

Baldwin, James. *Collected Essays.* Ed. Toni Morrison. New York: Library of America, 1998.

Baldwin, James. *Giovanni's Room.* London: Penguin, 1990.

Baldwin, James. *Going to Meet the Man.* London: Penguin, 1991.

Baldwin, James. *Go Tell It on the Mountain.* London: Penguin, 1991.

Baldwin, James. *Just Above My Head.* London: Penguin, 1994.

Baldwin, James. *The Price of the Ticket: Collected Nonfiction, 1948–1985.* New York: St. Martin's, 1985.

Baldwin, James, Romare Bearden, et al. *Perspectives: Angles on African Art.* Interviews by Michael John Weber. Introduction by Susan Vogel. New York: Center for African Art, 1987.

Benetta, Jules-Rosetta. *Black Paris: The African Writers' Landscape.* Foreword by Simon Njami. Urbana: University of Illinois Press, 1998.

Bergman, David. *Gaiety Transfigured: Gay Self-Representation in American Literature.* Madison: University of Wisconsin Press, 1991.

Bondy, François. "James Baldwin, as Interviewed by François Bondy." *Transition* 12 (1964).

Brown, Joseph A. "'I, John Saw the Holy Number:' Apocalyptic Visions in *Go Tell It on the Mountain* and *Native Son.*" *Religion and Literature* 27 (1995).

Campbell, James. *Talking at the Gates: A Life of James Baldwin.* London: Faber and Faber, 1991.

Champion, Ernest A. *Mr. Baldwin, I Presume: James Baldwin—Chinua Achebe: A Meeting of the Minds.* New York: University Press of America, 1995.

Cleaver, Eldridge. *Soul on Ice.* New York: Ramparts, 1968.

Cullen, Countee. *Color.* New York: Harper, 1925.

Dyson, Michael Eric. *Race Rules: Navigating the Color Line.* Massachusetts: Addison-Wesley, 1996.

Eckman, Fern Marja. *The Furious Passage of James Baldwin.* London: Michael Joseph, 1966.

Ezenwa-Ohaeto. "Notions and Nuances: Africa in the Works of James Baldwin." In Ojo-Ade, *Of Dreams Deferred.*

Field, Douglas. "Pentecostalism and All that Jazz: Tracing James Baldwin's Religion." *Literature and Theology* 22, no. 4 (December 2008): 436–57.

Holmes, Carolyn L. "Reassessing African American Literature through an Afrocentric Paradigm: Zora N. Hurston and James Baldwin." In Carol Aisha Blackshire-Belay, ed., *Language and Literature in the African American Imagination.* Westport, Conn.: Greenwood Press, 1992.

Hurston, Zora Neale. *Jonah's Gourd Vine.* Reprint, with afterword by Holly Eley. London: Virago, 1993.

Hurston, Zora Neale. *The Sanctified Church.* Foreword by Toni Cade Bambara. New York: Marlowe, 1981.

Isaacs, Harold. "Five Writer and Their Ancestors Part 2." *Phylon* 21, no. 4 (1960).

Judson, Barbara, and Andrew Shin. "Beneath the Black Aesthetic: James Baldwin's Prime of Black American Masculinity." *African American Review* 32, no. 2 (1998).

Leeming, David. *James Baldwin: A Biography.* New York: Alfred Knopf, 1994.

M'Baye, Babacar. "African Retentions in *Go Tell It on the Mountain.*" In Carol E. Henderson, ed., *James Baldwin's* Go Tell It on the Mountain: *Historical and Critical Essays.* New York: Peter Lang, 2006.

Macey, David. *Frantz Fanon: A Biography.* New York: Picador, 2000.

Nationalism, Colonialism and the United States: One Minute to Twelve. A forum sponsored by the Liberation Committee for Africa on its First Anniversary Celebration. June 2, 1961. New York: Photo-Offset Press, 1961.

Nwankwo, Chimalum. "Richard Wright: A Dubious Legacy." In Ojo-Ade, *Of Dreams Deferred.*

Ojo-Ade, Femi, ed. *Of Dreams Deferred, Dead or Alive: African Perspectives on African-American Writers.* Westport, Conn.: Greenwood Press, 1996.

Shockley, Ann Allen. *Say Jesus and Come to Me.* Florida: Naiad Press, 1987.

Sivan, Miriam. "Out of and Back to Africa: James Baldwin's *Go Tell It on the Mountain.*" *Christianity and Literature* 51, no. 1 (2001).

Standley, Fred. L., and Louis H. Pratt, eds. *Conversations with James Baldwin.* Jackson: University of Mississippi Press, 1989.

Tinney, James S. "The Blackness of Pentecostalism." *Spirit* 3, no. 2 (1979).

TWELVE

James Baldwin and Chinua Achebe

Transgressing Official Vocabularies

ELEANOR W. TRAYLOR

Perhaps I can begin with an Ibo proverb embedded in Chinua Achebe's *Things Fall Apart*. It reads:

> A man who calls his kinsmen to a feast does not do so to save them from starving. They all have food in their own homes. When we gather together in the Moonlit Village ground it is not because of the moon. Every man can see it in his own compound. We come together because it is good for kinsmen to do so.[1]

This proverb not only points to the desire, design, and method of Achebe's novel, as we shall see; it profoundly underscores one of the most remarkable aesthetic events of the latter twentieth century, now patent: the emergence of a denationalized literary landscape called *diasporo*, transgressing traditional boundaries, be they geographical, generic, or political; destabilizing referents of any kind, canceling metaphorical invisibilities, and calling into being metonymic constructions of identity still awakening. Joseph Harris's *Global Dimensions of the African Diaspora*, published in 1982, the most comprehensive study of the African diaspora extant, stimulates ever-developing explorations of how *diasporo* as a "conceptual and methodical comparative approach clearly has potential for the reconstruction of African history."[2] Its potential for the reconstruction of literary histories is most recently demonstrated by Curdella Forbes's *From Nation to Diaspora: Samuel Selvon, George Lamming and the Cultural Performance of Gender.* In kinship with this fertile potential, I situate an exploration of textualities in African American narrative that opens unprecedented generic spaces as a consequence of *diasporo* (continuing) awareness. I argue that before the lexicon descriptive of postmodern textual acts, a commemorative aesthetic has prevailed in literature of the referenced *diasporo* to extend existing vocabularies of "kinship" and "intimacy" as applied, particularly, to African American narrative approaches. Such acts of extension pivot *diasporo* (meaning new space for being) as a broader, more inclusive framework for embracing theoretical and cultural concepts than *post*modern or *post*colonial.

Brilliantly highlighting this new *situs* of being—*diasporo*, with its discovered and ever-discovering filiations—is the readerly and writerly kinship expressed by Chinua Achebe and James Baldwin. In fact, it contextualizes descriptive referents such as "kinship" and "intimacy" to signify the broader sense of *diasporo.* As Achebe tells us:

> When I read *Go Tell It on the Mountain* in 1958, I knew here was a *brother.* And so I immediately proceeded to the American Information Service in the city where I lived [Enugu] to borrow some more books by Baldwin. Unfortunately, there were no other books by Baldwin or anybody like him, in that library. And so I asked, "How come . . . ?" I must say in fairness to the people concerned, they were moved and that situation was changed.[3]

Similarly, Baldwin tells us:

> When I read *Things Fall Apart* [Achebe's first novel] which is about an Ibo tribe in Nigeria, a tribe I never saw, a system—to put it that way—or a society, the rules of which were a mystery to me, I recognized everybody in it. And that book was about *my father.*[4]

"Filiation," "affiliation," and "difference," chords touched here, resound throughout the fiction and essays of both these writers, riffing especially around the question of language itself. When Achebe discovered Baldwin in 1958, he might also have read that author's transgressive collection of essays *Notes of a Native Son* (1955), where he enunciates the premise on which postcolonial or postmodern aesthetics turns. Achebe might have also noted Baldwin's reinscription of the so-called international theme in American literature (or the theme of the American traveler abroad)—a theme popularized earlier than Henry James. That disruptive reinscription occurs in Baldwin's *Giovanni's Room* (1956). And by 1964, Chinua Achebe testifies to the consequence of his textual kinship with Baldwin in his instructive essay "The African Writer and the English Language," included in his beautifully titled collection *Morning Yet on Creation Day* (1975). In this essay, he quotes Baldwin, who, writing in the *London Observer*, says:

> My quarrel with the English language has been that the language reflected none of my experience. But now I began to see the matter in another way. . . . Perhaps the language was not my own because I had never attempted to use it, had only learned to imitate it. If this were so, then it might be made to bear the burden of my experience if I could find the stamina to challenge it, and me, to such a test.[5]

To this Achebe replies:

> I recognize, of course, that Baldwin's problem is not exactly mine, but I feel that the English language will be able to carry the weight of my African experience. But it will have to be a *new* English, still in full communion with its ancestral home but altered to suit its new African surroundings.[6]

This "new," by 1964, has not the chime of the modernist "making it new," which both authors had considered and reconsidered in their voyage texts. Each accomplishes but exceeds the modernist project of sifting his narrative to retrieve a usable past. For in *Things Fall Apart*, *Notes of a Native Son*, and *Giovanni's Room*, both these writers had begun the approach that now prevails to define contemporary fiction the world over. Situated within the (European and American) traditional scaffolding of the bildungsroman, *Things Fall Apart* and *Go Tell It on the Mountain* test and force the logocentric boundaries within which they must operate. Not only do these narratives erect a house of tales formerly unconstructed in novels set in Africa or in the neighborhoods-cum-ghettos of black America; they also displace the language by which these zones had been characterized. This language had closed a space that these narratives opened. If, in fact, the once-prevalent Hegelian-Conradian grand narrative of Africa as "heart of darkness" had closed from view its "bright savannahs green,"[7] then the harvest feast at Mbanta in *Things Fall Apart* undermines the conceptual lexicon by which such narratives are written. Likewise, if Bigger Thomas had once prevailed as symbol for the American other, then the fourteenth birthday of a child growing up in *Go Tell It on the Mountain* has troubled ever since the modal naturalistic claim to authority and exposed the failures of generic namings such as "protest."

One might argue that the method of reading and writing the world in representational texts so exemplary of recent narrative and pedagogy is the intertextual method formalizing the structures of *Things Fall Apart* and *Go Tell It on the Mountain.* This method of inclusion, much later named by Julia Kristeva, is embellished by what I call a commemorative desire not only parodic or signifying but, like a jam session, inviting prior texts to a dialogical conversation that addresses in present time another time, another place, another country.

Moreover, each novel unveils "experiences in family and intimate relationships that particularize a self as that self is shaped by a specific cultural heritage and as that self uniquely finds its being within and against the group."[8] But more, if such relationships produce a "displacement of symbol . . . creating a crisis for any concept of authority based on recognition," "a problematic" occurs.[9] Forty-one years after the publication of *Go Tell It on the Mountain* and thirty-five years after the publication of *Things Fall Apart*, Homi Bhabha names the strategies practiced by Achebe and Baldwin—hybridity and mimicry—in the creation of fiction whose desire and design is to decolonize the English language.

When Achebe looks into the mirror of *Go Tell It on the Mountain,* he sees no "other"; neither does he discover the Lacanian jolt of a split self. He sees neither "self" nor "other"; he sees "kin," or, to borrow Alice Walker's much later term, he sees a "familiar." What James Baldwin discovers through the mirror of *Things Fall Apart* is exactly that, "a familiar." Nor is this, dare I say, global awareness, produced by textual encounter, unique to their discovery. Two examples are germane. One is the response of a sophomore student in Humanities 014—a world literature course—at Howard University, where I teach. So enchanted was my student by a scene from Achebe's novel that her one-sentence proclamation innocently erased an entire century's portraiture of Africa as sign for "the other." I am certain that my student had not read, for example, Joseph Conrad or Joyce Carey or Edgar Rice Burroughs, though as one of the animated cartoon-viewing generation, she may have come to *Tarzan* (still an entry on the late-night television menu in the United States) with such an eye. No, my student's response to the scene of the gathering in chapter 6 of *Things Fall Apart* was as unassuming as the response of residents of Washington, D.C., where I live, to the Eastern Market. There on Saturday mornings one may find anything from a lost and seemingly irreplaceable button to a life-sized Ndebele doll, the freshest fowl for next day's dinner, or a scratch of cardamom for tea, hand-blown glass from Florence, or a delicate silk-screen; yet the language of negotiation—the motif of the market—including the drums, the blues man's horn, guitar, and voice, the city poets reciting their latest inspiration, the distinct accents of vendors and the haggle of their buyers, underscores the rhythmic movement of the place as congressmen from the Hill and Georgetown are edged aside by no-nonsense women of the valley who co-opt the butcher's attention by sheer persistence. So just as we say, as we do, "Go early if you go, for the world lives at the Eastern Market on Saturday morning," my student responded confidently and guilelessly to the scene in chapter 6, which reads:

> The whole village turned out on the ilo, men, women and children. . . . The young men . . . dashed about. . . . The people surged forward . . . Old men nodded to the beat of the drum. . . . The huge voice of the crowd then rose to the sky and in every direction.[10]

"All the world is *Umuofia*," said my student. I have no sense that she intended a comment on universality. My strong impression is that her reply was triggered by a purely local, immediate moment of pleasure as she witnessed something as familiar as the excitement of an athletic event—in this case, a wrestling match—in Achebe's *Things Fall Apart*.

Nor is awareness of the familiar less enthusiastically expressed by the ubiquity of readerly response to the much-written-about nightclub scene in James Baldwin's "Sonny's Blues," which, notwithstanding the widespread continuing reception of *Go Tell It on the Mountain* and the now New American Library Classic *Giovanni's Room*, is the most frequently anthologized, course-packeted, and requested-for-permission-to-print of the fictional oeuvre of the author. Considering its translation into Continental languages (as is also true of Achebe's *Things Fall Apart*), one might hypothesize that the world has sat sipping scotch or whatever libation at the Baldwin welcome table in the "defamiliarized" nightclub of "Sonny's Blues." The nightclub scene presents a different kind of wrestling match from that on the "ilo" of the Achebe novel. Here, in the midst of a similar knowing, expectant, diverse audience, a young musician—a student—struggles "to use" but not "to imitate" a language—"to test," to negotiate, to (re) "make" it "to carry the weight of [his] experience."[11]

"Sonny's Blues" is a story about kinship and reading and writing: "*I read about it*" is the sentence that opens "Sonny's Blues,"[12] and in the four-sentence first paragraph of that story—a tale of a very private and public engagement—the word "read" appears three times. The word "write" receives similar repetition in the pivotal scene of the story where Sonny and the unnamed narrator, his older brother, reconnect after an estrangement of years:

NARRATOR: I didn't *write* Sonny or send him anything for a long time. . . . When I finally did . . . he *wrote* me back a letter that made me feel like a bastard. . . .
SONNY: I wanted to *write* you many times . . . but I didn't *write*. . . .
NARRATOR: Then I kept in constant touch with him.[13]

Perhaps it is this emphasis that prompts a reading of "Sonny's Blues" as a story not only about reading and writing but also about acquiring a language. In the story, this language evolves from the wide vocabulary of the blues-jazz musicians whom Sonny and, finally, his brother seek to access:

NARRATOR: What kind of musician do you want to be?
SONNY: (laughing) How many kinds do you think there are?
NARRATOR: Be serious . . . do you want to be a concert pianist, you want to play classical music and all that, or . . . what?
SONNY: (laughing) I don't want to be a classical pianist. That isn't what interests me. I mean . . . I'll have a lot of studying to do, and I'll have to study everything. . . . I want to play with jazz musicians.[14]

The blues-jazz musician, suggests Baldwin, is a contemporary artist who reviews the past according to an urgent interest in the present and an investment in the future:

> "Well, Sonny," I said gently, "you know people can't always do exactly what they want to do—"
>
> "No, I don't know that," said Sonny, surprising me. "I think people ought to do what they want to do, what else are they alive for?"

> "You getting to be a big boy," I said desperately, "it's time you started thinking about your future."
>
> "I'm thinking about my future," said Sonny, grimly. "I think about it all the time."
>
> I gave up.[15]

Now the brother, the narrator, the teacher—not Sonny—is in trouble. His language fails him: "I didn't know what to say to that."[16] His language does not send the message of his concern or what is most important to him, his love for Sonny. He does not realize that his vocabulary of acceptance based on the grand narratives for living is now powerfully confronted by Sonny's vocabulary of denial. As Baldwin puts it elsewhere:

> The argument has nothing to do with language itself (*langue*) but with the role of language. Language, incontestably, reveals the speaker. Language, also far more dubiously, is meant to define the other—and, in this case, the other is refusing to be defined by a language that has never been able to recognize him.[17]

Sonny's struggle for language emerges in that liminal space that, years later, Stuart Hall would identify as "a space between." In Sonny's case that space exists between the legitimated standard or classic and the undiscovered unknown syncopations of a new vocabulary (*diasporo*). The utterance elicited from Middle Passage crises enunciates as hollers, howls, hoots, moans, shouts, bebops, raps, and riffs to be sounded and resounded again and again, each time incrementally different. What Sonny hears is what Alla Tovares, following Mikhail Bakhtin's evocation of internally polemic discourse, identifies as "self talk . . . a specific type of dialogic discourse [or] verbalized internal polemic." Focusing on "how endurance athletes verbalize their inner conversations during rigor, with an emphasis on how they employ an array of different voices to (re)construct their experiences in verbal . . . accounts," she offers, as example, the experience of Liz speaking of her mile race, saying: "Like I didn't know you could have two voices in your head like literally talking to each other, but they f*****g do."[18] Sonny's emergent language is situated in that in-between space of becoming (midpassage) where, as Nkonko Kamwangamalu theorizes, not only is "language intimately linked to an individual's or group's social identity [but] where language is assigned not one but multiple identities at various times in its social history."[19]

The identities arising from Sonny's blues-jazz idioms embarrass binaries like either/or as multicomplex possibilities of being appear, among them: a *soul* man, a *hoochie-koochie* man, Shine, John Henry, an *ice* man, a *watermelon* man, a mill-man, as in:

> Now lady I ain't no mill man
> Just the mill man's son
> But I can do your grinding
> till the mill man comes.[20]

Even yet a "Cowboy on the Boat of Rah," a "Wardrobe Master of Paradise," "Papa Labas," "Satin Doll," "Stella by Starlight," a "Sophisticated Lady" . . . discrete or all in one.[21] Sonny's language is the language of *diasporo*—a denationalized zone existing beyond flags, armies, or churches. Its distinguishing feature is kinship traversing time, ever discovering filiations amid crises of displacement.

Of his growth to maturity, Baldwin has said:

> I didn't know who I was, but I knew what I was determined not to become. I had not descended into the pit of self-contempt, though this odor rose sometimes, sharply, to my nostrils. No. I was at war with, was completely unable to accept the assumptions of the official vocabulary into which I had been born, which assumptions, it had been supposed would guide my life—and keep me in my "place."[22]

That official vocabulary, of course, is a school. By its terms, someone else leads; you follow. Someone else names "classical music"; you answer. The cathedral of culture not even in your land is where you worship; your church is exotic. Land? What land? The official vocabulary, suggests Baldwin, is a school: an overwhelming volume of various disciplines and accepted belief—a vocabulary that, finally, betrays, abandons the teacher and plunges the student into the void of homelessness.

NARRATOR: Sonny, you haven't even finished school. And if you really want to be a musician, how do you expect to study if you're not in school?

SONNY: I *ain't learning nothing in school.* . . . Even when I go . . . At least, I ain't learning nothing you'd want me to learn.[23]

Baldwin:

> For the basis of the vocabulary into which . . . we were born is that white Christians, aided, perhaps by a few Jews, are the authors and custodians of Civilization and History: a delusion validated only by the action and reality of white power. Now that that power is being contested, the moral basis of our vocabulary is being revealed and it is not an ennobling sight. . . . The gates of our cities are barred and Famine, Danger and Death are the ruling citizens. It is time to re-examine the principles of the vocabulary which has led us to this place.[24]

If it is true that, according to Baldwin, "a language comes into existence by means of brutal necessity, and the rules of the language are dictated by what the language must convey,"[25] then the language of the blues proves the rule. "What joins all languages, and all [people]," argues Baldwin, "is the necessity to confront life, in order, not inconceivably, to outwit death."[26] The price for this is a negotiation, requiring a transgression of all manner of constituted or conventional boundaries of hearing and understanding: an attempt to explore new possibilities of being in a present moment. This is the negotiation, the method, of the jazz musician, the contemporary artist that Sonny becomes. And when he plays, the narrator tells us:

> Sonny went all the way back, he really began with the spare flat statement of the opening phrase of the song. Then he began to make it his. It was very beautiful because it wasn't hurried and it was no longer a lament. I seemed to hear with what burning he had made it his, with what burning we had yet to make it ours, how we could cease lamenting. Freedom lurked around us and I understood, at last, that he could help us to be free if we would listen, that he would never be free until we did.[27]

This new freedom that the narrator-brother-teacher feels and hears through Sonny's piano is a release from a vocabulary of proscription. Sonny, the student, has achieved a vocabulary that is his. He is now leading, naming, and situating himself, and he is teaching others that they can do this too. He has learned from his chosen peers—the best jazz musicians in the world—that "deep water and drowning [are] not the same thing."[28] Sonny, like the best teachers in the world, says the narrator,

> hit something in all of them, he hit something in me, myself, and the music tightened and deepened . . . and . . . began to tell us what the

> blues were all about. They were not about anything very new. He and his boys up there were keeping it new, at the risk of destruction, madness, and death in order to find new ways to make us listen.
>
> For while the tale of how we suffer, and how we are delighted, and how we may triumph is never new, it always must be heard. There isn't any other tale to tell; it's the only light we've got. . . .
>
> And this tale according to that face, that body, those strong hands on those strings has another aspect in every country, and a new depth in every generation.[29]

This remarkable revelation coming from the narrator-brother-teacher, who has now become the prophet of salvation and not doom, is made possible because he now understands what very wise old jazz musicians like Louis Armstrong and Bessie Smith had played and sung and what W. E. B. Du Bois had formulated as a pedagogy:

> If we make money the object of man [and woman] training, we shall develop money-makers but not necessarily men and women; if we make technical skill the object of education, we may possess artisans, but not, in nature, men and women. Men and women we shall have only as we make manhood/womanhood the work of the schools—intelligence, *broad sympathy, knowledge of the world that was and is and our relation to it.*[30]

"Broad sympathy" is a vocabulary of kinship ("the power of association") and intimacy ("engagement with the world")—a pedagogy—wide enough and skillful enough to extend beyond *quartiers* to embrace the world.

When Baldwin's Sonny and Achebe's Nwoye voluntarily eschew an institutionalized vocabulary that fails or breaks faith with kinship (connections) and obscures intimacy ("knowledge of the world that was and is and our relation to it"), they head straight into Middle Passage experience. If they endure that hideously fragmented agonistic encounter, which is never assured, then, like Chinua Achebe and James Baldwin, they will own a language that, as profound as it is playful, will dare to strip away the mask of the *egwugwu;* look the ancestor right straight in the eye; face alone *ogbuagali-odu;* expose to all the world the murderous bond-price of Ikemefuna; fly in the face of consensus to honor the joyous, war-hating music of Unoka and seat him in the place of heroes; burn down the hallowed place of the missionary but guard the rites of passage of the young; rejoice in the nation's strength and glue in Okonkwo, show his tenderness and great care, but weep at and oppose the steely, unbending assumptions of the patriarchy. Such language will call out the liars, the hypocrites, the greedy, the petty; honor the wisdom of the stories that reach beyond consciousness to tell truths that pump the heart and warm and chill the blood of human life—the stories with music and dance that tell "of the men and women who have embodied and exemplified the meaning of the [village],"[31] that "show what a good person is like and . . . the virtues that define such character."[32] They "will also tell painful stories of shared suffering that sometimes create deeper identities than success . . . stories [these stories tell] not only of suffering received but of suffering inflicted—dangerous memories, for they call the community to alter ancient evils."[33]

By the mid-twentieth century, such language shaped by Chinua Achebe and James Baldwin had restaged profound insights that shatter idols of the clan and had made visible spaces that liberate discourses of the wonderful, such as *diasporo*.

NOTES

1. Achebe, *Things Fall Apart*, 166–67.
2. Harris, *Global Dimensions of the African Diaspora*, 63.
3. Tsuruta, "In Dialogue to Define Aesthetics," 211 (emphasis added).
4. Ibid. (emphasis added).
5. Achebe, "African Writer and the English Language," 103.
6. Ibid. (emphasis added).
7. Angelou, "Child Dead in Old Seas," 110.
8. Ellison, "Charlie Christian Story," 234.
9. Bhabha, *Location of Culture*, 162
10. Achebe, *Things Fall Apart*, 46–49.
11. Achebe, "African Writer and the English Language," 103.
12. Baldwin, "Sonny's Blues," 82.
13. Ibid., 92–93 (emphasis added).
14. Ibid., 97–98.
15. Ibid., 99.
16. Ibid., 106.
17. Baldwin, "If Black English Isn't a Language," 89.
18. Tovares, "Internal Polemic as an Intertextual Resource."
19. Kamwangamalu, "Mother Tongues and Language Planning," 734.
20. Reed, "Neo-HooDoo Manifesto."
21. The first three of these references are to Ishmael Reed and thence, respectively, to Duke Ellington and Billy Strayhorn; to Victor Young (and later to different versions: to Charlie Parker, Stan Getz, Bud Powell, Stan Kenton, Miles Davis, Dexter Gordon, Ray Charles, Ella Fitzgerald); and to Duke Ellington and Irving Mills.
22. Unpublished Baldwin manuscript, reproduced here with permission from the Baldwin estate.

23. Baldwin, "Sonny's Blues," 100–101 (emphasis added).
24. Unpublished Baldwin manuscript, reproduced here with permission.
25. Baldwin, "If Black English Isn't a Language," 321.
26. Ibid.
27. Baldwin, "Sonny's Blues," 116.
28. Ibid., 120.
29. Ibid., 115.
30. Du Bois, "Talented Tenth," 31 (emphasis added).
31. Bellah, *Habits of the Heart*, 133.
32. Ibid.
33. Ibid.

BIBLIOGRAPHY

Achebe, Chinua. "The African Writer and the English Language." In *Morning Yet on Creation Day*. London: Heinemann, 1975.

Achebe, Chinua. *Things Fall Apart*. New York: Anchor Books, 1959.

Angelou, Maya. "Child Dead in Old Seas." In *The Complete Collected Poems of Maya Angelou*. New York: Random House, 1994.

Baldwin, James. "If Black English Isn't a Language, Then Tell Me, What Is?" 1979. In Theresa Redd, ed., *Revelations: An Anthology of Expository Essays by and about Blacks*. Boston: Pearson Custom Publishing, 2004.

Baldwin, James. "Sonny's Blues." In *Going to Meet the Man*. New York: Dell, 1965.

Bellah, Robert N. *Habits of the Heart: Individualism and Commitment in American Life*. New York: Harper and Rowe, 1985.

Bhabha, Homi. *The Location of Culture*. London: Routledge, 1994.

Du Bois, W. E. B. "The Talented Tenth." 1903. In Booker T. Washington, et al., *The Negro Problem: A Series of Articles by Representative Negroes of To-Day*. Miami: Mnemosyne, 1969.

Ellison, Ralph. "The Charlie Christian Story." In *Shadow and Act*. New York: Random House, 1953.

Forbes, Curdella. *From Nation to Diaspora: Samuel Selvon, George Lamming and the Cultural Performance Of Gender*. Mona: University of the West Indies Press, 2005.

Harris, Joseph E. *Global Dimensions of the African Diaspora*. Washington, D.C.: Howard University Press, 1982.

Kamwangamalu, Nkonko. "Mother Tongues and Language Planning in Africa." *TESOL Quarterly* 39, no. 4 (2005).

Reed, Ishmael. "Neo-HooDoo Manifesto." In *New and Collected Poems 1964–2006*. New York: Carroll and Graf, 2006.

Tovares, Alla V. "Internal Polemic as an Intertextual Resource in Everyday Interaction." Lecture presented at American Association for Applied Linguistics, Montreal, Canada, July 2007.

Tsuruta, Dorothy Randall. "In Dialogue to Define Aesthetics: James Baldwin and Chinua Achebe." 1981. In Fred R. Standley and Louis H. Pratt, eds., *Conversations with James Baldwin*. Jackson: University Press of Mississippi, 1989.

Afterword

HORTENSE SPILLERS

I had never thought to count the ways that I miss James Baldwin, but they must powerfully add up, insofar as his absence to me feels comprehensive—all over everywhere, all the time, and shadowing national and global events as the genial insight that I will not now have. What would Baldwin say, for example, about the Obama presidency and the apparent boomerang that it provoked in certain quarters less than a year into the life of the new American administration? How would he feel about the prospects for peace and prosperity—these old-fashioned concepts that seem more fantastical now than ever before—among African nations? Or an effective response to the ongoing Palestinian-Israeli conflict? How would he gauge the global impact of the massive deterritorializations of world cultures and banking systems and the breakdown of regulated financial markets, tethered to the unbridled, unapologetic luxuriance of a new moneyed class, and at our feet the wrack of religious idols and institutions, brought on by the unprecedented proximity between the pulpit and protocols of greed? Dwight McBride's *James Baldwin Now*, to which the editors of this volume refer, not only gestures toward the durability of his body of work but also captures the urgency of its coeval appeal: this canon inscribes an excess of influence that forces Baldwin to the forefront of our consciousness more decisively than most writers living today. We might as well call it the "Baldwin effect," and I have spent a couple of decades trying to account for it with a modicum of precision and for sure assessing its role in shaping my own "sentimental education." To do all that is no easier now than it was in 1963, when, in the midst of radical change on the landscape of national life, I "discovered" *The Fire Next Time.* For all its relative brevity of scope, this essay, for example, sings the democracy and criticizes it at once in an amazing dialectical movement that opens fully onto the stage of national culture. Cora Kaplan and Bill Schwarz, in calling this collection *James Baldwin: America and Beyond,* bring together the principal venues of Baldwin's most passionate concern—the human possibility in the world of contending powers—as these sites (although "beyond" would qualify as a site plus) are interwoven into a single skein of focus. What we miss today is not only the clear and compelling force of his arguments, but moreover the long view that he took of human history that envisions struggle against the clotted darkness of our common ignorance as the redemptive element of both our individual and our collective habitation. As far as I can tell, Baldwin, unlike Faulkner, never said that we would endure, might even "triumph," but I believe that he thought so.

It would be difficult to overestimate the primary source of the amalgam of elements that apparently fired Baldwin's deepest impulses as a writer; I would even say that the outcome is virtually inimitable, insofar as his writerly moves are absolutely distinctive to his witness. In other words, there is no Baldwin "school" of writing as there might have been, for instance, and at least for a while, an "anxiety of influence" in reference to Hemingway style—the gambit of the *démeublé.* Indeed, we cannot easily imagine those Baldwinian periods in their pristine *resonance of sound* repeated anywhere. Perhaps we could even go so far as to say that Baldwin style—what happened when the boy preacher became a man and took up the pen for real—could only have emerged in the cultural context of the United States with its peculiarly religious-sanctioned nativism that springs directly from the freewheeling, nonhieratical traditions of the Protestant church of North America—often enough, people in congregations over a couple of centuries making it up as they go along, utterly enamored of the diction of the King James–commissioned translation of holy scripture. The rhetoric of the Protestant church, inspired by the poetry of the early seventeenth-century Bible, was, at one time, common as dirt to the language of the everyday, and it maintained both its beauty and dignity of bearing—the stentorian full sentence—and the communicative potential of the needful, ordinary message, made interesting or memorable because it had something of the old poetic attitude in it. When the extraordinary ordinary became poetry, it translated, for example, into the language and oracular force of the Reverend Martin Luther King Jr., who really did "move mountains" in accents familiar to every black schoolkid I know who grew up between VE, VJ Day and the 1965 passage of the new Voting Rights Act in the United States. But this language and its mental inward commotions, sieved through table-talk at Closerie de Lilas, say, or as the editors point out in their introduction, through the *lexis* and mental agitations of Parisian intellectual cadres in the immediate postwar period, might yield "Jimmy" Baldwin, or exactly, "America *and* Beyond." In brief, black preaching and praying meets French philosophy in a foreign metropolis on one of the heights of the "death of God."

Baldwin, then, remained true to what otherwise might have been a stark, if not an untenable, contradiction, except that his giftedness worked it out as the seamless fabric of a prophetic commitment, evinced across his career, in fiction and the essay in equal measure. Secularist and cosmopolitan adept, he sustained, as well, an infallible ear for the accents and timbres of his natal culture's first poets; nowhere is the convergence—almost magical in its seductive feature—more powerfully executed than in the closural motifs of his writings—the ineluctable finality of a fully comprehended and shareable insight:

> Everything now, we must assume, is in our hands; we have no right to assume otherwise. If we—and now I mean the relatively conscious whites and the relatively conscious blacks, who must like lovers, insist on, or create, the consciousness of the others—do not falter in our duty now, we may be able, handful that we are, to end the racial nightmare, and achieve our country, and change the history of the world.[1]

Beyond the sensuality of his language, Baldwin was able to make profound appeal to the "better angels of our nature," perhaps to be described as movement in one's sense that she is being summoned to strive toward the company of her own visionary potential; this standing in the space of the moral order is precisely the vocation that our politics most usually eschew, but that the work of art sometimes accomplishes, and Baldwin persistently engaged with this ambition. Each of the facets of Baldwin's project invites its own particular study in this regard, from *Go Tell It on the Mountain* and *Another Country*, in confronting the implications of a sexual and racial politics, as well as the latter's intramural disposition; to *Giovanni's Room* and its forthright homoerotic explorations; to *Just Above My Head* and *If Beale Street Could Talk*, with their penetrating, occasionally scary investigations into a familial politics of intimacy; to *The Price of the Ticket*, which shows the quite stunning range of Baldwin's grasp of the cultural problematic over nearly four decades of labor. Even abroad—and perhaps especially abroad—Baldwin's characters are preoccupied by what might be called a "transgenerational haunting" that arises from the soil of the culture of origin, yet nevertheless is taken over by the characters' psychic disposition as their own "stuff," as it were; the movement is repeated autobiographically as the Parisian essays, penned early on in his career, project a protagonist who, thanks to the blessings of distance, can now take up the rank agonism that the American life world evokes as a sickness unto death. In other words, it appears that Baldwin, fleeing the American Diner back in New Jersey during the war years, could only have figured out what the danger was then and how lethally he had been accosted by it when well beyond its reach. But even the drama of the diner is not Baldwin's alone, but rather emanates from the society at large, as if sickness embedded in the moral order widely reverberates through the comings and goings of individual social subjects. What the American political order failed to solve in the nineteenth century, which Baldwin parodies in "Notes on the House of Bondage," one of the late essays, "returns" in the twentieth and the twenty-first as the unfinished business of the democratic project.

Writers at midcentury, especially Ellison and Baldwin, kept the eye fixed on the symptoms of movement toward the fulfillment of promise. But in a very real sense, the realpolitik in Baldwin's view actually translates into a kind of eschatological riff made subtle by the context of the message:

> If we do not now dare everything, the fulfillment of that prophecy, recreated from the Bible in song by a slave, is upon us: *God gave Noah the rainbow sign, no more water, the fire next time*![2]

The dramatic "I" of the streets of Harlem, Paris, and the Swiss village, small and isolated enough to render black skin exotic, adopts as *persona* an ancient observer of Western history and politics from which perspective he, Baldwin, announces the *refusal* and the *indictment*. In that regard, America, as a world historical site of recent vintage, elaborates the career of the unfolding of a truth much older than itself. The advantage of the latter is that Baldwin never explicitly spells it out but circumnavigates "it" as the breath or flicker of a fundamentally moral universe whose "laws" are inescapable. His conception, then, of a prophetic dimension would be borne out in the democratic promise as the route to the achievement of "our country": one that is no longer based on skin color, but rather on consciousness, the personal stakes of which are hinted at in the previous quotations.

Baldwin achieves a quite remarkable coherence between big bumbling abstractions like truth, love, justice, maturity, and the individual location of the virtues, so that more than any other post–World War II writer in English, to my mind, Baldwin insists on the personal stakes of consciousness and that the latter is imperative. The negotiation that Baldwin effects between the abstract sentiment and the reality of practice demonstrates at once intellectual rigor and existential urgency that configure a calculus of motives that relate: (1) person to person; (2) person to state and institutions; (3) institutions in light of their proclaimed values over and against their actual performance; and finally, (4) person to self. Baldwin puts in motion all sides and levels of this calculus at the same time, insofar as the outcome "feels" three-dimensional—the richness of perspective and the sense of the impossibility of separating out these strands of experience from each other. Baldwin, the stylist, then, makes it difficult for the critic to limit an understanding of his writings to a predictable range of meaning. For instance, the recurrence of the race thematic in his work is, therefore, contextualized or conditioned by a larger sense of the *human* and the requirements of *humanitas.*

Baldwin's insistence that we make new—"We have come to the end of a language and are now about the business of forging a new one"—is asserted from his position as a moralist of the highest order.[3] By "moralist," I do not mean "moral-monger," but, rather, the moralist as one who emphasizes the significance of *conduct* as the primary question of an ethical project—what is at stake in the human and how we come to *humanization,* which demarcates the realm of culture. As a result, Baldwin holds substantial membership, I believe, in a "visionary company" stretching back through the ages of Western thought that founded its chief "cognitive object" on and in the human. If we would locate a "bottom line" in Baldwin, it is writ here, inflected by the currents of his particular biographical and autobiographical detail. My fear is that with his passing, they "broke the mold," but the prospect of a new one would not have disheartened him a bit!

NOTES

1. Baldwin, *Fire Next Time,* 141.
2. Ibid.
3. Baldwin, "Notes on the House of Bondage," 675.

BIBLIOGRAPHY

Baldwin, James. *The Fire Next Time.* New York: Dell, 1964.
Baldwin, James. "Notes on the House of Bondage." In *The Price of the Ticket: Collected Nonfiction, 1948–1985.* New York: St. Martin's, 1985.

Contributors

KEVIN BIRMINGHAM is a Lecturer in History & Literature at Harvard. His dissertation, "The One-Drop Aesthetic," considers Baldwin as part of a Faulknerian strand in U.S. literature that includes Thomas Pynchon and Gloria Anzaldúa. His article about Baldwin's relationship to the South appears in *African American Review*, and he is currently writing a book about the fight to publish James Joyce's *Ulysses*, forthcoming with Penguin Press.

DOUGLAS FIELD is senior lecturer in contemporary literature at Staffordshire University. He has published articles on African American literature and culture in *Callaloo*, *Literature and Theology*, *Genre*, and the *Guardian*. He is the editor of *American Cold War Culture* (Edinburgh University Press, 2005) and *A Historical Guide to James Baldwin* (Oxford University Press, 2009). He is the author of *James Baldwin* (Northcote Press, 2011) in the series Writers and Their Work, and he is writing a monograph on James Baldwin that explores the writer's political and religious work.

KEVIN GAINES is director of the Center for Afroamerican and African Studies and professor of history at the University of Michigan. He is author of *American Africans in Ghana: Black Expatriates and the Civil Rights Era* (University of North Carolina Press, 2006) and *Uplifting the Race: Black Leadership, Politics and Culture during the Twentieth Century* (University of North Carolina Press, 1996), which was awarded the John Hope Franklin Book Prize of the American Studies Association in 1997. He was elected president of the American Studies Association in 2008.

BRIALLEN HOPPER received her PhD from Princeton in 2010 and is a lecturer in English at Yale. She has studied religion at Yale as a Class of 1952

Scholar and Samuel Slie Fellow. She has taught classes at Princeton, Boston University, Southern Methodist University, and Yale, and has published essays on Frederick Douglass and on post-Katrina New Orleans in Hollywood film. She is working on a manuscript on the ethics of political emotion entitled "Feeling Right in American Reform Culture."

CORA KAPLAN has held chairs of English at Rutgers University and at the University of Southampton, and has recently been visiting professor of English at Queen Mary, University of London. She is a feminist critic with a specific interest in race and class. Her books include *Genders* (with David Glover) (Routledge, 2009) and *Victoriana—Histories, Fictions, Criticism* (Edinburgh and Columbia, 2007).

D. QUENTIN MILLER is associate professor of English at Suffolk University in Boston. He is the author of *John Updike and the Cold War* (University of Missouri Press, 2001) and has edited *Re-Viewing James Baldwin* (Temple University Press, 2000) and *Prose and Cons: New Essays on Contemporary U.S. Prison Literature* (McFarland, 2005). He is also one of the editors of the *Heath Anthology of American Literature* and of two composition textbooks, *The Generation of Ideas* (Heinle, 2004) and *Connections* (Houghton Mifflin, 2008). His articles have appeared in many journals, including *American Literature, Forum for Modern Language Studies, Legacy, American Literary Realism*, and the *Hemingway Review*, and in a variety of books and reference volumes. He is currently completing a manuscript on James Baldwin in the context of the law.

VAUGHN RASBERRY completed his PhD in the Department of English at the University of Chicago in 2009. After spending a year as a Fulbright lecturer at the Humboldt-Universität Berlin, he is now an assistant professor in the Department of English and Center for Comparative Studies in Race and Ethnicity at Stanford University.

ROBERT REID-PHARR is Presidential Professor of English and American Studies at the Graduate Center of the City University of New York. His latest book is *Once You Go Black: Choice, Desire, and the Black American Intellectual* (New York University Press, 2007).

BILL SCHWARZ teaches in the School of English and Drama at Queen Mary University of London. The first part of his three-volume *Memories of Empire* is due out shortly from Oxford University Press. Most recently he has edited *Caribbean Literature after Independence: The Case of Earl Lovelace*

(Institute for the Study of the Americas, 2008) and, with Susannah Radstone, *Mapping Memory* (Fordham University Press, 2010).

GEORGE SHULMAN teaches at the Gallatin School of New York University. His second book is *American Prophecy: Race and Redemption in American Politics* (University of Minnesota Press, 2009).

HORTENSE SPILLERS is Gertrude Conway Vanderbilt Professor in the Department of English at Vanderbilt University. She is the author of *Black, White, and in Color: Essays on American Literature and Culture* (University of Chicago Press, 2003).

COLM TÓIBÍN is a novelist, short story writer, and essayist. *The Master* (2004) was winner of the *Los Angeles Times* Novel of the Year and of the Prix du Meilleur Livre Etranger and was shortlisted in the UK for the Man Booker prize. He has published five volumes of nonfiction and writes for the *New York Review of Books*, the *London Review of Books*, and the *Dublin Review*. He has lectured and had visiting posts at numerous universities, most recently at Stanford and Princeton. He has been fellow at the Cullman Center for Scholars and Writers at the New York Public Library, where he researched Baldwin's unpublished writings, on which this chapter is based; in March 2008 he was among those paying tribute to Baldwin at the library. His latest novel is *Brooklyn* (2009).

ELEANOR W. TRAYLOR is graduate professor of English and chairs the Department of English in the College of Arts and Sciences at Howard University. She has published work on Larry Neal, Henry Dumas, Toni Cade Bambara, Margaret Walker, James Baldwin, Toni Morrison, and Richard Wright. Among the texts that she has produced are *Broad Sympathy: The Howard University Oral Traditions Reader* (Simon and Schuster, 1996), *The Humanities and Afro-American Literary Tradition* (DC Community Humanities Council, 1988), and a multimedia piece entitled *The Dream Awake: A Spoken Arts Production* (1968), as well as biographical and cultural scripts for the Smithsonian Institution's Program in Black American Culture. She is currently working on a book on the pedagogy of African American literature.

CHERYL A. WALL is Board of Governors Zora Neale Hurston Professor of English at Rutgers University and author of *Worrying the Line: Black Women Writers, Lineage, and Literary Tradition* (University of North Carolina Press, 2005) and *Women of the Harlem Renaissance* (Indiana University

Press, 1995). She has edited several books, including the writings of Zora Neale Hurston, *Novels and Stories* (1995) and *Folklore, Memoirs and Other Writings* (1995) for the Library of America. Her current project is a study of the African American essay.

MAGDALENA J. ZABOROWSKA has taught and been a visiting scholar at the University of Oregon, Furman University, Aarhus University in Denmark, Tulane University, and the University of Michigan, where she is currently professor and Director of Graduate Studies in the Program in American Culture and the Center for Afroamerican and African Studies. Her books include *James Baldwin's Turkish Decade: Erotics of Exile* (Duke University Press, 2009; winner of the MLA William S. Scarborough Prize) and *How We Found America: Reading Gender through East European Immigrant Narratives* (University of North Carolina Press, 1995), as well as the edited and coedited collections *Other Americans, Other Americas: The Politics and Poetics of Multiculturalism* (Aarhus University Press, 1998), *The Puritan Origins of American Sex: Religion, Sexuality, and National Identity in American Literature* (Routledge, 2001), and *Over the Wall/After the Fall: Post-Communist Cultures in the East-West Gaze* (Indiana University Press, 2004). Her new projects include a monograph on the twentieth-century black novel, race, and gender, "James Baldwin in the Company of Women," and a mixed-genre piece on the proliferation of American notions of race and sexuality in post–Cold War Eastern Europe, "Racing Borderlands."

Index

Abu-Jamal, Mumia, 161
Achebe, Chinua, 3, 222, 230, 238; "African Writer and the English Language, The," 231; *Morning Yet on Creation Day*, 231; *Things Fall Apart*, 77, 213, 222, 229, 230, 231–33
Actors Studio, 203, 204
Adorno, Theodor, 10, 88
Africa. *See also under individual countries*
Africa: International Business, Economic and Political Magazine, 222–23
African Literature Association, 222
"African Writer and the English Language, The," Achebe, C., 231
"Alas Poor Richard," Baldwin, J., 71
All That Is Solid Melts into Air, Berman, M., 92
Als, Hilton, 204
Ambassadors, The, James, H., 57
Amen Corner, The, Baldwin, J., 162, 189, 191, 199, 203
American Dilemma, Myrdahl, G., 118
American Novel and Its Traditions, The, Chase, R., 49n5
Anderson, Robert M., 212, 215
Another Country, Baldwin, J., 6, 53, 54–55, 59, 74, 84, 92, 94–95, 160, 176, 178, 181–86, 189, 202, 243
Appeal to the Coloured Citizens of the World, Walker, D., 37
Arendt, Hannah, 25n20, 86, 116, 121
Armstrong, Louis, 238
Arnold, Matthew, 136
Atatürk, Kemal, 28n74
Auchinloss, Eve, 222
"Autobiographical Notes" (Go Tell It on the Mountain), Baldwin, J., 71, 72, 74
"Autobiographical Notes" (Notes of a Native Son), Baldwin, J., 71, 72 , 210
Avedon, Richard, 204; *Nothing Personal* (with Baldwin, J.), 24n8
Avi-Ram, Amitai, 215

Badiou, Alain, 85–86, 102n5, 102n6
Baker, Josephine, 193, 200
Baldwin, David, 210
Baldwin, James: "Alas Poor Richard," 71; *Amen Corner, The*, 162, 189, 191, 199, 203; *Another Country*, 6, 53, 54–55, 59, 74, 84, 94–95, 97, 160, 176, 178, 181–86, 189, 202, 243; "Autobiographical Notes" (*Go Tell It on the Mountain*), 71, 72, 74; "Autobiographical Notes" (*Notes of a Native Son*), 71, 72, 167–68, 210; "Black Girl Shouting," 126–27, 133; *Blues for Mister Charlie*, 24n8, 189,

Baldwin, James (*continued*)
199, 203, 204; "Color and American Civilization," 64; "Crusade of Indignation, The," 73, 100; "Death of a Prophet," 59, 60, 212; *Devil Finds Work, The*, 79, 221; "Discovery of What It Means to Be an American, The," 9, 15, 26n44, 35, 36, 41; "Down at the Cross: Letter from a Region in My Mind," 40, 160; "Easy Rider," 94–95; "Encounter on the Seine: Black Meets Brown," 93–94, 163, 210, 216, 217; "Equal in Paris," 162, 163, 164–66, 167, 170–71; "Everybody's Protest Novel," 69, 70, 71, 72, 80–81, 168; "Evidence of Things Not Seen, The," 128, 130, 132–36, 160; *Fire Next Time, The*, 6, 20, 23, 25n20, 39, 40, 42, 75, 87, 88, 96, 97, 108–9, 122, 123n24, 129, 142–43, 144, 149, 151, 152–53, 189, 190, 221; *Giovanni's Room*, 6–7, 7–8, 65, 74, 84, 129, 160, 162, 176, 178–81, 195, 203, 220, 231, 243; "Going to Meet the Man," 24n8, 59, 74–75, 189; *Go Tell It on the Mountain*, 55, 56, 59, 71, 72, 74, 77, 129, 148, 160, 162, 165, 210, 213, 214, 215, 230, 231, 232, 243; "Here be Dragons," 190; *If Beale Street Could Talk*, 199, 243; "In Search of a Majority," 219; *Just Above My Head*, 190, 199, 222, 224, 243; "Many Thousands Gone," 72, 168, 219; "Mass Culture and the Creative Artist," 62; "Negro in Paris, The," 216; *New Story*, 214; *No Name in the Street*, 15, 17, 23, 36, 40, 41, 42, 44, 45–48, 91, 141, 160, 162, 174, 179, 189, 193, 202, 219, 221, 223; *Nobody Knows My Name*, 5, 10, 24n14, 36, 37, 39, 91, 165; *No Papers for Mohammed*, 193; *Notes of a Native Son*, 11, 21, 39, 40–41, 44, 49n9, 50n20, 54, 71, 72, 89, 90, 162, 163, 167, 168–69, 170, 210, 212, 230–31; "Notes on the House of Bondage," 244; *Nothing Personal* (with Avedon, R.), 24n8; *One Day When I Was Lost*, 189; "Outing, The," 213, 214 , 216; *Perspectives: Angles on African Art*, 223–24; "Preservation of Innocence," 49n16; "Previous Condition," 59, 162; *Price of the Ticket, The*, 190, 244; "Princes and Powers," 46, 146, 175, 196, 211, 216, 218, 219, 221; "Question of Identity, A," 40, 148, 163; "Sonny's Blues," 233–37; "Stranger in the Village," 35, 38, 46, 89–90, 148, 163, 218, 223; "Take Me to the Water," 42–45; *Tell Me How Long the Train's Been Gone*, 189, 202–3, 204; "This Morning, This Evening, So Soon," 69, 74–75, 76; "To Be Baptized," 42, 47; *Welcome Table, The*, 188–90, 191–200, *192*, 202, 204; "White Problem, The," 63–64
Balfour, Lawrie, 90–91
Balzac, Honoré de, 49n15
Baraka, Amiri, 154, 221
Barthes, Roland, 128
Bauman, Zygmunt, 102n14; *Modernity and the Holocaust*, 88–89
Beam, Joseph, 190, 205n10
Beauvoir, Simone de, *Second Sex, The*, 13
Belafonte, Harry, 204
Bellow, Saul, 12
Berman, Marshall, *All That Is Solid Melts into Air*, 92
Bhabha, Homi, 232
Bigsby, C. W. E., 147
Birmingham, Kevin, 20
Black Boy, Wright, R., 13, 147, 148, 151, 218
"Black Girl Shouting," Baldwin, J., 126–27, 133
Black Metropolis, Drake, St. C., Cayton, H., 88
Black Orpheus, Sartre, J.-P., 145
Black Panthers, 47
Black Power, Wright, R., 27n59, 211

Black Scholar, 20
Black Skin, White Masks, Fanon, F., 13, 177
Bloch, Marc, 1, 2
Blues for Mister Charlie, Baldwin, J., 24n8, 189, 199, 203, 204
Boudin, Kathy, 161
Bowling Green State University, Ohio, 76, 77, 211, 222
Brando, Marlon, 204
Brooks, Gwendolyn, 217
Brown, Joseph A., 215
Brown, Wendy, 116, 120
Brown v. Board of Education, 97
Buber, Martin, 119
Burroughs, Edgar Rice, 232

Cain, James M., 41, 49n16; *Postman Always Rings Twice, The*, 58
Caldwell, Erskine, *Sure Hand of God, The*, 58
Campbell, James, 49n15, 51n36, 210; *Exiled in Paris*, 162–33
Camus, Albert, 15
Capote, Truman, 12
Carby, Hazel, 128–29
Carey, Joyce, 232
Caribbean diaspora, 27n58
Caster, Peter, 168
Cavell, Stanley, 107, 119
Cayton, Horace, *Black Metropolis*, 88
Césaire, Aimé, 13, 14, 87, 145, 146, 216; *Discourse on Colonialism*, 27n61
Cezzar, Engin, 18–19, 189, 202, 204–5
Champion, Ernest, 213, 222
Chandler, Raymond, 41, 49n16
Charles, Ray, 21, 53, 54, 64
Chartres cathedral, France, 46, 92, 93, 148, 223
Chase, R., *American Novel and Its Traditions, The*, 49n5
Cheever, John, 161
Chekhov, Anton, *Cherry Orchard, The*, 190, 199
Cherry Orchard, The, Chekhov, A., 190, 199
China, 100
Christian-Suggs, Jon, 169
Churchill, Winston, 27n61
CIA (Central Intelligence Agency), 46, 174, 217
Civil Rights Movement, 12, 15, 16, 36, 41, 43, 46, 64, 107, 129, 189, 204
Clark, Kenneth, 100, 171n6
Cleaver, Elridge, 154; *Soul on Ice*, 161, 221
Cold War, 18, 23, 36, 85, 97–98, 100–101, 121, 154, 175, 176
"Color and American Civilization," Baldwin, J., 64
Color Curtain, The, Wright, R., 27n59
Commentary, 58–59, 98
Confessions of Nat Turner, Styron, W., 43, 50n25
Confessions of Nat Turner: Ten Black Writers Respond, 50n25
Congress for Cultural Freedom, 174
Conrad, Joseph, 232
Cook, Mercer, 217
Cooper, Anna Julia, *Voice from the South, A*, 36
Cooper, Gary, 64
Counts, Dorothy, 173, 174
Crane, Gregg, D., 169
Crawford, Cheryl, 204
"Crusade of Indignation, The," Baldwin, J., 73, 100
Cullen, Countee, 211

Dakar, 153, 157n37, 219, 220
Dallas, Walter, 191, 199–200
Damas, Léon-Gontrand, 216–17
Davis, John A., 217, 218
Davis, Miles, 21, 53, 54, 61
Davis, Sammy, Jr., 204
Day, Doris, 64
"Death of a Prophet," Baldwin, J., 59, 60, 212
Delbanco, Nicholas, 200–202
Denning, Michael, 36
Dennis, Patrick, *Genius*, 53
Derrida, Jacques, 212

Descartes, René, 215
Deux Magots, Les, 12
Devil Finds Work, The, Baldwin, J., 79, 221
Dickens, Charles, 21, 41, 54, 72; *Tale of Two Cities, A*, 71, 79
Dien Bien Phu, battle of, 15
Diop, Alioune, 13, 145, 146, 216, 217
Dis-Agreement, Rancière, J., 119, 121
Discipline and Punish, Foucault, M., 166
Discourse on Colonialism, Césaire, A., 27n61
"Discovery of What It Means to Be an American, The," Baldwin, J., 9, 15, 26n44, 35, 36, 41
Dixon, Melvin, 204
Douglas, Ann, 100
Douglass, Frederick, "What to the Slave Is the Fourth of July?" 37
"Down at the Cross: Letter from a Region in My Mind," Baldwin, J., 40, 160
Drake, St. Clair, *Black Metropolis*, 88
Drury, Allen, *Shade of Difference, A*, 53
Du Bois, W. E. B., 87, 131, 156n24, 176, 238; "Of Alexander Crummell," *Souls of Black Folk, The*, 45; *Phylon*, 84
Dudziak, Mary, 100, 101
Dunbar, Paul Laurence, *Sport of the Gods*, 96
Dupee, F. W., 96
Düşenin Dostu. See *Fortune and Men's Eyes*
Dyson, Michael, 215

"Easy Rider," Baldwin, J., 94–95
Eckman, Fern, 220
Edwards, Brent, 137
Elgrably, Jordan, 223
Ellison, Ralph, 38, 211, 244
Emerson, Ralph Waldo, 36, 49n18
Encounter, 46, 146, 174, 175, 217
"Encounter on the Seine: Black Meets Brown," Baldwin, J., 93–94, 163, 210, 216, 217
"Equal in Paris," Baldwin, J., 162, 163, 164–66, 167, 170–71
Eschen, Penny von, 137
Essence, 65–66
Evers, Medgar, 43, 47
"Everybody's Protest Novel," Baldwin, J., 69, 70, 71, 72, 80–81, 168
"Evidence of Things Not Seen, The," Baldwin, J., 128, 130, 132–36, 160
Exiled in Paris, Campbell, J., 162–63
Ezenwa-Ohaeto, 211, 216, 221, 224n8

Fanon, Frantz, 86, 131, 179; *Black Skin, White Masks*, 13, 177
Faulkner, William, 56
Faure, Jeanne, 193, 206n21
Feidelson, Charles, *Symbolism in American Literature*, 49n5
Field, Douglas, 19; *Historical Guide to James Baldwin*, 3
Fire Next Time, The, Baldwin, J., 6, 20, 23, 25n20, 39, 40, 42, 75, 87, 88, 96, 97, 108–9, 122, 123n24, 129, 142–43, 144, 149, 151, 152–53, 189, 190, 221
First Negro Writers and Artists Congress, 13, 19, 24n14, 92, 94, 146, 151, 173–74, 175, 176–78, 181, 186, 216–19, 221
Fitzgerald, F. Scott, 21, 56, 93; *Great Gatsby, The*, 55
Flaubert, Gustave, 49n15
Forbes, Curdella, *From Nation to Diaspora: Samuel Selvon, George Lamming and the Cultural Performance of Gender*, 230
Fortune and Men's Eyes, Herbert, J., 188, 189, 199, 202
For Whom the Bell Tolls, Hemingway, E., 56
Foucault, Michel, 118; *Discipline and Punish*, 166
Franklin, H. Bruce, *Victim as Criminal and Artist, The*, 160–61
Freud, Sigmund, 134, 142, 154n2
From Nation to Diaspora: Samuel Selvon,

George Lamming and the Cultural Performance of Gender, Forbes, C., 230
Furnas, J. C., *Goodbye to Uncle Tom*, 73

Gaines, Kevin, 2, 103n25
Garvey, Marcus, 87, 211
Gates, Henry Louis, Jr.,193, 200; *Annotated Uncle Tom's Cabin, The*, introduction to, 70, 80–81
Genius, Dennis, P., 53
Ghana, 157n37
Gillespie, Dizzy, 26n49
Giovanni's Room, Baldwin, J., 6–7, 7–8, 65, 74, 84, 129, 160, 162, 176, 178–81, 195, 203, 220, 231, 243
Glaude, Eddie, 50n24
Glazer, Nathan, 98
Global Dimensions of the African Diaspora, Harris, J., 229
"Going to Meet the Man," Baldwin, J., 24n8, 59, 74–75, 189
Goldstein, Richard, 7
Gorky, Maxim, 58, 60
Go Tell It on the Mountain, Baldwin, J., 55, 56, 59, 71, 72, 74, 77, 129, 148, 160, 162, 165, 210, 213, 214, 215, 230, 231, 232, 243
Great Gatsby, The, Fitzgerald, F. S., 55
Greenwich Village, New York, 5, 10, 27n58, 94, 181–82
Griffith, Paul, 155n3
Guardian, 129
Guinea, 150, 157n37, 220
Gülriz Sururi and Engin Cezzar Theater, Istanbul, 188
Guthrie, Tyrone, 199

Hall, Stuart, 137, 235
Hansberry, Lorraine, *Raisin in the Sun*, 204
Happersberger, Lucien, 179
Harlem, New York, 4, 5, 8, 27n58, 39, 43, 68, 123, 148, 162, 175, 181–82, 203
Harlem Renaissance, 39, 211
Harris, Joseph, *Global Dimensions of the African Diaspora*, 229
Hassel, Bernard, 193
Hemingway, Ernest, 21, 49n15, 56, 57, 163; *For Whom the Bell Tolls*, 56; *Sun Also Rises, The*, 55, 57
Herbert, John, *Fortune and Men's Eyes*, 188, 189, 199, 202
"Here be Dragons," Baldwin, J., 190
Himes, Chester, 12
Historical Guide to James Baldwin, Field, D., 3
Hoetis, Themestocles, 164
Holliday, Billie, 73
Holmes, Carolyn, 213
Holocaust, 88–89, 150, 152
Hook, Sidney, 98
Hoover, J. Edgar, 154
Hopper, Briallen, 20, 21
Horkheimer, Max, 88
Horne, Lena, 204
"How Bigger Was Born," Wright, R., 70
Howe, Irving, 98
Hughes, Langston, 84
Hurston, Zora Neale, 212, 213; *Jonah's Gourd Vine*, 213, 214–15

If Beale Street Could Talk, Baldwin, J., 199, 243
"In Search of a Majority," Baldwin, J., 219
Irele, Abiole, 145
Isaacs, Harold, 209, 210, 211, 220
Israel, 18, 22, 144, 149–50, 151, 152
Istanbul, 10, 18–19, 20, 28n74, 188, 189, 190, 191, 202
Ivory Coast, 220

Jackson, George, *Soledad Brother*, 161
James, C. L. R., 27n58, 131
James, Henry, 1, 8, 21, 22, 40–41, 49n18, 54, 57, 62, 93, 154n2; *Ambassadors, The*, 57; *Notes of a Son and Brother*, 41

James Baldwin Now, McBride, D. A., 2–3
James Baldwin's Turkish Decade: Erotics of Exile, Zaborowska, M. J., 3, 18, 28n74
Jarrett, Thomas D., 84
jazz music/musicians, 12, 38, 53–54, 55, 218, 235, 236, 237. *See also under individual entries*
J.B., MacLeish, A., 203
Jews/Judaism, 18, 87, 88–89, 149, 150, 151, 152, 157n33
Jim Crow laws, 85, 86, 87, 90, 99, 101, 102n15, 107
Jonah's Gourd Vine, Hurston, Z. N., 213, 214–15
Joyce, James, 74
Judson, Barbara, 222
Jules-Rosette, Bennetta, 218
Just Above My Head, Baldwin, J., 190, 199, 222, 224, 243

Kamwangamalu, Nkonko, 235
Kaplan, Amy, 137
Karefa-Smart, Frank, 220
Kazan, Elia, 203, 204, 207n39
Kenan, Randall, 204
Kennedy, J. F., 28n74
Kenya, 157n37, 221
King, Coretta Scott, 191
King, Martin Luther, Jr., 9, 17, 43, 45, 47, 98, 120, 161, 171n5, 171n6, 174, 242–43; "Letter from a Birmingham Jail," 37, 161
King James Bible, 21, 41, 54, 72, 79, 242
Kitt, Eartha, 193
Klein, Kerwin Lee, 155n10
Kristeva, Julia, 232

Lamming, George, 24n14, 177–78, 179, 186; "Negro Writer and his World, The," 177
Lasebikan, M., 217–18
Lawd Today!, Wright, R., 211
Lawrence, Jacob, 85
Lear, Jonathan, 121
Le Baron, Bentley, 145
Leeming, David, 9, 20, 24n8, 50n31, 156n24, 160, 162, 200, 202, 203, 220
"Letter from a Birmingham Jail," King, M. L, 37, 161
L'étudiant noir, 216
Lewis, Ida, 220
Lewis, R. W. B., *American Adam, The*, 49n5
"Liberalism and the Negro" (*Commentary*, 1964), 98–100
Lincoln, Abraham, 121
Liston, Sonny, 60, 61
Locke, Alain, 84
Loèche-les-Bains, 148
London Observer, 231
Lori-Parks, Suzan, 204
Los Angeles Times, 65, 67
Lynch, Nancy, 222

Macey, David, 12, 217
Machine in the Garden, The, Marx, L., 49n5
MacLeish, Archibald, *J.B.*, 203
Magpie, 127, 132
Mailer, Norman, 12, 39, 161
Malcolm X, 43, 47, 160, 161, 171n5, 171n6, 174, 189
"Many Thousands Gone," Baldwin, J., 72, 168, 219
Marx, Leo, *Machine in the Garden, The*, 49n5
"Mass Culture and the Creative Artist," Baldwin, J., 62
Matthews, Victoria, "The Value of Race Literature," 39
Matthiessen, F. O., 36
Maynard, Tony, 47, 160
M'Baye, Babacar, 213
McBride, Dwight A., *James Baldwin Now*, 2–3, 241
McCarthy, Mary, 49n15
Mead, Margaret, 143
Mercer, John, 218

Miller, D. Quentin, *Re-Viewing James Baldwin: Things Not Seen*, 3
Miller, Henry, 49n15
Modernity and the Holocaust, Bauman, Z., 88–89
Monrovia, 220
Morning Yet on Creation Day, Achebe, C., 231
Morrison, Toni, 21, 25n18, 91, 92–93, 124n35
Muhammad, Elijah, 40, 120, 123n24, 151, 160
Mumford, Lewis, 36
Murray, Albert, 92
Myrdahl, Gunnar, 98; *American Dilemma*, 118

National Association for the Advancement of Colored People (NAACP), 17
Nationalism, Colonialism and the United States: One Minute to Twelve, Liberation Committee for Africa, 221
Native Son, Wright, R., 69, 77, 78, 169–70
"Negro in American Life, The," U. S. Information Agency, 101
"Negro in Paris, The," Baldwin, J., 216
New Leader, 58, 60
New Story, Baldwin, J., 214
Newton, Huey, 47, 200
New York, 3, 7, 49, 92, 129, 132, 146, 153, 162, 164, 165, 181; Greenwich Village, 5, 10, 27n58, 94, 181–82; Harlem, 4, 5, 8, 27n58, 39, 43, 68, 123, 148, 162, 175, 181–82, 203
New Yorker, 149, 150, 220, 221
New York Post, 20
New York Review of Books, 3, 59
New York Times, 23, 53, 56, 57–58, 61, 64–65
New York Times Book Review, 36, 51n31
Nichols, Charles H., Jr., 84
Nietzsche, Friedrich, 114, 116, 117
Nigeria, 157n37
Nobody Knows My Name, Baldwin, J., 5, 10, 24n14, 36, 37, 39, 91, 165
No Name in the Street, Baldwin, J., 15, 17, 23, 36, 40, 41, 42, 44, 45–48, 91, 160, 162, 174, 189, 193, 202, 219, 221, 223
No Papers for Mohammed, Baldwin, J., 193
Notes of a Native Son, Baldwin, J., 11, 21, 39, 40–41, 44, 49n9, 50n20, 54, 71, 72, 89, 90, 162, 163, 168–69, 170, 210, 212, 230–31
Notes of a Son and Brother, James, H., 41
"Notes on the House of Bondage," Baldwin, J., 244
Nowlin, Michael, 70
Nwankwo, Chimalum, 211

"Of Alexander Crummell," Du Bois, W. E. B., 45
Ojo-Ade, Femi, 211
One Day When I Was Lost, Baldwin, J., 189
"Outing, The," Baldwin, J., 25n21, 214, 216

Packard, Vance, *Pyramid Climbers*, 53
Page, Gerry, 200
Painter, Mary, 193
Paris, 5, 7, 10–11, 12, 13, 14, 16, 27n66, 45–46, 93–94, 129, 145–46, 162, 163, 166, 211
Patterson, Floyd, 60–61
Peltier, Leonard, 161
Perspectives: Angles on African Art, Baldwin, J., 223–24
Phillips, Caryl, 129–31, 133
Phylon, 84
Pierson, Ann, 204
Playboy, 62, 63, 66–67
Plimpton, George, 223
Podhoretz, Norman, 98, 99
Poitier, Sidney, 204
Porter, Horace A., 82n6
Postman Always Rings Twice, The, Cain, J. M., 58
Poyrazoğlu, Ali, 188, 189, 205n3

Présence africaine, 13, 217
"Preservation of Innocence," Baldwin, J., 49n16
"Previous Condition," Baldwin, J., 59, 162
Price of the Ticket, The, Baldwin, J., 190, 244
"Princes and Powers," Baldwin, J., 46, 146, 175, 196, 211, 216, 218, 219, 221
Pyramid Climbers, Packard, V., 53

"Question of Identity, A," Baldwin, J., 40, 148, 163

Raisin in the Sun, Hansberry, L., 204
Rancière, Jacques, *Dis-Agreement*, 119, 121
Reagan, Ronald, 2
Redding, Bertice, 193
Reporter, The, 216
Re-Viewing James Baldwin: Things Not Seen, Miller, D. Q., 3
Rogin, Michael, 116
Rose, Jacqueline, 22
Ross, Marlon B., 6; "White Fantasies of Desire," 50n20
Roth, Philip, 12
Russia. *See* Soviet Union

Sartre, Jean-Paul, 12, 41, 146; *Black Orpheus*, 145
Schaub, Thomas, 85
Schmitt, Carl, 116, 119
Schwarz, Bill, 86
Seale, Bobby, 200
Second Sex, The, Beauvoir, S. de, 13
Second World War, 27n61, 87–88, 89, 98, 99, 132, 145
Senegal, 150, 151, 157n37, 219, 220; Dakar, 153, 157n37, 219, 220
Senghor, Léopold, 13, 19, 26n58, 145, 146, 147, 151, 157n37, 216, 218
Shade of Difference, A, Drury, A., 53
Shagaloff, June, 204
Shawn, William, 220–21
Shin, Andrew, 222
Shulman, George, 22, 23
Sierra Leone, 150, 157n37, 211, 220
Simone, Nina, 193
Singh, Nikhil Pal, 85, 98
Smith, Bessie, 35, 62, 95, 185, 238
Soledad Brother, Jackson, G., 161
"Sonny's Blues," Baldwin, J., 233–37
Sorbonne, Paris, 13, 14, 173
Soul on Ice, Cleaver, E., 161, 221
Souls of Black Folk, The, Du Bois, W. E. B., 45
South Africa, 22
Soviet Union, 58, 67, 100, 101
Spillers, Hortense, 70
Spivak, Gayatri, 37, 48n3
Sport of the Gods, Dunbar, P. L., 96
Stein, Solomon, 49n9, 132
Stevens, Wallace, 117
Stevenson, Robert Louis, 60
Stewart, Jacqueline, 94
Stowe, Harriet Beecher, 69, 70, 71, 81, 82, 154n2, 168; *Uncle Tom's Cabin*, 20, 22, 69, 70–74, 76–80, 81, 169
St. Paul-de-Vence, 20, 189, 190, 193, 200–202, *201*
"Stranger in the Village," Baldwin, J., 35, 38, 46, 89–90, 91, 148, 163, 218, 223
Strasberg, Lee, 204
Strawbridge, Mary, 204
Styron, William, 66; *Confessions of Nat Turner*, 43, 50n25
Sun Also Rises, The, Hemingway, E., 55, 57
Sundquist, Eric, 70
Sure Hand of God, The, Caldwell, E., 58
Sururi, Gülriz, 193
Sweet Bird of Youth, Williams, T., 201
Symbolism in American Literature, Feidelson, C., 49n5

"Take Me to the Water," Baldwin, J., 42–45
Tale of Two Cities, A, Dickens, C., 71, 79

Tell Me How Long the Train's Been Gone, Baldwin, J., 189, 202–3, 204
Things Fall Apart, Achebe, C., 77, 213, 222, 229, 230, 231–33
Third Annual Conference of African Culture (1960), 209
"This Morning, This Evening, So Soon," Baldwin, J., 69, 74–75, 76
Till, Emmett, 204
Tillman, N. P., 84
Time magazine, 130, 160, 200
Tinney, James, 212–13
Tiyatro, 188
"To Be Baptized," Baldwin, J., 42, 47
Tóibín, Colm, 3, 21, 22, 41, 49n18
Tovares, Alla, 235
Traylor, Eleanor, 19
Turkey, 9, 19, 28n74, 156n28, 188, 189, 190, 191, 202, 205n3. *See also* Istanbul

Uncle Tom's Cabin, Stowe, H. B., 20, 22, 69, 70–74, 76–80, 81, 169
Uncle Tom's Children, Wright, R., 70

"Value of Race Literature, The," Matthews, V., 39
Ventura, Michael, 215
Victim as Criminal and Artist, The, Franklin, H. B., 160–61
Vietnam, 16, 27n63, 44, 47
Voice from the South, A, Cooper, A. J. 36

Walker, David, *Appeal to the Coloured Citizens of the World*, 37
Wall, Cheryl A., 5, 21–22, 22–23
Warren, Kenneth, 70
Watkins, Mel, 51n31
Weber, Max, 88
Weber, Michael John, 223
Welcome Table, The, Baldwin, J., 188–90, 191–200, *192*, *201*, 202, 204
West, Cornel, 165
West Africa, 144, 150, 213
"What to the Slave Is the Fourth of July?," Douglass, F., 37
"White Fantasies of Desire," Ross, M. B., 50n20
White Man, Listen!, Wright, R., 27n59
"White Problem, The," Baldwin, J., 63–64
Whitman, Walt, 36, 179
Wideman, John Edgar, 161
Williams, Billy Dee, 47
Williams, Connie, 27n58
Williams, Tennessee, *Sweet Bird of Youth*, Williams, T., 201
Williams, Wayne, 133, 136, 160
Wilson, Edmund, 58
Winthrop, John, 36
World War Two. *See* Second World War
Worth, Eugene, 186
Wright, Richard, 12, 41, 69–70, 77, 81, 89, 94, 113, 154n2, 163, 168, 173, 211, 217; *Black Boy*, 13, 147, 148, 151, 218; *Black Power*, 27n59, 211; *Color Curtain, The*, 27n59; "How Bigger Was Born," 70; *Lawd Today!*, 211; *Native Son*, 69, 77, 78, 169–70; *Uncle Tom's Children*, 70; *White Man, Listen!*, 27n59

Yarborough, Richard, 70

Zaborowska, Magdalena J., *James Baldwin's Turkish Decade: Erotics of Exile*, 3, 18, 28n74